I0098573

Forty Days in the Valley

of the Shadow of Death

Tough Answers to the Tough

Questions Christians Ask

Michael K. Pasque

Copyright 2013 Michael K. Pasque

If you had responded to my rebuke,
I would have poured out my heart to you
and made my thoughts known to you.

—Proverbs 1:23

Copyright 2013 Michael K. Pasque

Preface In Prayer

Heavenly Father, with all my heart I want everything that you have to offer.

I want it all.

I don't just want it all, I want even more than all you were planning to give me.

I desperately want you to fill every moment of the life that I have left with absolutely as much of the knowledge of you that you are willing to impart.

And yet I am completely powerless, hopelessly inadequate, and utterly helpless in the task of getting there myself.

I need you to flood my life with your grace if I am to have any chance of getting everything that you have to offer.

Please don't hold back even a tiny morsel of all that my weak and limited human mind, spirit, heart, and body can handle—for in my extraordinary weakness is your power made extraordinarily complete.

Give me everything.

Make me shudder in fear in your *Presence*.

Make me regret—to the point of revulsion—my every transgression as I fall on my face before your perfect holiness and your merciful love.

Hurt me as much as you must to get me there.

Violently rip from my heart the idols that I harbor there.

And have no mercy upon those principalities, powers, and authorities to whom I have—in my sin—given control over my life.

Utterly destroy them my Redeemer.

Help me.

And let me know (in that magnificent way that you do) of the depth of your compassionate mercy and love for me.

Copyright 2013 Michael K. Pasque

Please help me.

I can't get there—where I desperately want to be—without you.

Enthrall me with your beauty, stun me with your righteousness, discipline me with your justice, give me a taste of your knowledge, fill me with your compassion, and help me know the infinite depth of how you love me with all of your heart.

I want to feel your delight for me by the knowledge of you that you will share with your humble servant.

Copyright 2013 Michael K. Pasque

Introduction

While we are submerged and overwhelmed by the fury and fluff that fills the minutes of our every day, our tendency is towards never coming to understand, acknowledge, or even recognize the real mechanisms that are at work in our life. These are the mechanisms behind all of the things that leave us in wonder, amazement, and awe—or that make us worried, anxious, or fearful. An understanding of the mechanisms behind the things that happen to us, especially things that occur in response to our actions, is the only thing that can keep us from spending our lives hopelessly railing and mindlessly flailing against the people and things that we incorrectly hold responsible for that which is happening to us.

Until we can stand above it all and see it like it really is, we are like rats in a maze—all that we see are walls. But when we come to understand that our life has a pattern with purpose, we are no longer relegated to wandering aimlessly, staring at the walls, and wondering where the exit might be. Instead, when we view the maze from above, we can see that there is an exit from the confusion, a solution to our problem. From this new perspective, from the eternal perspective of God, the solution is easily seen to be Jesus. What a sad sight it is to see a man or woman approaching their twilight years having never understood what life is really all about, why things happen the way that they do, and the potential practical life impact of an eternal perspective.

Authors Note: This book is not written like any book you have ever read. It is written—and should be read—as a summary outline. I have attempted to write each sentence *as a paragraph*, as an independent statement that can stand alone, but one that maintains its dependence upon the statements that precede it. Above

Copyright 2013 Michael K. Pasque

all, it is critical that the reader avoid skipping over the Biblical text that is abundantly scattered throughout the book. Your job is to check the theology found on these pages against its only true metric: the Bible, the written Word of God.

Repetition is used extensively in this book. I realize that many would call this bad editing. I would propose otherwise. Taking the biblical writers as my example, I repeat to emphasize. I have written these chapters as God has given them to me. When I repeat facts in multiple different manners, it is—in my mind—with great purpose. It is to drive home the central theme from as many vantage points as possible. In this regard, my writing attempts to be a conveyance of the facts of God in a *multi-parametric* manner. By approaching the facts of God from as many vantage points as possible, my hope is to strike chords that resonate the deep inner heartstrings of every potential reader's heart. My multi-parametric manner of conveying these thoughts is in recognition that every reader's heart is, by the gracious and artistic hand of God, magnificently personal in regard to the unique combination of chords that resonate their deep inner heartstrings. If I didn't believe that every heart should feel the resonance of these facts of God, I would not have written this book. I hope you will bear with me and be willing to put up with a little repetition while I attempt to speak to every reader's heart in its unique language.

Copyright 2013 Michael K. Pasque

Day 1

We All Believe In God—So What's So Important About Jesus?
Jesus Plus Nothing

It is all about Jesus.

Despite the fact that in every single day of our life we are relentless in our attempts to make it all about us, it is nonetheless still all about Jesus.

And yet the mighty, omnipotent, omniscient Son of God—the Master of the Universe—cherishes us so dearly as to choose to somehow subserviently and sacrificially make it all about us.

Whether we acknowledge it in this life or not, the very first reality that we will face when we take that final life step into eternity is that every single moment of our life—and of every life—was about only one thing: Jesus Christ.

Can it be any other way?

In no uncertain terms, He claimed to be the only Son of God.

A discussion regarding His status, His importance in our life and in the world in general (as *the* Son of God) simply cannot be a casual conversation.

The eyewitnesses have clearly documented that Jesus claimed to be the Son of God, so He must be either absolutely nothing—a joke, a creep, a psycho, a liar, a great big zero—or He must be absolutely everything.

There can be no middle ground in this, the most critical of all of our life discussions.

Copyright 2013 Michael K. Pasque

If Jesus is the Son of God as He claims, His impact in our day-to-day life cannot be anything less than all-pervasive through every moment, every facet of our life.

> He is the **image** of the invisible God, the **firstborn** over all creation. For by him **all** things were created: things in heaven and on earth, visible and invisible, whether thrones or powers or rulers or authorities; **all** things were created **by** him and **for** him. He is **before all** things, and **in** him **all** things hold together. And he is the **head** of the body, the church; he is the **beginning** and the **firstborn** from among the dead, so that in **everything** he might have the **supremacy**. For God was pleased to have **all** his fullness dwell **in** him, and **through** him to reconcile to himself **all** things, whether things on earth or things in heaven, by making peace through his blood, shed on the cross. (Colossians 1:15-20; emphasis added)

Indeed, every single day we can praise God for the magnificent complexity of the situations that we find ourselves in—and yet likewise also praise Him for the utter simplicity of the solution to every one of them.

This logical and obligatory all-pervasiveness of Jesus in our life means that in every difficulty (and delight), in every storm (and sunny day), in every frenzy (and calm), in every heated battle (and peaceful moment), in every darkened night (and new light) we know—there is no hidden mystery here—exactly to Whom we can and must turn.

Jesus is always there and He is always the answer.

Always.

Copyright 2013 Michael K. Pasque

Even in the difficulties we face this very day, we can be assured that Jesus is all we need for this (and every) situation.

In addition to His day-to-day impact in our life, we can also be assured of His importance in the single most important aspect of this life: our eternal salvation.

It is Jesus plus nothing for our salvation—the most eternally important mission and purpose of this life of ours.

In regard to our salvation, the verdict is clear: even with a full life of toil—even if we are the nicest person in the whole world—we, by ourselves, have zero impact on our salvation and can add absolutely nothing to what Jesus has already done for us in this regard.

And in this regard—in the matter of our salvation—belief *"in God"* is incomplete—and in that incompleteness, utterly fatal.

Fatal.

Without belief in Jesus specifically, all is lost.

> *Moreover, the Father judges no one, but has entrusted all judgment to the Son, that all may honor the Son just as they honor the Father.* **He who does not honor the Son does not honor the Father, who sent him.** *(John 5:22-23; emphasis added)*

With Jesus we get everything.

Without Jesus we get nothing.

The Bible is clear in its revelation that you can have the most sincere belief "in God" without belief in Jesus—and in that state you are utterly and hopelessly lost.

> *You believe that there is one God. Good! Even the demons believe that—and shudder. (James 2:19)*

Copyright 2013 Michael K. Pasque

The impact of Jesus in our life is so pervasive that we can be assured whenever we find ourselves in trouble that the trouble has invariably occurred as a result of our taking our eyes off of Jesus—and putting them on ourselves.

In fact, in this life we should never worry about ourselves at all.

We should never concern ourselves with our lives, our accomplishments, our happiness, our fulfillment—or even our heavenly rewards.

We should concern ourselves with bringing glory to Jesus by the expression of His subservient, sacrificial love through us and directed toward those individuals He has brought into our life—and let Him worry about everything else (including our heavenly rewards).

Actually, it is wonderfully comforting—almost *freeing*—to know that it is not about us, or what we must do, but rather, is all about Jesus and what He has already done.

There is nothing that we can do to impact the love that Jesus already has for us—we cannot make it increase and we cannot make it decrease.

Instead, we can relax—there is no competition—if we are in Jesus Christ.

It is not about us, it is about Jesus Christ.

It is also Jesus plus nothing for our sanctification—the second most eternally important mission and purpose of our life—to be made into the very likeness of Jesus Christ.

> Let us **fix our eyes on Jesus, the author and perfecter of our faith,** who for the joy set before him endured the cross, scorning its shame, and sat down at the right hand of the throne of God. (Hebrews 12:2; emphasis added)

Copyright 2013 Michael K. Pasque

It is Jesus plus nothing that solves every situation that we could ever find ourselves in—this is our sanctification—for all situations were known, planned, and created by God, the Master of the creation of the universe, such that every moment is, in fact, *about* Jesus.

Jesus is thus the answer to every question.

He is the Savior in every battle.

He is the way out of every trap.

He is the rescuer for every captive.

He is the shelter in every storm.

He is the water in every drought.

He is the bread in every famine.

He is the light in every moment of absolute darkness.

He is the only truth in the sea of untruth in which we are hopelessly submerged.

He is the only satiation of every deep craving of our heart.

He is the only voice that answers the deep cry of our heart.

He is the only True North by which to chart the course of our life.

His is that hand that reaches down and firmly grabs our hand as we sink for the last time into the dark lagoon of our self-deception.

He is our redemption, our only salvation.

Jesus is not "part" of the solution to anything—He is the whole solution to everything.

Jesus plus nothing satisfies our hungry heart.

It is Jesus plus nothing—in every moment of our lives.

Jesus is our only hope.

Jesus is the entirety of our eternity and our eternity is our only hope.

Copyright 2013 Michael K. Pasque

We will romp with Jesus through the adventures of eternity dressed immaculately in the pure white righteousness of His perfect life, perfect death, and glorious resurrection, just as if we had never committed a single rebellious offense against the perfect holiness of the uncreated, mighty, and Most Holy God—and all this utterly and only by the work of Jesus Christ.

For whenever the Father looks at us, He will see us through Jesus!

Only through Jesus—always and everywhere and only—and that for all eternity!

For when Jesus became a man forever, He agreed to become the mediator of a new covenant between, the intermediary between, the connection between created man and the Uncreated God.

> *Therefore, when Christ came into the world, he said: "Sacrifice and offering you did not desire, but **a body** you prepared for me; with burnt offerings and sin offerings you were not pleased. (Hebrews 10:5-6; emphasis added)*

Jesus is our interface, our connection, our only link to the eternal, uncreated, infinite God.

Jesus, fully man and fully God, is the One and Only Mediator that connects us to God.

He has been that *always*.

He will be that *forever*.

> *Jesus Christ is the same yesterday and today and **forever**. (Hebrews 13:8; emphasis added)*

Copyright 2013 Michael K. Pasque

He is that seemingly impossible link between the temporary and the Eternal, the created and the Uncreated, the finite and the Infinite, the unrighteous and the Most Holy.

Jesus is our hope and in that hope, our joy, and in that joy, eternal life—life as we can never imagine it now.

We are simply and utterly unable to even imagine the magnificence of the eternity that God has planned for us in Jesus Christ.

Do you think that I have overstated the case for Jesus Christ?

It is outside of the mental, emotional, and spiritual capacity of any man or woman to exceed reality in his or her description of the glory ascribed to Jesus Christ.

It is Jesus *plus nothing*—yesterday, today and for all eternity in every setting, every time and always.

Copyright 2013 Michael K. Pasque

Day 2

What Can We Really Know About God And Does It Really Matter?
A Brief Summary That Will Save Your Life: The Attributes Of God

God is Love

Because our Creator God *is* love, our deepest heart desire (and the entire purpose of our creation) is to *subserviently, sacrificially love God*—for God made us in His own image—and to thereby join into the eternal fellowship of the Triune Godhead

God is Infinitely Creative

The magnificent creation we see around us—from microscopic detailed intricacy to the vast galaxies—is nothing compared to the eternal landscape in which the heirs to the kingdom of Heaven will eternally experience God's loving fellowship.

God is Perfect

God's perfection mandates that He cannot settle for 2nd best in anything, including His eternity.

Thus those who spend eternity with Him will have the exact nature and attributes that God desires in eternal companions and will have acquired the

Copyright 2013 Michael K. Pasque

knowledge of God that is the critical foundation for joining the eternal loving fellowship of God.

God is Mysterious

Mysteriously, our sinful nature—that nefarious tendency toward rebellion against the righteous authority of God—is God-ordained and therefore critical to our perfection as eternal heirs of the kingdom of God.

God is Holy

The infinitely pure and holy love that exists in eternity between the three Persons of the Trinity, by its very nature, cannot exist in eternity between Them and the those whose love is not infinitely pure and holy (those defiled by sin— even the smallest sin yet still representing heinous rebellion against God).

Therefore, God Has a Problem!

Accordingly, one of the attributes that God therefore mandates in us as eternal heirs to His kingdom, in fact, excludes us from ever becoming that.

Our God-ordained nefarious tendency toward heinous rebellion, which God obviously desires (and by His perfection, will have) in His eternal sons and daughters, is the precise thing that in fact excludes us from ever becoming that for which we were created and for which is our deepest heart desire.

God is Perfectly Just

God's perfect justice mandates that evil have consequence (we would not want it any other way!).

Consequently, He can't "just forget" our sin.

Copyright 2013 Michael K. Pasque

Perfect eternal life is lost (because of our sin); perfect eternal life must (in perfect justice) be given.

God is Merciful

Mercifully, God does not immediately destroy us when we rebel against Him—we are given every chance to accept the only pathway back to our creation purpose and deep heart desire (love and fellowship with God for eternity).

In finding and traveling that pathway is found our perfection as a critical part of God's perfect eternity.

God *is* Subservient, Sacrificial Love (Grace is inherent to His nature)

Perfect eternal life (fulfilling our deep heart desire and creation purpose) must be paid for our redemption—a price that we are utterly unable to pay because we are not—by our sinful nature—capable of a perfect life.

Jesus does that which we are utterly unable to do in regard to solving our dilemma: in the cataclysmic moment of our eternal redemption, Jesus sacrificed (for the first and only time in all eternity) that which He already possessed, perfect eternal life in the loving fellowship of the Trinity.

God is Glorious

It is God's infinite glory that assigns infinite value to perfect eternal *life* in His presence.

This is what is lost by our sin and, therefore, what must be paid for our redemption.

Thus the price paid for our redemption (the perfect eternal life of His Son) demonstrates our infinite worth to God.

Copyright 2013 Michael K. Pasque

[Was there nothing short of the death of Christ that could have paid our ransom?

Is death really the necessary price that must be paid?

This seems harsh to us—after all, *we* only execute murderers and you and I are not murderers!

Death seems like a high price for our seemingly small sins.

By this admission, we show that we have no clue regarding the bright white glory of God's pure and infinite holiness.

If we did, if we could be in His glorious presence for the fraction of a moment, we would know why even a tiny sin is a catastrophic affront to the holiness of God.

We would know why death—loss of true life in the presence of God—must be paid for what is lost.

Besides, the price of redemption is not determined by the gravity of the sin forgiven, but rather by that which is lost because of even the tiniest of our sins—our eternal destiny as sons and daughters of God.

Because of our sinful rebellion, perfect eternal life in the presence of God has been lost and is owed.

This is exactly the price paid by Jesus.

It is God's glory that assigns value to this perfect eternal *life* in His presence.

The price paid for our redemption demonstrates our infinite worth to God.]

God is Love (once again)

We are back to *love* yet a third time.

In the infinite gift of our free will, God gave us the ultimate demonstration of His love for us—the right to determine our eternal fate.

Copyright 2013 Michael K. Pasque

In this free will is found the only chance for those who would be eternal children of God to *"overcome"* (Revelation 21:7) their naturally nefarious tendency to rebel against God and choose to be found only in the shed blood of the sacrifice of His Son Jesus on the cross of Calvary.

It is in that choice that we volitionally choose to romp through the adventure, exhilaration, passion, romance, and love of an eternity of glorious *life* with God.

And in this free will is also found a stark reality: that the majority of us will simply refuse this free gift and instead spend eternity frustrated in obtaining our one true destiny and deep heart desire—with utterly no hope of our condition ever changing.

All free, all paid for, all simply for the asking—and yet it fully meets the perfect demands of God's justice, holiness, mercy, and love.

The choice is yours—and, very literally, everything depends on it.

Copyright 2013 Michael K. Pasque

Day 3

Why Do We Exist?
Our "Creation Purpose"

We exist because God is love.

For all eternity the three Persons of the Triune Godhead live *life*—as it is perfectly defined—in an existence that is best described as *love*, an existence founded in an eternal fellowship of love with each other.

The foundation of that loving fellowship is the volitional and perfectly subservient and sacrificial nature with which each of the three Persons of the Triune Godhead glorifies each of the other two Persons of the same Godhead— that very same subservient, sacrificial, glorifying fellowship to which we are called.

> *We proclaim to you what we have seen and heard, so that you also may have fellowship with us. And our fellowship is with the Father and with his Son, Jesus Christ. (1 John 1:3)*

For all of eternity, each of the three Persons of the Trinity has refused to upstage the other two.

This is why the Triune Godhead has been called an eternal *dance* of love— because if one of them were to stop moving toward sacrificially serving the others and became still, the others would by their very nature voluntarily, immediately

Copyright 2013 Michael K. Pasque

rush to revolve around Him in subservient sacrificial love (See writings of C. S. Lewis and Tim Keller).

This decision to stop and let the others circle around Him would, by definition, establish the immobile Person as the dominant, central, primary figure of the Triune Godhead—a position that none of the Trinity is willing to assume because of their glorifying, sacrificial love for one another.

This, the truest of love, naturally seeks a position of subservience.

This is unconditional love in its purest form.

To our dark world the unconditional love shared by the Trinity is the brightest of bright light and completely unknown in the inherent nature of man—except in the knowledge of Jesus Christ.

The Triune Godhead—three Persons in a single God—could not exist without this unconditional, subservient, sacrificial love.

For instead of stopping and saying, "Focus your love on me," each Person of the Triune Godhead moves continually with purpose toward lifting up the other two—never ceasing in this quest and therefore never standing still and therefore never elevating Himself (by centering Himself) such that the others would rotate around Him.

And thus we can logically conclude that which has already been revealed in the written Word of God: *"God is love."*

*This is why we can know that God really is love. Dear friends, let us love one another, for love comes from God. Everyone who loves has been born of God and knows God. Whoever does not love does not know God, because **God is love**. (1John 4:7-8; emphasis added)*

God is love.

Copyright 2013 Michael K. Pasque

Love can only exist as an entity that is shared between individuals.

Thus only a Triune Godhead—three Persons in one God—could embody love—could claim to *be* love—*before* the creation of other individuals.

The God of the Christian Bible, *unlike any other god of any other religion, is* love.

No other religion has a deity who can even make the claim to *be* love.

This amazing eternal existence of God in eternal perfect love lacks nothing.

God did not create us to fill any need of His.

Our creation did not come about for a purpose or to fill a desire—but rather as *a consequence*.

In other words, our creation came about as an inherent, natural, direct consequence of the serving, sharing nature of God's love.

It simply could not happen any other way.

It is and always has been, for all eternity, God's pure and perfect will—as a direct consequence of His inherent nature—to *share* the perfect loving fellowship of the three Persons of the Triune Godhead.

This sharing of God's love is a natural, innate outpouring of the inherent glory and magnificence of the love of God.

And we are the result of this glorious and magnificent love.

God loves to love.

He can't help it.

It is His very nature to love.

We are the objects of His love.

As we discuss God's plan for us, we will see that an intense sacrificially subservient love for us is revealed in every step of the gospel of Jesus Christ.

Copyright 2013 Michael K. Pasque

Just as each Person of the Trinity shares subservient, loving fellowship with the other members of the Trinity, so also do they desire to share the very same subservient loving fellowship with us.

And so, God created.

God did not create us to love Him because He somehow has a deep need that can only be filled by us loving Him.

God has never and will never *need* us.

He is infinitely complete in every way.

God has no needs except to be utterly true to Himself.

God does not ask us to obey and serve and love Him because He needs or desires or has an unfulfilled void in these areas.

God did not create us to love Him because He needs to be loved or even because He loves to be loved.

Quite the opposite is true.

God created us so that *He* could subserviently sacrificially love *us*.

God created us because He loves to love—and we are the eternal objects of His love.

God created all that has been created, including the very special creation of our heart.

Our heart is the greatest of His creations and is very specially designed to God's exact specifications.

Because He loves us, God created us *in His image*.

Since we are created in His image, we also—in the deepest recesses of the most holy place of our heart—*love to love*.

Just like the deepest desire of His heart is to love, so also did God give our hearts (since we are made in His image) this same deep desire to love.

Copyright 2013 Michael K. Pasque

We desire to subserviently, sacrificially love God just like He subserviently, sacrificially loves us—this is the way God created us.

Thus, God does not ask us to serve Him because He is a demanding, egocentric despot whose deep need is to have created beings cower before Him.

The truth is in fact the exact opposite of this Satanic lie.

Instead, God asks us to serve and obey Him because He knows that serving and obeying someone is how you love someone—and He created us to love!

Thus, God asks us to serve and obey because He knows that *only* this will fulfill our creation purpose and our deepest heart desire.

In other words, God asks us to serve Him because He loves us.

How can this statement be logical?

It is logical because God knows our hearts.

He knows that we love to love and therefore our deepest heart's desire is in fact to love Him.

We love Him and fulfill our deepest heart's desire and creation purpose when we obey and serve Him because that is how we subserviently, sacrificially love— and *that is why He asks us to serve and obey Him.*

Christ's obedient death on the cross, His ultimate demonstration of servanthood to the Father (and to us), eliminates our sinful imperfection and in so doing ultimately frees us to attain our deep heart desire to love God by serving God:

> How much more, then, will the blood of Christ, who through the eternal Spirit offered himself unblemished to God, cleanse our consciences from acts that lead to death, **so that** we may **serve** the living God! (Hebrews 9:14; emphasis added)

Copyright 2013 Michael K. Pasque

Loving is obeying.

Loving is serving.

So, God asks us to obey and serve Him, and thereby love Him.

He asks us this because He knows that we were made to subserviently sacrificially love because we are made in His image and He loves to subserviently sacrificially love.

So God created man in his own image, in the image of God he created him; male and female he created them. (Genesis 1:27)

And we were made that way because God is that way and because subservient, sacrificial love is the deepest and greatest and highest and widest and most profound of all existence.

It is, because God is that way; and God is that way, because it is.

Thus, we, like God, seek to subserviently, sacrificially love because God first subserviently and sacrificially loved us.

We love because he first loved us. (1John 4:19)

Do you want proof that He first loved us?

Just look at the cross of Christ.

In the cross of Christ, all three Persons of the Triune Godhead subserviently and, very definitely, sacrificially loved us.

Our deepest heart desire to subserviently and sacrificially love is undeniable and insuppressible.

Copyright 2013 Michael K. Pasque

So we make it our goal to please him, whether we are at home in the body or away from it. (2 Corinthians 5:9)

We fulfill this deepest heart desire by subserviently, sacrificially loving God and we subserviently, sacrificially love God by subserviently, sacrificially loving the individuals that God brings into our life.

In other words, by subserviently, sacrificially loving one another, we subserviently, sacrificially love God—which is our creation purpose and deepest heart desire.

> Loving one another in a subservient, sacrificial manner is therefore precisely the achievement of that which we were created for (to love God), is the only way to fulfill the deepest desire of our heart (to love God), and is thus the single most important thing that we do.

Thus, God created us because the desire to share this loving fellowship of the Trinity is the relentless, undeniable, unstoppable, and therefore inevitable consequence of the glorious explosion of subservient, sacrificial love that is inherent in the nature of God and therefore the foundation of God's eternity.

In other words, God created because He could do nothing less (and nothing more) by His very nature and for the purpose of His glory through loving fellowship.

The purpose of God's creative effort was therefore singular:

> To bring into existence—through the process of creation, salvation, and sanctification—the precise individuals with whom He wanted to spend eternity in loving fellowship.

God did not want to spend eternity with just anyone.

Copyright 2013 Michael K. Pasque

Instead He brought about the creation exclusively for the purpose of creating, identifying, calling, sanctifying, and eternally glorifying the precise and very unique individuals who would be the exact sons and daughters of God—the princes and princesses of His eternal kingdom—who will be (upon the completion of His work) endowed with *the* perfect natures, personalities, wills, emotions, spiritual makeup, and bodies for an eternity of loving fellowship with the three Persons of the Trinity—and with each other.

This purpose is precisely why we were created the way we are and why we go through what we go through.

> *"Come, let us return to the* LORD. *He has torn us to pieces but he will heal us; he has injured us but he will bind up our wounds. After two days he will revive us; on the third day he will restore us,* **that we may live in his presence.** *(Hosea 6:1-2; emphasis added)*

We—all who are saved by the perfect sacrificial atonement provided by the cross of Jesus Christ and perfected by the grace that is the product and power of His death and resurrection—are perfect (only by the work that Jesus has already completed) eternal children of God.

> *How great is the love the Father has lavished on us, that we should be called children of God! And that is what we are! The reason the world does not know us is that it did not know him.*
>
> *Dear friends, now we are children of God, and what we will be has not yet been made known. But we know that when he appears, we shall be like him, for we shall see him as he is. (1John 3:1-2)*

Copyright 2013 Michael K. Pasque

We are the perfect eternal children of God and by the perfect plan of God we will be a critical—and perfect—part of His eternity.

Copyright 2013 Michael K. Pasque

Day 4

What Is The Primal Desire Of Man's Heart?
Man's Deepest "Deep-Heart Desire"

Accordingly, there is a primal desire deep in the heart of every created human being.

As we have discussed, our Creator placed this primal desire there in the heart of every man and every woman.

As the *primal* desire of our hearts, this desire is the root of (it causes, it is the source of, it is behind) all other desires.

In its unadulterated form, this primal desire is *of God*, having been created by God to His glory and our eternity.

In its undefiled form, this desire is pure light, pure good, pure righteousness.

In its pure form, this primal desire is the image of God in which we were created.

This primal desire is not *for love*.

It is most certainly not *to be loved*.

It is not even *to be loved by God*.

For indeed *to be loved* is not God's primary desire—He does not desire or *seek* love...and it is not our primary desire either (for, once again, we are made in His image).

Instead, each individual Person of the Triune Godhead has spent eternity glorifying and loving the other two—not trying to *be glorified by* or trying *to be loved by* the other two.

Copyright 2013 Michael K. Pasque

Since each Person of the Triune Godhead has spent eternity seeking to love His Partners in an unconditional, subservient, sacrificial fashion, so also—by our God-created nature—do we.

We have no choice in this matter.

It is what is written on our hearts.

Thus our primal desire mirrors God's primal desire.

We are indeed made in His image.

God's primal desire is to love—God *is* love.

Man's primal desire is also to love.

More specifically, just as by their very nature, each Person of the Trinity desires to love the other members of the Trinity, so also do we seek to love the Persons of the Trinity.

What a man desires is unfailing love; (Proverbs 19:22a)

Unfailing love is what we desire and unfailing love is found only in loving God unfailingly.

The *primal* desire of every man and every woman is therefore *to love God*.

Copyright 2013 Michael K. Pasque

Day 5

How Do We Satisfy The Primal Desire Of Our Heart?
Loving God

We fulfill our primal desire, then, by loving God.

How do we love God?

Although it may not seem logical at first, God has told us precisely how to love Him: we love God by *serving* God.

> But if serving the LORD seems undesirable to you, then choose for
> yourselves this day whom you will serve, whether the gods your
> forefathers served beyond the River, or the gods of the Amorites, in
> whose land you are living. But as for me and my household, we will
> serve the LORD." *(Joshua 24:15)*

If this is true, then the words *love* and *serve* must be interchangeable.

If this is true, then we will spend eternity loving God by *serving* Him.

Many react poorly to the suggestion that it will be a *good* thing to spend eternity *serving* God.

This reaction is based in a lack of understanding.

To truly love someone is to love them unconditionally.

There is only one kind of real love and that is unconditional love.

The eternal love that literally explodes forth from the fellowship of the Triune Godhead—to which we have been invited by the fellowship of the cross of Jesus

Copyright 2013 Michael K. Pasque

Christ—is, has always been, and always will be 100% perfectly unconditional love.

To love unconditionally, by definition, is to *serve* unconditionally.

This is true because *serving* someone means that you place their needs and desires above your own—and *that* is the *definition* of unconditional love: to subserviently and sacrificially put the needs and desires of the object of your unconditional love above your own—at any cost (in other words, there are *no* conditions).

Any who have ever loved unconditionally know that when captivated by the throes of unconditional love, we become less important in our own eyes than the object of our unconditional love.

To illustrate the concept of true unconditional love being manifest by obedience and servanthood, we only need to think of the last time we *fell madly in love with* someone.

By falling in love, I mean head-over-heels, can't-get-them-off-our-minds, infatuated love!

Every desire of the heart of the object of our unconditional love indeed becomes *our* heart's desire.

We would do anything for them.

Anything = unconditional.

When in the midst of unconditional love, our only travail becomes the actual identification of the desires of our beloved's heart—desires that we *long* to fulfill.

Our hearts long to *serve* them by meeting these desires of their heart.

Our needs and desires become less important in our eyes than their needs and desires.

Thus, the very definition of unconditional love mirrors that of truly *serving* someone.

Copyright 2013 Michael K. Pasque

We really should have already drawn this conclusion since the only true and perfect example of unconditional love that we have ever even heard of involves the Trinity.

We know that the three Persons of the Triune Godhead have spent eternity loving each other by the continual and perfect subservient, sacrificial love—of which only God is capable.

So, if we desire to mimic them, then we love God by putting Him first, by making His will more important than ours, by acknowledging His importance as greater than our own, and by seeking to fulfill the desires of His heart.

In other words we place God's desires above ours and seek to obey and serve Him.

Thus, by clearly making His desires known to us by His very clear and concise commands, God has perfectly defined for us the pathway to loving Him.

Obeying His commands is serving God and that is, by definition, loving God—choosing to do His will in our life rather than our own.

We love God when we serve Him.

We serve God, we love God, when we acknowledge His expression in the Bible of His heart's desire for our behavior—and obey Him.

This is precisely why Jesus makes the statement that to love Him is to obey His command.

If you obey my commands, you will remain in my love, just as I have obeyed my Father's commands and remain in his love. I have told you this so that my joy may be in you and that your joy may be complete. My command is this: Love each other as I have loved you. (John 15:10-12)

Copyright 2013 Michael K. Pasque

Why is this important?

If we truly love someone, we will seek their will over ours.

If we truly love someone, we will seek to serve them.

It naturally and logically follows that if we truly love someone, we will *obey* their commands because their commands are a verbal statement of their will.

With the gospel of grace appropriately filling our sermons every Sunday, we become casual with obedience to God.

We relegate obedience to secondary status.

But obedience to God is not a secondary issue.

Obedience to God is the whole show, *but not for the sake of obedience*.

In other words, we should obey God as a result of our true love for God and not in an attempt to get what we want from God or out of fear of God.

Obedience is the whole show because *subservience* is what makes love unconditional.

If we are not obedient, we are not subservient.

If we are not subservient, then our love has conditions.

Thus, if we are not subservient, we do not unconditionally love God.

In other words, if we do not have a subservient heart, God's desires become our desires only when they fit our conditions.

If we pick and choose when to obey God's commands, then we have placed conditions upon our love for Him.

If *we* regard our obedience to the will of God as being dependent upon the conditions in our life surrounding that decision—instead of obeying continually and always and, thus, unconditionally—then we are making the will of God in our life subservient to our own will.

Copyright 2013 Michael K. Pasque

Bottom line: if we are not obeying God we are not loving Him.

And now we are back to the cross of Jesus Christ—where every discussion must end—because we have been shown this subservient, sacrificial love already.

In fact, we desire to love God and are enabled to love God because God first loved us.

We love because he first loved us. (1John 4:19)

God first loved us by subserviently, sacrificially serving *us*.

This subservient, sacrificial love was manifest in our redemption by the death and resurrection of Jesus, God's only Son.

There can be no question about this.

In the cataclysmic momentary disruption of the loving eternal fellowship of the Trinity that occurred in the timeless moment of the death of Christ on the cross of Calvary, all three Persons of the Triune Godhead suffered immeasurably and sacrificed infinitely in this act of the redemption of the sons and daughters of God.

Thus, we mimic God's love by loving Him—and we do this by seeking to subserviently, sacrificially obey and serve Him.

So, precisely how do we subserviently, sacrificially obey and serve God?

The answer is delightful in its simplicity (and its complexity).

It is simple because there really is only one way.

Jesus told us precisely how to do it, as recorded in multiple places in the Bible.

He had *only* one command.

By His use of the singular (non-plural) word *"command"* in John 15:10-12 (see above), Jesus clearly focuses our priorities by telling us that there really is

Copyright 2013 Michael K. Pasque

only one command to obey and by that alone to love God: We are to *"Love each other."*

This is why *"Love your neighbor as yourself"* is tagged on to the most important command to *"love the Lord your God with all your heart and with all your soul and with all your mind."*

> *Jesus replied: " 'Love the Lord your God with all your heart and with all your soul and with all your mind.' This is the first and greatest commandment. And the second is like it: 'Love your neighbor as yourself.' All the Law and the Prophets hang on these two commandments." (Matthew 22:37-40)*

You cannot do the latter without doing the former.

We subserviently, sacrificially serve Jesus by obeying His command.

We love the Lord our God when we love one another.

Thus, Jesus has told us how to love Him because He has told us how to serve Him because He has told us His will when He gave us His singular command to *"Love each other."*

Thus, to fulfill our eternal deepest heart desire to love God, we are to serve and obey Him by following His command to *"Love each other."*

And how do we love one another—by subserviently, sacrificially serving one another.

Precisely *who* falls into the category of "each other" or "one another"?

The familiar parable of the *good Samarian* tells us that we are to love any and all persons—without exclusion—whom God brings into our life.

This is the bottom-line:

Copyright 2013 Michael K. Pasque

To fulfill our creation purpose and attain our deepest heart desire, we are to subserviently, sacrificially love God by subserviently, sacrificially loving every person—without exclusion—whom God brings into our life.

Let's expand this statement to a series of summation statements:

1) The three Persons of the Triune Godhead subserviently, sacrificially love one another.

2) As a natural outpouring of their inherent nature, the Persons of the Divine Trinity invited us to subserviently, sacrificially love them by first subserviently, sacrificially loving us in the ultimate redemptive act of subservient, sacrificial love: the incarnation, death, and resurrection of Jesus Christ.

3) In this act, all three Persons of the Triune Godhead subserviently, sacrificially loved us to an infinite degree—thereby defining *our worth to them* as nothing less than infinite.

4) We demonstrate our acceptance of this offer to join this fellowship of the eternal kingdom of God by loving God.

5) God showed us how to love Him.

6) We are to mimic God's ultimate act of subservient, sacrificial love by subserviently, sacrificially loving Him by subserviently, sacrificially serving Him.

7) Jesus told us how to subserviently, sacrificially *serve* God since His commands are the expression of His will and we serve by seeking, surrendering to, and doing God's will.

8) God's will, as expressed by His direct (embodied in the words of Jesus) command, is that we *"Love each other."*

9) We mimic God's ultimate demonstration of subservient, sacrificial love when we subserviently sacrificially love Him by subserviently, sacrificially loving every single person that God brings into our life.

Copyright 2013 Michael K. Pasque

10) In loving the people that God brings into our life, we do what the three Persons of the Trinity have been doing for eternity and what they did for us in the incarnation, death, and resurrection of Jesus Christ.

11) God already did for us precisely that which is our deep heart desire to do for Him.

12) In loving the people that God brings into our life, we do nothing less than that which we will be doing for eternity with the three Persons of the Triune Godhead as princes and princesses of the eternal kingdom of God.

Thus we answer those who complain that God is self-serving because He repeatedly tells us to obey God, to serve God, and to love God.

Nothing could be further from the truth.

In fact, that line of thought is precisely 180 degrees in the opposite direction of the truth.

God has not asked anything of us that He, as described in detail above, has not already done for us—and that *to an infinite degree!*

God asks us to serve and obey and love Him because in reality those three words are essentially three separate descriptors of exactly the same thing—and that thing characterizes the relationship that the three Persons of the Triune Godhead have had with each other for eternity.

In asking us to serve Him, God is extending an invitation to us to join Him in fellowship forever.

In asking us to serve Him, God is extending an invitation for us to do precisely what the three Persons of the Trinity have been doing for eternity.

He is, in fact, extending an invitation for us to do precisely what our heart desires the most.

In other words, in asking us to serve Him, He is offering us the opportunity to get precisely what we most want.

Copyright 2013 Michael K. Pasque

That doesn't sound self-serving to me.

In fact, God has gone to extreme measures at extreme personal cost to assure that we get exactly what we most want!

Gloriously—and by the grace of Christ alone—we have been asked to fulfill that for which we were created and attain that which is our deepest heart desire by joining into this glorious eternal love relationship—and all of this by simply obeying God's request that we subserviently, sacrificially love one another.

God is complete in every way.

We cannot add to Him in any way.

He does not need us or our servitude or our obedience or even our love to *complete* Him—God is complete in every respect.

The glorious love shared for eternity by the three Persons of the Trinity is complete—without us—in every respect.

Instead, God asks us to serve, obey, and love Him because, amazingly, He created us in His image and He knows precisely that for which we were created— the craving, desire, and need of our deepest heart—and that is to join into this fellowship of subservient, sacrificial love.

Our love of God—the purpose for which we were created and in which we will find utter and eternal and infinite and complete joy—is complete only when the needs and desires of the object of that love are placed above our own.

Obey, serve, and love—all are words describing that which is the currency of the timeless and eternal relationship of the fellowship of the Trinity.

And we have been asked to learn precisely those relational skills and to become magnificent members of that eternal Fellowship.

And that is what our life is all about—learning the relational skills that really matter, that are eternal, that will be used in the kingdom of God, and that help us attain a perspective that mirrors God's perspective.

Copyright 2013 Michael K. Pasque

Those very people that are brought into our life every single day are brought there for *this* purpose—to teach us obedience, servitude, and love and to develop in us the same eternal perspective with which God views our eternal relational interactions.

And this is the heavenly reward that seems to be spoken of so often—that which we learn in this life by assuming a *sacrificially subservient posture of unconditional love*, goes with us into eternity and is that which multiplies the joy of heaven that is available to the children of God.

And not one bit of any of this is doable or obtainable except by the grace—the direct intervention—of God in our life as manifest by the strength and power of the cross of Christ and His resurrection.

It always goes back to Jesus.

In this most important act of the attainment of our deepest heart desire, to love God, we are eternally and entirely dependent upon Jesus Christ, our eternal mediator.

All love—all love—in its purest unconditional, subservient, sacrificial form is embodied in and exists in the Person of Jesus Christ.

We have no chance of truly, unconditionally, subserviently, and sacrificially loving one another (and thereby loving God) without the presence of Jesus Christ in our hearts.

No chance.

No Jesus = no unconditional, subserviently sacrificial love.

Without the grace that exploded through the creation in the moment of the death and resurrection of Jesus Christ and that now permeates every created atom and every created moment of time, we are utterly and hopelessly lost because we cannot attain that for which we were created—eternal fellowship with the three

Copyright 2013 Michael K. Pasque

Persons of the Triune Godhead and with each other—or our deepest heart desire to subserviently, sacrificially love God and each other.

Copyright 2013 Michael K. Pasque

Day 6

From Where Does The Power To Satisfy Our Primal Deep-Heart's Desire Come?
The Gap Between Created And Uncreated

As we have discussed, the fulfillment of our deep heart's one true desire mandates that we, the created, spend eternity in loving fellowship with God, the Uncreated.

The gap between the created (mankind) and the Uncreated (God) is unfortunately very literally infinite in its length, width, and depth.

This is because of the infinite nature of God.

All of God's attributes are by definition infinite in nature.

God is infinitely wise, infinitely powerful, infinitely capable, and infinite in His compassion, mercy, and love—to name just a few of His known attributes.

All of our attributes, as created beings, are by definition finite in nature.

Since we are infinite in precisely nothing, the gap between God (Who is infinite in precisely everything) and us is, therefore, very literally *infinite*.

As we have discussed, this is unfortunate because achieving our creation purpose and sating our primal deep heart desire require that we spend eternity in subservient and sacrificial loving fellowship with God.

That eternal destiny for which we were created and thus the deepest desire of our heart—the knowledge and presence of God that can only be found in eternal loving fellowship—is thus separated from us by the infinite gap that differentiates created from Uncreated.

Copyright 2013 Michael K. Pasque

We, *the created*, cannot by wisdom, knowledge, strength, power, authority, cunning, or guile even come close—by our own effort—to spanning this infinite gap between God and us.

The created cannot become Uncreated.

The created cannot even approach the Uncreated.

Only the Greater can span the gap between the Greater and the lesser.

Thus, God *alone* can be (and is in the Person of Jesus Christ) the only link, connection, bridge, or mediator that spans the infinite gap between the created and the Uncreated (and thus between us and the achievement of our creation purpose and the attainment of our deepest heart desire).

Only Jesus can span this gap because only He is both fully God (Uncreated) and simultaneously fully man (created).

Only Jesus is both inherently Greater and voluntarily lesser.

The very purpose of our creation and our deepest heart desire—to spend eternity as children of God in fellowship with God, knowing and loving and serving and glorifying Him—are thus obtainable only and exclusively through Jesus Christ.

By our nature and by the very nature of God, we are—through Jesus Christ alone—to God's glory.

Motivated by our deep heart desire to subserviently, sacrificially love God, we cannot help but pursue our God-ordained creation purpose to join each other in the loving fellowship of the three Persons of the Triune Godhead in the eternal kingdom of God.

By our very nature (God-ordained), we try to do this by trying hard to obey God and therefore in our minds justify ourselves before God.

We work hard to make ourselves worthy of our creation purpose as if our efforts could justify us by making up for our sinful rebellion.

Copyright 2013 Michael K. Pasque

The gospel of Jesus Christ tells us that all of the work of our justification—the *complete* elimination of the sin of our rebellion—has already been done by Jesus upon the cross of Calvary and that no further work on our part can add *in any way* to what Jesus has already done.

Thus, the achievement for us of our creation purpose and the attainment of our deepest heart desire have already been assured and guaranteed by the work of Jesus Christ on our behalf.

When we realize, therefore, that we are already glorified, already a child of God, already a son or daughter of God, and already a prince or princess of the eternal kingdom of God, then we cannot help but be filled with pure joy because of this hope that we have for our eternity of loving fellowship.

This whole messy life of ours is guaranteed to end well for us!

We get an eternity of joyous, rambunctious, exciting, enthralling, adventurous, passionate, captivating, fulfilling, compassionate, loving, and glorified life, while utterly avoiding a dark, cold eternity of hopeless denial of our creation purpose and deep heart desire as a palpable, sentient, feeling human being in hell.

The price paid for us—a cataclysmic momentary separation of Jesus from the eternal loving fellowship of the Trinity in which He had spent eternity with its associated infinite pain, infinite grief, infinite wrath—thereby defines our *worth* to God as *infinite*.

The price paid for us defines the depth of the subservient, sacrificial love of God for each of us as infinite.

Knowledge of this cannot help but fill our heart with joy.

Knowledge of this cannot help but assure us for the rest of our life that God's heart for us is *always* good because of the infinite love that He has for us.

Copyright 2013 Michael K. Pasque

The LORD will keep you from all harm—he will watch over your life;
(Psalm 121:7)

And we can therefore know that all of the God-ordained circumstances of our life are thereby declared *good*—no matter what they look like to us.

From God's eternal perspective, they are good.

And in this knowledge, which we build over our lifetime, is found the motivation for us to make Godly choices in our life—not because we must in order to achieve what has already been given us, but instead out of the thankfulness and love of a grateful and thankful child of God.

We obey because we place God's priorities above ours in sacrificial service—and by that obedience we love God.

No longer is our choice motivated out of our misguided effort toward self-righteousness, but rather out of the humble subservience of a grateful heart.

Then we realize that God's law was not put there to make our life miserable, but rather to reveal God's deep heart desire for the way that He wants us to live.

It is much easier to make Godly choices at each of the decision-points that God has orchestrated into our lives when we acknowledge both 1) His sovereign control of our life and 2) His loving heart for us—and thus that the circumstances that we find ourselves in *were sent by God for our eternal good.*

And we find the strength to get through these circumstances at the foot of the cross of Christ where we find His grace and power that emanate from there being manifest in our life as He stands back-to-back with us in every situation.

When we *get* this, we no longer strive to be good in misguided self-righteousness, but rather as the natural consequences of a heart that is thankful for all that has already been done for us.

Copyright 2013 Michael K. Pasque

Day 7

For What Part Of My Salvation Am I Really Responsible?
Defining "Hopeless"

So, do you still believe that you had anything to do with your salvation?

Well, you did.

Kind of.

But not really.

If you have any questions in this regard, the second chapter of Ephesians, among many similar Bible chapters, is definitive in this regard.

It repeatedly tells us that prior to our rescue, we were just like all the other people who we now look down upon (in our arrogance) as *unsaved unbelievers*.

We were utterly lost.

> As for you, you were **dead** in your transgressions and sins, in which you used to live when you followed the ways of this world and of the ruler of the kingdom of the air, the spirit who is now at work in those who are disobedient. *(Ephesians 2:1-2; emphasis added)*

Do you understand the expanse of knowledge found in the meaning of the word *"dead,"* above?

It means *dead*—deader than a doornail.

Copyright 2013 Michael K. Pasque

That doesn't *just* mean that we had no future in the kingdom of God—which it clearly does mean, for we truly had no future as heirs to the kingdom.

It also means that we were utterly helpless in regard to our lost state.

It means that we had no hope.

It means that, just like all *"dead"* people, we could not move, could not think, could not will ourselves out of our predicament—we were *"dead."*

The use of the word *"dead"* means far more than a cursory reading of this chapter might lead us to believe.

It conveys in both its literal and figurative senses the purest form of utter hopelessness.

> … *remember that at that time you were separate from Christ, excluded from citizenship in Israel and foreigners to the covenants of the promise,* **without hope** *and without God in the world. (Ephesians 2:12; emphasis added)*

"Without hope" means exactly what it says.

"Without hope" means that we could not save ourselves.

"Without hope" means that despite the fact that the door was open, we could not even find the door by our own hard work, skill, intelligence, wisdom, motivation, desire, or efforts.

"Without hope" means that we had no chance of ever finding our way to God without *outside* help.

This is confirmed in the very next verse in Ephesians 2.

Copyright 2013 Michael K. Pasque

But now in Christ Jesus you who once were far away **have been brought near** *through the blood of Christ. (Ephesians 2:13; emphasis added)*

The phrase *"have been brought"* clearly implies that we did not bring ourselves *"near,"* but instead were *"brought"* by someone else—that being Jesus and the grace that is manifest in the power of His cross.

In other words, it emphasizes, in the most emphatic terms available, our utter inability to affect—in any way—our condition.

It means that if we had mustered all of our intelligence and wisdom and willpower and strength and power, we still had no chance of changing our predicament.

And, most importantly, this was not because Christ had not already opened the gate to heaven—He had.

Surely this magnificent first step was critical.

Without Christ opening to us the door to eternity—to the kingdom of God—all would be lost; there would not even be a door for us to try to find.

But Christ's death and resurrection did so much more than just open the door.

It not only opened the door to those who would believe in His Name, but it also became the focal point of the power needed *to go get those individuals.*

There was nothing passive about the cross of Christ and there was nothing passive about His salvation of the saints who will joyfully populate the eternal kingdom of God.

He did not just open the door and say, *"There it is, its open. I have done my part. Now see if you can find your way in."*

He did so much more.

Copyright 2013 Michael K. Pasque

The second chapter of the book of Ephesians, among many other great chapters in the Bible, tells us that we were so given over to the world's way of thinking that we had no chance of *ever* finding that door that was so spectacularly opened by the work of Jesus.

It could not be any clearer.

We were like all the rest, wandering around in the world, completely given over to its way of thinking and its way of treating others.

> *As for you, you were dead in your transgressions and sins, in which you used to live when you followed the ways of this world and of the ruler of the kingdom of the air, the spirit who is now at work in those who are disobedient. (Ephesians 2:1-2)*

We were utterly lost.

We can know the true depth of that description of our lost state at that time because we are called *"objects of wrath."*

> *All of us also lived among them at one time, gratifying the cravings of our sinful nature and following its desires and thoughts. Like the rest, we were by nature **objects of wrath**. (Ephesians 2:3; emphasis added)*

God does not pour down His wrath on any except the utterly lost.

Not by any effort or any righteousness on our part—because we're incapable (because of the unrighteous condition of our minds and hearts) of generating the wisdom and understanding necessary to find the door to eternity by ourselves— *Jesus comes after us.*

There is nothing passive about this process.

Copyright 2013 Michael K. Pasque

Jesus isn't just sitting around waiting to see if anyone can find the gate; He is running hard after each of us.

He isn't waiting for us to find our way out of the morass of sin and debauchery because He knows that even an eternity would not be enough time for us to find our way out.

He is not waiting around in the comfort of His Father's heavenly throne.

He is hunting us down.

He is down in the dirt, in the middle of a street fight, in the debauchery of our world.

He is here to rescue us.

Jesus is, in His basic nature, a rescuer.

Rescue is the purest form of subservient, sacrificial love because it calls for subservient sacrifice on the behalf of those who would be rescued.

And the cross of Christ was the ultimate in sacrifice.

That which was surrendered by Christ on the cross of Calvary is unfathomable to us.

And from this infinite subservient sacrifice by God comes infinite power from God.

And in that infinite power is found our salvation.

In that infinite power is found not only the opening of the door to the eternal kingdom of God, but also the strength to go out and get the utterly lost children of the kingdom.

There is nothing passive about our rescue.

Jesus did not stop at opening the door.

He came into the world and He came back for those who were lost.

He came back for every single one of us who *believes* in the Name and sacrifice of Jesus Christ.

Copyright 2013 Michael K. Pasque

Thankfully, He did not just wait on His throne for us to find our way to the kingdom.

For just like our inability to open that door in the first place, we could not even find that door on our own.

> And God raised us up with Christ and seated us with him in the heavenly realms in Christ Jesus, in order that in the coming ages he might show the incomparable riches of his grace, expressed in his kindness to us in Christ Jesus. (Ephesians 2:6-7)

So, truth be told, we have nothing to do with our salvation.
Nothing.
It was pure Grace that came down, became one of us, kicked that door open, and drug us—kicking and screaming—through that open door.

> For it is by grace you have been saved, through faith—and this not from yourselves, it is the gift of God—not by works, so that no one can boast. (Ephesians 2:8-9)

God is clear in the Bible in regard to the source of the faith that saves us.
Most Christians believe that the *"faith"* part is *our* part.
They believe that we come up with that saving faith on our own.
I like that.
I like that because it seems to make it all about me.
And I like it being all about me.
There is only one problem with that theology, however.
It has nothing to do with the written Word of God.

Copyright 2013 Michael K. Pasque

The statement above, *"and this not from yourselves, it is the gift of God"* clearly refers to that which immediately precedes it: *"faith."*

Our faith is a gift from God.

A gift is not *earned* or it would not be a gift, it would be wages.

> *Now when a man works, his wages are not credited to him as a gift, but as an obligation. (Romans 4:4)*

We earn nothing by our efforts, not even our faith.

Our salvation—both the opening of the door to eternal life and the strength to find and walk through that door—is completely the gift of God in the work of Jesus Christ.

If you are not convinced by my interpretation of the first part of this blessed passage from Ephesians, you only have to read a little bit further.

In the words of this passage, we are told that our salvation was not attained by our thoughts or efforts (our *"works"*)—and then puts the final nail in the coffin by telling us that therefore, *"no one can boast."*

Boasting always occurs in regard to accomplishments.

If there is no boasting on our part, then there must be no accomplishments on our part.

Case closed.

We are then told in 1st Corinthians that indeed there is boasting to be done, but only boasting in regard to He who actually performed the work for that which has been achieved.

All credit and therefore all glory—and therefore all boasting—is in Christ alone.

Copyright 2013 Michael K. Pasque

But God chose the foolish things of the world to shame the wise; God chose the weak things of the world to shame the strong. He chose the lowly things of this world and the despised things—and the things that are not—to nullify the things that are, so that no one may boast before him. It is because of him that you are in Christ Jesus, who has become for us wisdom from God—that is, our righteousness, holiness and redemption. Therefore, as it is written: "Let him who boasts boast in the Lord." (1Corinthians 1:27-31)

Sorry, but we have nothing to do with our salvation.

Nonetheless, if *you* have *not* accepted Christ and claimed the title of an eternal child of the eternal kingdom of God, you can do that right now.

This is the wonderful conundrum of the gospel of Jesus Christ.

It is 100% by the grace of God that we are saved, and yet if you want to be saved, you can do that right now.

All you have to *do* is accept the free gift of the salvation offered in belief in the Name and shed blood of Jesus Christ.

And when you do this and take that spectacular step into eternity, it will seem as if *you* will have done something to effect your eternal salvation.

And I applaud your efforts in this regard.

But, both you and I will still know that your effort was only achievable in the power of the cross of Christ.

Your effort in belief was only achievable because Jesus not only opened the door that you acknowledged as being open in your statement of faith, but also because He came back and drug you through that door.

Copyright 2013 Michael K. Pasque

And in the moment that you acknowledge this, you will say, "Ah, yes, for sure" as you remember the utter hopelessness of the condition of your mind and heart in achieving salvation before He came and got you.

And you will never again hold your salvation over those who are not saved as if you have done something and therefore deserve credit for something that you did not do.

You will never look down your nose at them again.

You will never boast in your decision for your salvation, you will boast in the cross of Christ.

And you will know the true meaning of the phrase, "There, but for the grace of God, go I."

And you, instead of comfortably sitting on your throne that you think you earned by your belief, will accept the invitation of Jesus to join the rescue effort.

You will accept the invitation to be like Jesus in your stepping down off of your throne and walking down in the dirt of the world as a member of the rescue team.

You will accept the invitation to become a member of the rescue team that acknowledges that even *your* strength in these rescue efforts is found solely in the power of the cross of Christ.

Jesus is a rescuer.

We are being made into the likeness of Jesus Christ in our salvation and sanctification.

In the ultimate act of rescue, He subserviently and sacrificially gave up everything to open the unopenable door and to pull us through it.

And in our efforts to assist in the rescue of others, we have only praise.

Nothing more—only praise.

Copyright 2013 Michael K. Pasque

Day 8

Why All This Emphasis On "Obeying" God?
What "Obeying" Really Means

The Bible, both Old Testament and New has a central theme that is expressed in one way or another on almost every page: *Obey God*.

We humans seem to be inherently endowed with a natural loathing toward being told to obey someone.

We just naturally do not like to be told to *do* anything.

We surely do not like it when it comes in the form of a command.

This aversion to being told to do something defines that naturally rebellious attitude with which every man and women is endowed by their Creator.

This emotion forms the core of our sinful nature.

In fact, this rebellious nature almost defines *being human*.

God's infinitely wise decision to give us a rebellious nature was somehow critical in defining our potential to become an eternal heir to the kingdom of God and forms the crux of our eternal dilemma—for it is this rebellious nature that stands in the way of precisely that.

It is very important that we understand the nature of God's request that we obey Him.

God is asking for obedience of our heart.

As we have reviewed, obedience has to do with serving.

Serving has to do with placing the needs, desires, wishes, and commands of the object of our service above our own.

Copyright 2013 Michael K. Pasque

When this is done out of affection (and specifically not out of oppression), then this is the foundation of love.

True unconditional love is found only in the emptying of our heart of all of our own desires such that the object of our love becomes the center of our existence and that person's (in this case, God's) needs, desires, wishes, and commands become the focus of our consciousness.

In other words, we become their servant, always seeking to fulfill the desires of *their* heart, not ours.

Only at that point can our love be offered without conditions.

Unconditional love is, therefore, serving.

And thus we find the definition of unconditional love—as defined in its perfection in the cross of the Son of God, Jesus Christ—as being subservient, sacrificial love.

It is in this light that the command to obey God is seen from the appropriate perspective.

In asking us to obey Him, God is really asking us to love Him.

Since subserviently, sacrificially loving God is our deepest heart desire (just like His also is to subserviently, sacrificially love—for we are made in His image), in asking us to obey Him, God is inviting us to fulfill nothing less than our deepest heart desire.

> It is perhaps the finest demonstration of the mastery of God's eternal plan for His creation that in seeking to meet the deep heart desire of God by seeking to meet the desires of the individuals God places in our life, we also meet our own deepest heart desire.

This requested love of God, this obedience of God—for they are one and the same when the love is subserviently sacrificial—is not that of the oppressed.

Copyright 2013 Michael K. Pasque

We do not love God by obeying Him because He is standing over us in a threatening stance waving a stick as if to smite us.

That is not the love or the obedience for which God is looking.

That is not the love that God wishes to share with us for eternity.

In fact, God's request for us to obey comes from the deepest core of his love *for us*.

As we have discussed, the love that the three Persons of the Trinity have shared for eternity is subservient, sacrificial love and is given voluntarily and by free choice.

That is the very love that God—in all three Persons—has already shown us in the sacrifice of Jesus Christ on the cross of Calvary.

And it is in recognition of the fact that God has already loved us that we now love Him.

We love because he first loved us. (1John 4:19)

God doesn't want our love in any context other than that one.

In other words, we do not love and obey God out of oppressive fear.

We love and obey God because we experience the magnitude of His love for us in acknowledging that which was given up by God and that which has been obtained for us by the voluntary, purely loving, subserviently sacrificial acts of the crucifixion, death, and resurrection of Jesus Christ.

And thus the Bible admonishes us to love God because He first loved us.

We make ourselves sacrificially subservient in the obedience of God because He first made Himself sacrificially subservient to us in the ultimate act of love on the cross.

We obey God not out of fear, but out of love.

Copyright 2013 Michael K. Pasque

That is the obedience that God seeks.

God has given us a free will—we are not asked to obey God forcibly in oppression.

We can do whatever we want.

Thus God's focus for this life is to give us literally thousands upon thousands of opportunities to love Him by subserviently, sacrificially obeying Him.

And in every case, we have the free will choice to do whatever we want.

We can love or not love.

We can sacrifice or not sacrifice.

We can obey or not obey.

We can put God's desires above our own or put ours above His—it is all our free choice.

And thus in every case—at every decision-point that God orchestrates in our daily life—it is not the forced obedience of the oppressed that God seeks.

He seeks obedience that comes from the volitional subservience that comes from the voluntarily surrendered heart of the individual who has been told of the cross of Christ and has recognized that it obtains for them the eternal life they cannot obtain on their own.

And in the subservient sacrificial love that results is found the currency of eternity.

God seeks the surrendered heart that has realized that its eternal purpose is to love Him as His royal heir—a prince or princess—of the eternal kingdom of God and that this eternal purpose could not be obtained on its own, but only by the free gift of righteousness that is found only in the blood voluntarily, subserviently, and sacrificially shed by Jesus on the cross of Calvary.

God seeks the obedience of the heart surrendered out of love.

And this has nothing to do with forced oppression.

Copyright 2013 Michael K. Pasque

For in our recognition of the infinite extent of what was given up, what is prevented, and what is made available by the grace extended in the sacrifice of Jesus on the cross of Calvary, the last thing on our mind is forced oppression.

We give because He gave.

We serve because He served.

We sacrifice because He sacrificed.

We obey because He obeyed.

And we love because He first loved us.

And we do all of this not because we have to, but because we want to.

Not because we are being forced to, but because it is the deepest desire of our hearts.

Thus, God commands us to love Him because He loves us.

He knows our heart.

He knows what our heart desires.

He knows what is best for our hearts.

By commanding us to love Him, God is telling us that we were made in His image, with a heart whose deepest desire it to subserviently sacrificially love God.

What does subserviently, sacrificially loving God look like?

It looks like seeking to know God's mind and His deep heart desires—which we then make our own.

When God's deep heart desires are substituted for our own and become our focus, then obedience is automatic—not only does it come easily and naturally, we run hard after it!

Thus God knows that our eternal creation purpose and our deepest heart desire are both fulfilled when we obey Him—and that is the *only* reason He asks us to obey.

Copyright 2013 Michael K. Pasque

Every activity of God toward us has our eternal good as its only motivation.

*As for the saints who are in the land, they are **the glorious ones in whom is all my delight**. (Psalm 16:3; emphasis added)*

In God's command to obey Him we see no deviation from that path.

God is just telling us what we—deep in our hearts (and recognized or not)—desperately desire.

And all of this finds its foundation, once again, in the cross of Christ.

New Testament or Old, the truth is the same.

In the Old Testament, God's command was still the same, despite the fact that the literal crucifixion had not yet occurred.

Once again, God was not asking for the mandatory forced submission and obedience of the oppressed.

He asked for their voluntary subservient obedience based not upon fear, but upon that which He had already done for them.

Admittedly, one could perceive God's later Old Testament warnings as threats, but they weren't—they were loving warnings in which God told the Israelites that things simply could not go well for them when they continued to oppose the Creator God of the Universe.

More importantly, in all cases, God refers back to that which He had already done for the Israelites.

That is why the Exodus is so critical in the history of Israel.

It is not just for its very literal analogous reflection of the sacrifice of Christ on the cross, but also because in the Exodus, God acted powerfully to free the oppressed from their oppressors.

God freed the Israelites.

Copyright 2013 Michael K. Pasque

Not only that, but God blessed and prospered the Israelites in every imaginable way.

And He simply asked them—as documented repeatedly, in nearly every circumstance—to simply *remember* what He had done.

For in remembering that which had been lovingly and powerfully done for them, their hearts would seek to serve their loving Savior not in a forced, legalistic manner, but as a loving response to the love that He had already shown them.

Sound familiar?

Throughout the Old Testament history of the Israelites, God repeatedly reminded the Israelites to *remember*—especially when their train was off the tracks—and He then repeatedly saved them from their oppressors.

He did it repeatedly right before their very eyes—and all He asked was that they remember.

> *He asked that they remember because He knew that then they would obey out of love, not out of fear.*

He had repeatedly miraculously saved them from their enemies right in front of their eyes—the response to which can only be love.

And Jesus became more subservient than anyone of us ever could, sacrificed more than any of us could sacrifice, and bought for us that which we could not buy—eternal life as a child of God—the response to all of which *can only be love.*

And in those love responses, our personal desires become secondary to the desires of the One that we love and sacrificially, subserviently obey.

And that is why the Israelites had to be reminded by God's repeated saving intervention.

Copyright 2013 Michael K. Pasque

After all, it was God who sent their oppressive neighbors against the Israelites in the first place—God was trying to convince them that He could be trusted and therefore should be the first they call upon in any difficult situation.

Sound familiar?

This is also why *we* must be repeatedly taken back by God's intervention in our life—as always—*to the cross of Christ*.

God asks us—just like He repeatedly asked the Israelites—to simply remember.

This act of *remembering* is what communion—the bread and the wine—is all about.

In communion, we remember the magnitude of that which has been done for us.

God asks us to remove our focus from what we *can do* for Him to gain His favor and instead remember what He has *already done* for us.

He asks us to, instead, place our focus upon—and to simply remember—that which has already been done for us by Jesus on the cross of Calvary.

When we are there at the foot of the cross, it is easy to obey, sacrifice, and serve—and thereby to love—God.

Not from the fear of the oppressed, but from the grateful heart of the gracefully blessed.

Just remember.

Copyright 2013 Michael K. Pasque

Day 9

What Is Satan's Plan Of Attack?
Our "Worthiness" To Love God

We have defined our *primal* deepest deep heart desire.

In the deepest recesses of our heart, an unquenchable (in this world) desire wells uncontrollably to the surface: *We desire to subserviently, sacrificially love God as He has subserviently, sacrificially loved us.*

This desire is the one behind all of the other good desires that we have, as well as the other not-so-good desires that we, in our sinful nature, come up with.

So, why is this discussion important?

It sounds theological without day-by-day practical implications.

It is theological, but it is anything but impractical.

Why?

Because, we have an enemy.

Satan desires to thwart our attainment of our primal desire (and, therefore, the realization of our creation purpose).

We, nonetheless, must remember that we—and our primal desire—are really not Satan's *primary* targets.

He couldn't care less about us except as he can use us to strike at his primary target.

Satan's whole existence is consumed with his desire to strike at the very heart of God.

Copyright 2013 Michael K. Pasque

But Satan is a cleaver foe—He strikes at the tender heart of God in its only "weakness"—God's consuming love for us!

Satan's primary goal therefore is to take advantage of God's intense love for us in order to try to hurt God.

He does this by targeting the derailment of our attainment of our purpose, destiny, and heart's desire.

This strike at us is, therefore, a strike at God.

But Satan is craftier still.

Our enemy, Satan, does not strike directly at this desire of ours—this strength of our heart—for that desire is God-ordained as the deepest heart desire of every man and every woman.

As such, God protects that deep heart desire in the hearts of His believers.

Even though this desire can be covered over, it can never be extinguished—it is eternal in every one of us—believers and non-believers, alike.

It is precisely in this fact that we see heaven and hell defined.

For those who are found in Jesus, this desire will be continually and infinitely sated for all eternity—this being precisely what makes heaven, heaven.

The fulfillment of this desire is that which we call joy.

And similarly, for those who deny Jesus, this desire will be continually and infinitely and hopelessly frustrated for all eternity—this being precisely what makes hell, hell.

The frustration of this desire is that which is called the burning fire of hell.

It is in the fact that this deep heart desire is—by God's ordination—the strength of our heart that we are encouraged.

Unfortunately, Satan knows of this God-given strength of ours.

Satan is smart enough to know that he has no strength there against this God-ordained deepest desire of our heart.

Copyright 2013 Michael K. Pasque

So, just as any great strategist would devise, Satan's plan avoids our strength and instead strikes right at our weakness...and that, with all of *his* strength.

His strength is deception.

Rather than striking at the heart of the issue, Satan instead tries a flanking maneuver.

Surely Satan's deep heart desire is to make sure that we never realize ours.

And the way that he attempts to achieve his goal is not to directly attack our desire to love God, but instead, our worthiness to love God.

Thus, his deception questions not our impenetrable, unchangeable desire or ability to love God, but rather our *worthiness* to love God.

It is in this curve ball that Satan reveals that he knows something very important about our human nature.

He knows that *to love God*, we need to feel that what we have to offer is of value; that it actually *matters* to God that we in fact love Him.

And precisely here in the determination of the worthiness of our love for God is where—because of Satan's direct attack—the train of our Christian walk often comes right off its tracks.

The beginning of our problem is found when—because of Satan's temptation—we lose our focus on God.

Our loss of focus upon the Person of Jesus Christ is the root of all sin.

We are simply and utterly unable to sin if the true focus of our heart is kept on Jesus.

This is, in fact, how Jesus led a perfect life; He—through the Holy Spirit—never lost His focus on the Father—not just in His life on earth, but for all eternity.

Copyright 2013 Michael K. Pasque

In a similar vein, *in the pursuit of the fulfillment of our primary desire*, our loss of that focus on Jesus is fatal.

For instead of going to God—Who is the only *true* Judge of our value and the only source of meaningful judgment in this regard—to find this "worth" that we seek, we instead—because of the diversion of the focus of our heart—turn to other judges of our worth.

Our misdirected quest is bound to frustration right out of the chute because it is entirely self-centered.

In other words, in trying to prove our worthiness, we try to assign value to that which we *are* or *do* for God—instead of focusing on God and what He is to us and what He has done for us.

In other words, we ignore the Gospel of Jesus Christ and what it tells us about our true value.

It tells us that we can have no value outside of God.

It tells us that we can have no value outside of Jesus—who was indeed the true measure of our worth.

It tells us that only as we resemble Jesus—and that only by His grace—do we have any chance in achieving our primal desire to love God.

This is because all real love is centered in the only human being who is capable of truly loving God and that Person is in fact a Person of the Triune Godhead, Jesus Christ.

Thus, the only way that any human being can achieve their creation purpose and satisfy the primal desire of their heart is to have Jesus present in and loving the Father through their heart.

In other words, they must be *in* Jesus Christ.

And, in that same cross of Christ (that is the focal point of this relationship and the center of all love) is in fact found the answer to the question with which Satan

Copyright 2013 Michael K. Pasque

taunts us: *"Are you of any value to God such that your love would even matter to Him?"*

The price paid for us in the death of Christ on the cross of Calvary tells us that in Jesus, we in fact have infinite worth.

We cannot assign, attain, obtain, or earn any eternal value on our own outside of Jesus.

So once again it goes back to God—He alone is the only arbiter of value in the universe.

In our self-centered delusion, we try to hijack—from God—the ability to assign value.

Despite the fact that so many of us work our entire lives to prove the contrary, there simply is no value to be found outside of God.

It is not about us.

It is not about what we bring to God.

It is about Jesus.

We are nothing, do nothing, think nothing, attain nothing, know nothing, achieve nothing, and earn nothing without God's direct, palpable, and undeniable decree in the first place—all are gifts from God.

So, the key to thwarting this most dastardly of attacks on our primal desire (via our perception of our own self-worth) is to, once again, refocus the attention of our heart upon the cross of Christ.

In the cross of Christ is found the only true measure of our worth.

We spend a huge portion of our lives seeking valuation in the creation rather than in the Creator.

We spend a huge amount of time and effort and angst trying to measure up—in our work, in our relationships, in our community, in things devoid of any true worth—instead of *resting* in the worth assigned us by Jesus.

Copyright 2013 Michael K. Pasque

And in that worth is found the hope of the eternity that is ours.

The bad news, therefore, is that all of our efforts to prove our worth through our efforts can only be described as utterly futile.

And the good news is also that all of our efforts to prove our worth through our efforts are utterly futile!

In other words, the bad news is that we can't do anything to *increase* our worth in the eyes of the only One who matters.

But, because this means that our standing with God is not in our hands at all—we have no control over it whatsoever—then the good news is that the opposite of the above statement is also true.

In other words, the good news is that we also can't do anything to *decrease* our worth in the eyes of the only One who matters.

And both of these statements bring us the joy of knowing that we can't mess this up because it, very simply, is not dependent upon us.

Jesus has already proclaimed from the mountaintop the extraordinary value that He sees in you and in me.

Our worth is infinite to Him, and so our love for Him is of infinite value to Him.

And in that thought is immeasurable joy.

And that joy is all by the infinite grace found in the cross of Christ.

It is not about us—it is about God and that which He has graciously given to us.

The gospel of Jesus Christ teaches us that in regard to our true value, *grace* is indeed the only operative word.

Our deluded quest to define our value elsewhere is futile—and yet we are all relentlessly drawn to make it the focus of our lives.

Copyright 2013 Michael K. Pasque

We appoint ourselves (and those in the world around us) as judges of our worth, our value.

And it is here where the catastrophic fatality of our initial small step off of the path of righteousness comes to full fruition as we try to prove to ourselves (and to those around us) that our love matters because we have value, because we matter.

We try to prove that we matter.

If we would only turn to God for this answer, all would be perfectly resolved—for God went to great pains to provide an answer.

We famously ignore that answer despite the fact that the answer comes in the form of the most stupendous, improbable, and yet glorious rescue by way of the greatest single example, in all history, of subservient, sacrificial love.

Despite the ready availability of this most extraordinary of answers, we do not seek of God our true valuation.

We do not seek of God to know that we matter.

Instead, we spend every day of our life trying to prove to ourselves and to those around us that because we matter, our love matters.

Seeking this assurance from within ourselves uniformly leads to pride and self-absorption, and the answer supplied is never—can never be—good enough.

But deep in our hearts, even the most deluded of us knows enough to know that—by definition—we simply cannot be the judges of our own worth.

And in this knowledge, many of us take another step down the pathway of futility.

Since we cannot be the arbiters of our worth, we seek knowledge of our worth from others.

And this leads to relational self-centeredness as we try to get everyone else to focus on us.

Copyright 2013 Michael K. Pasque

We seek to persuade others to tell us that we matter and therefore that our love matters.

We seek to become the center-point around which they revolve.

And in this, we are doing precisely the opposite of what we are supposed to be doing.

Instead of seeking a position of subservient, sacrificial love for ourselves—just like the three Persons of the Trinity have so perfectly modeled for eternity—we are seeking that position for others.

Instead of lovingly serving others, we ask them to serve us.

Instead of actually fulfilling our deep heart desire by loving God by loving others, we are heading 180-degrees in the opposite direction.

We have become the antithesis of that for which we were created.

In this most nefarious of activity, we have thrown off the mantle of our creation purpose, destiny, and deep-heart desire.

We have recreated the sin of Satan.

Behind it all is the misguided belief that if others love us then we are proved *worthy* of their love—and thus we must matter, we must have value—and therefore our love matters.

Our logic is stunningly twisted and could not be more incorrect.

In fact, we have it precisely backwards.

This focusing on others seems so righteous.

After all, the attention is on them, not us.

But this is anything but righteous.

It is in fact self-righteous.

It really is not about them, for in this activity, we have made it all about us.

Copyright 2013 Michael K. Pasque

Thus we spend the greater part of our life trying to gain the approval of the people in our life whom we have designated as *significant* and therefore surrogate judges of that which only God can judge—our worth.

And in this is the greatest tragedy of life.

For as we have discussed, God Himself has already answered the question of our worth—in fact already describing us as being of infinite value, such that no further question in this regard can even be posed.

He defined our worth as being of *infinite* value by the only true metric of worth: the price that He had to pay to save us—to redeem us—to *buy* us back.

That *infinite* price is defined in the very act of the uncreated God becoming created man (to become our Mediator), forever, and in this incarnation literally travelling across an infinite divide, for there is an infinite distance, an infinitely wide barrier, an infinitely powerful resistance between the Uncreated and the created.

> *And it was not without an oath! Others became priests without any oath, but he became a priest with an oath when God said to him: "The Lord has sworn and will not change his mind: 'You are a priest forever.'" Because of this oath, Jesus has become **the guarantee** of a better covenant. Now there have been many of those priests, since death prevented them from continuing in office; but **because Jesus lives forever**, he has a **permanent priesthood**. Therefore he is able to save completely those who come to God through him, **because he always lives to intercede for them**. (Hebrews 7:20-25; emphasis added)*

Copyright 2013 Michael K. Pasque

In fact, there can be no other better definition of *infinite* than the distance between Uncreated God and created mankind—the distance travelled by Jesus in the rescue of mankind.

Even then, after traveling an infinite distance in the incarnation, Jesus travelled a second infinite distance in His death upon the cross—the act of allowing mankind, which He created, to torture and murder Him so that He could save them.

And in that death He suffered the second death—the separation from the loving fellowship of the Trinity.

That separation of one eternal member of the Triune Godhead from the loving fellowship of the others represents the singular most cataclysmic event in all eternity—and this is the price willingly offered and fully paid for us!

So, do you think we have value?

Do we have value to the only One who really matters?

Do we have worth on the only scale of true worthiness?

We are of infinite value to the only judge and of infinite worth by the only metric.

So, if we are of infinite value and worth, does our love matter?

Infinitely.

These are the primal questions arising from the primal desire and they—like everything else in this world—all go back to the cross and back to the One who gave everything that we might have an answer.

Only in the cross of Christ can we ever have hope of fulfilling the primal desire of our heart.

Once again, with the cross of Christ we get everything.

Without the cross of Christ, we gain only an eternity of frustration.

Copyright 2013 Michael K. Pasque

As the proof of our worth, the cross of Christ is the gateway to *life*—to the eternal sating of our primal desire.

For indeed, this question of our worth is the only obstacle blocking our ability to love God.

This is why in this life there is no other *way* other than the cross of Christ.

By answering with finality the question of our worth, only the cross of Christ frees us to love God—and precisely in that is found our creation purpose and the sating of our primal desire.

Copyright 2013 Michael K. Pasque

Day 10

Who Is The Judge And What Is The Metric By Which Our Worth Is Determined?
Practical Implications

This whole concept of a primal desire behind all other human desires is critical to understanding, developing, and implementing a practical theology that truly encompasses our day-to-day interaction with the Living God.

To further illustrate this critical concept, let's look at the idea of a life-governing primal desire in a slightly different manner.

As discussed, the foundational principle is that to love we must feel that the love that we offer is of value to whomever it is being offered.

For our love to be of value, *we* must be of value—the love we give must be coming from someone who is of value to whomever it is being offered, to the object of that love.

This is best illustrated by practical examples from our daily life.

Think of how you felt the last time that you discovered that someone *loved* you.

When you do not feel particularly close to or attracted to that person, it is nice to be loved by them, but their love is not of great value to you.

But, when the lifelong unrequited love of your heart suddenly expresses love toward you—in other words one who (for whatever reason) you truly value expresses their love to you—well, then, that is the source of immeasurable joy!

Copyright 2013 Michael K. Pasque

In other words, it is essential to *the one who loves* that the object of their love values *the one who loves*.

And so we seek to know that we are valued in the eyes of the one we seek to love.

Thus, to carry out our destiny—the fulfillment of our deep-heart desire to love God—we seek to know that we are of value...to God.

This becomes our lifelong quest—to be found to be *of value* in the eyes of the object of our love.

Unfortunately, as we have discussed, this is where we run into trouble, for the object of our love is, on a superficial level, perceived to be *unavailable* to us.

We don't see God—He is not visible.

We don't hear God—He does not speak audibly to us.

We don't smell God.

We cannot touch God.

In other words, except in extraordinary circumstances, the normal human being does not directly and palpably interact with God every day.

The consequence of having a non-visible, non-audible, non-palpable God is obvious and critical: it is not easy to actually *experience* God.

On a day-to-day basis, we don't feel as if God is there to answer that critical question of our valuation (because we ignore the cross of Christ) and so we seek our valuation from someone other than *the One we love*—someone we can actually see.

In so doing, however, we have—by definition—taken our eyes off of the One that we seek to love—Jesus.

Only He really has the answer to the question in our heart.

As we have discussed, He, the only true Judge of our value, has already made the most profound statement of our truly infinite value.

Copyright 2013 Michael K. Pasque

But most of us just don't see this (except in those all-too-infrequent moments where God makes His presence palpably known to us).

Instead, Satan and our sinful nature work to lure us into taking our eyes off of Jesus and place them on others in our world—the people that are visible and actually speak to us on a day-to-day basis.

This is not completely outlandish in its design since the Bible clearly teaches us that we in fact love God by fearlessly loving the people that God brings into our life.

But, instead of selflessly and fearlessly loving them as God has requested, we do the opposite—we try to get them to love us.

We don't seek their love in the mutual loving fellowship of the Trinity—which is based in selfless, subservient, sacrificial, and unconditional love—but instead we seek their love for our own selfish purpose.

In seeking for them to love us, we are asking them to assign value to us.

This is purely self-centered activity, for we are focused only on achieving our life's purpose through means that were never prescribed by God.

God prescribed a selfless love.

Truly selfless love can be defined as placing extraordinary value on another person—*extraordinary* being defined as a value greater than that which we place on ourselves.

So, instead of seeking to love God selflessly in the way that He prescribed—by loving the people that He sends into our lives—we instead spend our lives futilely trying to entice others into assigning value to us by loving us.

Thus we have placed ourselves at the center of our lives, at the center of our environment, at the center of the universe—we seek to scheme and manipulate others into rotating around and serving us as if the whole of creation was all about us.

Copyright 2013 Michael K. Pasque

For, if someone acknowledges our centering of ourselves and begins to rotate around and serve us, that person has assigned value to us.

What methods do we employ and what metrics do we utilize to entice the people in our environment to assign value to us?

This being the main goal of humankind, we have come up with a myriad of diverse ways.

One method of getting people in this world to assign the value that we crave involves the acquisition of wealth—for wealth is always acknowledged as being of value and people with wealth are therefore almost universally felt to be of value.

In fact, in our world, we learn at a very young age that people with wealth are always considered to be *of value*.

We notice them.

We defer to them.

We ask for their advice and opinions.

We value them.

Besides wealth, we also seek any number of other things that assign value to us, ranging from power to fame to an athletic body image to beauty to special knowledge or to special skills.

Note that all of the things that assign value have to do with getting a response from people.

This is because God made us entirely about relationships.

We must note that in seeking to have others focus their attention upon and serve us, we are now doing the exact opposite of our deep heart desire to focus our attention upon and selflessly love God.

We are also doing the exact opposite of that which Jesus did on the cross of Calvary where He took a position subservient to all of us.

Copyright 2013 Michael K. Pasque

And we are thereby doing the precise opposite of that which the three Persons of the Trinity have been doing for eternity—and that which they offer us in the Gospel of Jesus Christ.

Our desire is to love them—just like their eternal desire is to love one another and just like they have already loved us.

Thus our desire to get others to assign value to us by focusing their attention upon us has taken us in the exact opposite direction of our destiny to focus our attention subserviently and sacrificially upon God by subserviently and sacrificially loving the people that He sends into our life.

The train is totally off the tracks.

And the nature of the derailment is precisely the reason that nothing less than Jesus Christ resident in our heart can get us to focus—as *He* always has—upon subserviently and sacrificially serving others—as He did upon the cross of Calvary.

Everything always goes back to the cross of Christ.

The only way to avoid the derailment is to understand that Jesus—the very focus of our desire to love—has already assigned ultimate infinite value to us by His death for us upon the cross.

With this knowledge of our infinite value entrenched deep *in* our hearts by our resident Savior, we are thereby freed to love God by loving the people that He sends into our life.

This is why becoming a Christian involves the adoption of an entirely new paradigm.

This adoption of a new paradigm is not just a slight deviation from our *pre-belief* path.

Copyright 2013 Michael K. Pasque

Our meeting of the risen Savior and our asking Him to take command of our life is nothing less than a 180-degree turn.

We are then going in exactly the opposite direction that our prior life had taken us!

We stop demanding that others serve us and boldly begin to seek positions of subservience with those individuals that God has placed in our life.

This is—for every one of us—a radical 180-degree turn.

We cannot do this by ourselves.

The cross of Christ is our only chance.

Only by it do we have a chance to truly know and believe in our hearts that we are of value.

Thus only by the cross of Christ do we have any chance of recognizing our infinite value to the only One by whom we are judged, thereby freeing us to achieve our destination: our subservient, sacrificial loving of God.

The cheap value that we seek from the people in our world is easily seen as contrived by our deep heart.

Our deep heart is not so easily fooled.

All of our quests and striving to get the individuals of this world to focus upon us (and thereby assign value to us) are declared futile and destined to utter failure by the Judge who sits in the dark recesses of every human heart.

All of this makes sense when we stop to acknowledge that this resembles that which already occurs every day in our life—for only the object of our love (the one we seek to love) can be the "assigner" of value.

Logically, only Jesus—the One we seek to love—can be the judge, the arbiter of our value.

Think about it—if you are deeply in love with someone, ultimately it does your heart no good to be held in value by anyone other than that person.

Copyright 2013 Michael K. Pasque

Only Jesus can assign us value because only Jesus is the One Whom our deep-hearts desire to love.

Truly, our efforts in regard to having others assign value to us are utterly futile and a total waste of time.

In summary, Jesus is the only focus of our one deep-heart desire to love.

Therefore only Jesus can assign the value to us that frees us to love Him.

In the act of assigning that value to us, He demonstrated His love for us.

Love is essentially defined as the subservient and sacrificial act of assigning more value to someone else than you assign to yourself.

And that is precisely what He did on the cross.

In our quest to know our value and thereby be freed to love Jesus, we need to look no further than the literal *center* of the creation: Jesus Christ on the cross of Calvary.

Copyright 2013 Michael K. Pasque

Day 11

What Was The Point Of Our Creation?
Life!

We were created for *life*—real heart throbbing, palpable, compassionate, emotion-filled, thrilling, adventurous, passionate, joyous, and enraptured *life*!

We were created for the sole purpose of spending eternity as sons and daughters of God—and this is *life*.

> *"I will be a Father to you, and you will be my sons and daughters, says the Lord Almighty." (2Corinthians 6:18)*

As sons and daughters of God, we are *royal heirs*—princes and princesses—of the eternal kingdom of God—and this is *life*.

> *So you are no longer a slave, but a son; and since you are a son, God has made you also an heir. (Galatians 4:7)*

We were created for the sole purpose of spending eternity in loving fellowship with each other and with the three Persons of the Triune Godhead—and this is *life*.

Engulfed in this *life* we will *bring glory to* God for eternity *by* our service for, praise of, worship of, knowledge of, love of, and fellowship with the three Persons of the Trinity.

And in doing precisely this, we will have *life*.

Copyright 2013 Michael K. Pasque

And in doing precisely this, we will attain—to unknowable levels—the deepest desire of our heart and this is *life*.

This eternal *life* —which is centered in and upon the Person of Jesus Christ—is (in this world and in eternity) the stuff of legends.

This eternal *life* involves exploration of the unknown, fulfilling work, warm fellowship, thrilling adventure, tumultuous battle, captivating beauty, enlivening passion, tender romance, unknowable joy, and infinite unconditional and selfless love—everything for which we were created and find enrapturing in our current life.

But eternal *life* actually involves so much more—the fullness of which is only subtly hinted at by the things that we call *great* in this world.

We have no capacity to comprehend or even imagine the life that God has planned for us in eternity.

First of all, imagine life in 10 dimensions.

There is obviously a problem with that request.

There is no possibility that beings that exist in only 4 dimensions can even imagine life in 10 dimensions.

And yet the expansion of our dimensions is almost certainly a component of our eternity.

There are, in fact, very literally no superlatives in our language that are adequate to describe the eternal *life* God has planned for His children.

Imagine everything in this life to which you are in any way attracted.

Now multiply it in an infinite fashion.

These many things that capture our heart in this life—from the simple beauty of a flower to the magnificence of romantic love—are like the subtle flickering of a shade that renders a momentary glimpse at a tiny fraction of the brilliant light of the midday sun.

Copyright 2013 Michael K. Pasque

Our entrance into eternal *life* is based exclusively and only upon our true heart belief that Jesus is exactly who He says He is, the only Son of God.

If we enter into this belief, we enter into the eternal dance of the Trinity.

There is no entrance into the dance, save the belief that Jesus is the only true Son of God.

And the currency of that dance is—for eternity—subservient sacrificial love.

And in this is found the nature of the heaven that awaits us.

Imagine *life* as you know it now—except that the relationships that are the focus of this life (and the next!) and literally fill every moment with adventure, love, fulfillment, and passion are *all* then found exclusively and only in the setting of *pure*, subservient, sacrificial love.

Imagine every person that you encounter in your life right now—but instead imagine them almost exploding in subservience—and ever willing to make the love they offer sacrificial.

Imagine your life right now—except imagine the utter absence (in any person, including yourself) of any emotion other than subservient, sacrificial love.

Imagine intimately knowing and exploring and celebrating the inmost details of every life that you encounter—every one like you in many ways, but also so utterly different than you in so many other fascinating ways!

For there will be no secrets, no hiding, no manipulation, no duplicity, no animosity whatsoever because we will all be focused on each other by way of the Person of Jesus Christ—instead of ourselves—for that is the nature of the subservient, sacrificial love that is modeled in the cross of our Savior.

In the depth of our understanding of the *life* that God has planned for those who believe only and exclusively in His Son, Jesus Christ, our true deep-heart belief that Jesus is the only Son of God really does change everything.

Copyright 2013 Michael K. Pasque

Day 12

Does God Determine Who Spends Eternity In Heaven Or Do We?
The Foundational Dichotomy: God's Gift Of Free Will Versus His Perfect Sovereignty

God is the Creator of all that has been created.

All that has been created includes everything—and every individual—outside of the *Uncreated* (the three Persons of the Triune Godhead).

Central to the Theory of Relativity is the concept that all created matter has as one of its innate attributes the *time* within which that matter is observed.

All *time*—forever and ever—is therefore simply another intrinsic facet *of* the creation.

> The creation does not exist in time; time exists in the creation.

This means that in the act of the creation, God has already carefully planned and created every single moment in time for every single subatomic particle of every molecule of every type that exists in every solar system of each of trillions of galaxies throughout the entire universe—and that for all eternity.

This has great theological implications.

But great theological implications are not what we are about.

We, in this discussion, are pursuing the pragmatic.

> From a pragmatic point-of-view, the fact that God not only created the physical matter of the universe, but also the time within which that matter exists, is critical

Copyright 2013 Michael K. Pasque

since it means that God has, therefore, *already* carefully and perfectly planned and created every single moment of our life on earth.

He has also planned every single moment of our *life* in infinite eternity.

Only an infinite God with infinite capabilities has the capacity to have already planned all of eternity.

The fact that God has already created all matter and all of the time associated with that matter for all eternity delivers a critically pragmatic message to us: God is *absolutely, infinitely, and perfectly sovereign* over every single moment of time and atom of matter with which we are composed, engulfed, come in contact with, or are in any way affected by for the totality of our life on earth and our eternity.

> *Are not two sparrows sold for a penny? Yet not one of them will fall to the ground apart from the will of your Father. (Matthew 10:29)*

The utter sovereignty of God over all created matter, space, and time logically means that *He could not help but determine the eternity of every created man and every created woman.*

After all, every created man and woman finds their existence entirely included within the confines of the matter, space, and time of the creation.

Thus, God has already determined who will spend eternity in heaven and who will spend eternity in hell.

> *And we know that in all things God works for the good of those who love him, who have been called according to his purpose. For those God foreknew he also predestined to be conformed to the likeness of his Son, that he might be the firstborn among many brothers. And*

Copyright 2013 Michael K. Pasque

those he predestined, he also called; those he called, he also justified;
those he justified, he also glorified. (Romans 8:28-30)

This fact is further supported by scripture that tells us that some people are born as weeds with a predetermined destiny to be weeds and to suffer the eternal fate of weeds.

Then he left the crowd and went into the house. His disciples came to
him and said, "Explain to us the parable of the weeds in the field."

He answered, "The one who sowed the good seed is the Son of Man.
The field is the world, and the good seed stands for the sons of the
kingdom. The weeds are the sons of the evil one, and the enemy who
sows them is the devil. The harvest is the end of the age, and the
harvesters are angels.

"As the weeds are pulled up and burned in the fire, so it will be at the
end of the age. The Son of Man will send out his angels, and they will
weed out of his kingdom everything that causes sin and all who do
evil. They will throw them into the fiery furnace, where there will be
weeping and gnashing of teeth. Then the righteous will shine like the
sun in the kingdom of their Father. He who has ears, let him hear.
(Matthew 13:36-43; emphasis added)

The Apostle Peter confirms the fact that some are born destined to the fate of the wicked.

Copyright 2013 Michael K. Pasque

*But these men blaspheme in matters they do not understand. They are like brute beasts, creatures of instinct, born **only** to be caught and **destroyed**, and like beasts they too will perish. (2Peter 2:12; emphasis added)*

Paul adds his voice to this prophetic testimony.

The facts are clear: unbelievers *"are [born] to be"* slaves to the world and to never see an eternity of freedom as heirs—in the blood of Christ—to the kingdom of God.

*These things may be taken figuratively, for the women represent two covenants. One covenant is from Mount Sinai and bears children who **are to be** slaves: This is Hagar. (Galatians 4:24; emphasis added)*

I emphasize the words *"are to be"* because they are the hinge-point words of this passage.

They tell us that this has been predetermined, predestined.

It will happen exactly as the creator has planned it.

And yet we, in our limited understanding, find tension in the truths of the Bible.

For the Bible also emphasizes on essentially every page that God has given us a free will with the ability to freely choose our path in the many decision-points that have been built into the days of our life.

Thus, we are confronted during every moment of our existence with the unwieldy and confusing dichotomy that despite the undeniable sovereignty of God over every molecule of matter and millisecond of time that together comprise the

Copyright 2013 Michael K. Pasque

creation, it is our choice—right this second—whether we spend eternity in heaven or hell.

The Bible, the written Word of God, solidly and unrelentingly supports both facts, 1) the sovereignty of God and 2) the free will freedom of every individual to choose to believe in the Name of Jesus or not.

Acknowledgement of this dichotomy—that God before the creation determined your outcome combined with the fact that right this moment it *is your* choice—recognizes and allows for both the perfect sovereignty of God and the guarantee of our free will to choose God or not.

This dichotomy also completely eliminates any rationale for our boasting, our raising ourselves above anyone else, our judging one another, our pride, or our self-righteousness.

For if we accept the eternal salvation found exclusively in the work of Christ on the cross, it is only because God so ordained us—and yet right this minute, it is still our choice.

This dichotomy is the focal point of the magnificence of God's creation.

The fact that God has planned out every single moment and event of our life, nonetheless, does not make us robots and does not make our lives any less personal or our decisions any less our responsibility or their consequences any less eternal.

The fact that God has planned out every single moment of our life also does not lessen in any way our responsibility for that decision that determines our eternity—nor does it lessen in any manner the personal nature of the eternal consequences of that decision.

This is true because—right this moment—the decision is *ours*.

Copyright 2013 Michael K. Pasque

God has given us the very special gift of free will—which gives us the ability to change our eternity right this minute, or at any moment in our life.

The fact that God has planned out every single moment of our life also does not make our eternal *LIFE* in heaven any less joyful or our eternal life in hell any less horrible.

Just because God planned and foreknew every moment of our life does not lessen the intense personal joy that we will experience as a result of our decision to accept the eternal salvation purchased by the shed blood of Jesus Christ.

Just because God planned out every millisecond of our life does not mean that heaven will be any less physically, emotionally, or spiritually pleasing and joyful for us as eternal children of the kingdom of God.

Nor does the fact that God planned and foreknew every moment of the lives of those who would spend their whole life refusing God's offer of salvation lessen the very personal nature of the eternity of despair, cold darkness, and burning pain that they will endure without hope of rescue.

Just because God planned out every millisecond of our life does not mean that the burning fire of hell will be any less physically palpable and the despair any less hopeless for those who refuse to believe.

The fact that God planned every moment of our life does not free us from the eternal responsibility for our choice—God says precisely what He means and means precisely what He says in regard to our eternity and all is recorded in His Holy Word.

Whether God planned it or not, the decision is yours right this minute.

God planned it, but you have the power—right this minute—to take your life and your eternity, in either of two polar opposite directions.

You make the call.

Copyright 2013 Michael K. Pasque

Day 13

Does God Determine Everything That Happens To Us Everyday?
How God's Sovereignty Impacts The Way We Live Our Life

Since God has in fact already planned and created the nano-trajectories of every single atomic particle in the universe for every single nanosecond of eternity, we can safely assume that God has also planned and orchestrated every interpersonal life encounter of every single moment of our entire life.

> *Therefore, since we are surrounded by such a great cloud of witnesses, let us throw off everything that hinders and the sin that so easily entangles, and let us run with perseverance* **the race marked out for us***. (Hebrews 12:1; emphasis added)*

God orchestrates our every life encounter.

God has planned every moment, every encounter, every relationship, every *good* thing, every *bad* thing, every big event, every tiny event, every significant encounter, every "insignificant" encounter, every profound thought, every passing thought, every lifelong dream, every daydream, every great task, every insignificant task, every joy, every pain, every despair, every moment of hope, every hopeless moment, every optimism, every pessimism—every moment of every minute of every hour of every day of every week of every month of every year of our entire life.

Copyright 2013 Michael K. Pasque

All the days ordained for me were written in your book before one of them came to be. (Psalm 139:16b)

We, as humans who have grown up with a world perspective that celebrates the utter randomness of life, have difficulty with the reality of God's sovereignty in our life.

Sure, we all-too-readily acknowledge God's hand in some momentous events in our life.

We also readily accept the fact that God's hand is active in the broad strokes of the recognized *will of God* through the history of mankind, such as the salvation of those who accept the grace of the cross of Christ or the fulfillment of the empire-predicting prophecy of Daniel's statue vision (Daniel 2).

We may even recognize the broad strokes of God's will in our life, such as our personal salvation, marriage partner, or career—all of which we may readily attribute to God.

But we similarly seem so eager to dismiss the thought that God is right there with us in every single breath that we take, every glance of our eyes, every thought of our mind, every desire of our heart—large or small, profound or mundane, life-changing or seemingly inconsequential.

We dismiss the fact that God is ahead of, in the middle of, behind, and totally all over every one of these events—no matter how trivial.

Our belief in the *randomness* of life is bolstered by our observation of the billions of seemingly totally unpredictable human beings—all admittedly with the freedom to do whatever they please in every moment of their life—that fill our immediate living space as well as the entirety of the world that we live in.

Copyright 2013 Michael K. Pasque

It is precisely the unpredictable nature of the countless human beings that influence our life that indeed binds our intellect irretrievably to the logic of a totally random world and similarly binds our hearts to worship the false freedom to hold every one of those human beings accountable for the influence their decisions have on our life.

And yet it is God who knew, in infinite detail, every single one of their choices in every one of the decision-points that He orchestrated into their lives and then orchestrated those precise decisions of theirs into the fabric of *our* life.

In other words, clearly the individuals that God brings into our life exercise their free will in making the choices they do—even knowing that the consequences of their choice will hurt us—*but they have nothing to do with the time and the place of the position of their decision in our life* and therefore nothing to do with the fact that the mal-consequences of their actions impact *us and not someone else*—all of this being solely *in God's jurisdiction.*

Many are the plans in a man's heart, but it is the LORD's purpose that prevails. (Proverbs 19:21)

God orders the time and consequences and location of their decision and He is therefore directly responsible for the impact that their decision has in our life.

Without God's direct influence and direction, we would not even know their names!

Although this may seem logical in our perspective of the sovereignty of God, this is utter nonsense to the world.

The worldview holds that every one of the seemingly random and yet free will decisions that are made by the individuals who influence our life are theirs alone to make and therefore cannot be seen as anything other than entirely random

Copyright 2013 Michael K. Pasque

relative to the broad strokes of our life and the effects that these decisions have on our life.

In other words, the world sees the fact that we were born when we were born and to whom we were born and where we were born with the attributes we were born with as utterly random influences that just happened—by random happenstance—to affect our life and not the life of someone else.

This worldly perspective further emphasizes that when the individuals or organizations that impact our life make decisions that similarly impact our life, they should be *held responsible* for the impact that these decisions have on our life.

In fact, this worldly perspective doesn't just *allow* us to hold them responsible; it *demands* this action on our part!

Thus this worldly perspective displaces from God the responsibility for both the *good* and the *bad* that are clearly sent our way by the *direct and purposeful design* of the Creator God, and instead places it solely upon the individuals with whom we interact.

And this, in turn, frees us (by making it seem the logical conclusion) to respond to those individuals in any manner that we deem appropriate (once again, from a worldly perspective) to that which they have wreaked upon our life.

Anger, vengeance, retribution, and justice are the words we use to describe our *justified* response to these individuals.

There is only one problem with this worldly perspective.

It has, thereby, led us to respond to these individuals in a manner that is 180 degrees opposite of the way that God—as documented by the words of Jesus Himself—has asked us to respond to them.

Jesus told us not to just love those who love us, but to love everyone—including those individuals that our worldly perspective labels as our "enemies."

Copyright 2013 Michael K. Pasque

We are to love them all in every single circumstance and to trust God for the outcome.

The only way that this is possible is if we recognize that it is in fact God who is sending the *bad* stuff our way.

Then, this "bad" stuff is instead categorized as *discipline with a purpose*—God's purpose—in our life.

It was sent by God (with nothing except His infinite love as its motivation) into our life to make us more into the likeness of His Son—and thereby to prepare us for the glorious eternity of *real* life that God has planned for us.

> They preached the good news in that city and won a large number of disciples. Then they returned to Lystra, Iconium and Antioch, strengthening the disciples and encouraging them to remain true to the faith. **"We must go through many hardships to enter the kingdom of God,"** they said. (Acts 14:21-22; emphasis added)

We can be assured that in every single case, that which God is doing in our life—no matter how bad it may look or feel—is good and has the wellbeing of our eternal heart as its propellant into our life.

> Should it be said, O house of Jacob: "Is the Spirit of the LORD angry? Does he do such things?"
>
> "Do not my words do good to him whose ways are upright? (Micah 2:7)

Copyright 2013 Michael K. Pasque

Knowing, acknowledging, and incorporating this fact into our life perspective is the only way by which we can respond correctly to the challenging situations that God sends into our life in the process of our sanctification.

The worldly perspective that allows us to logically and self-righteously hold the individuals in our life responsible for the impact that their actions have upon our life is simply intolerant of the command to love our enemies, the most precious of the commands of our Savior Jesus.

Jesus has—in the written Word of God—therefore given us an alternative perspective to that which has been ingrained in us since the day of our birth.

It is so profoundly different—precisely opposite in fact—from that which is taught by the world around us that some of us react viscerally to its very mention.

But this perspective is, nonetheless, taught throughout the Bible.

This perspective assures us that despite the incredible complexity and seemingly intensely random nature of the events, circumstances, and social interactions that occur every minute of every hour of every day of our life, there is not a single part of it—from the tiniest detail to the grandest life vision—that did not have its origination, planning, ordering, and orchestration by the mind and hand of the Mighty and Sovereign God.

Once again, our first response of disbelief is fueled by the millions of free will decisions that are made literally every moment by each one of the billions of people in the world—many of which have a direct impact upon the actual events and circumstances of our life—that can only be adequately described as "wildly random" in the way that they influence our life.

But the truth is anything but that.

The eternal truth is that the omnipotent, omniscient God—the Creator of all that has been created—is not only the Origin of every nanoparticle of every

Copyright 2013 Michael K. Pasque

substance and every millisecond of time, but also every thought of every mind, and every desire of every heart.

He planned, created, orchestrated, and implemented every circumstance, every environment, every relationship, every job, and every social situation in which we could ever find ourselves.

> And he is not served by human hands, as if he needed anything, because **he himself gives all men** life and breath and **everything else.** From one man he made every nation of men, that they should inhabit the whole earth; and **he determined the times set for them and the exact places where they should live.** (Acts 17:25-26; emphasis added)

He already knew—before He created a single thing—every potential thought and action of every person who would live and interact with us (or the world around us) during every moment of our life.

He knew precisely what their choice would be to every possible situation that He might orchestrate in their lives—just like He knew yours and mine—because He created them, just like He created us.

He knew how they would respond to every one of the millions of decision-points that He could orchestrate into their lives—just like He already knew how you and I would respond.

He knew precisely how every possible person who would ever live would respond to all of the choices that each of *us* would make to the many decision-points that He would place in *our* lives.

Copyright 2013 Michael K. Pasque

And this is the most incredible part of God's incredible creation: God, with this full knowledge of every possible combination of every possible person in every possible set of life situations, circumstances, and relationships, then made the infinitely precise and perfect creation that would deliver those foreknown eternal sons and daughters of the eternal kingdom of God from the imperfection of this world and this life to the perfect eternity that He has planned for us.

We proclaim him, admonishing and teaching everyone with all wisdom, so that we may present everyone perfect in Christ. (Colossians 1:28)

The mandatory consequences of this perspective impact every moment of our life.

We can know as absolute fact that every single thing that comes at us as we move through the days of our life is from God and God alone.

God does not just "allow" all this stuff—both good and bad—to happen in our life.

He sends it.

He sends it all.

Not one single thing that happens in any of our lives occurs by random happenstance.

The word *allow* simply does not fit.

The use of the word *allow* suggests that someone other than God put the bad stuff in our lives, that God just acquiesces to their will, and that God is, therefore, simply a secondary responder.

Copyright 2013 Michael K. Pasque

That would, by definition, make God into something less than God (See A. W. Tozer, *The Knowledge of the Holy*).

The word *allow*, therefore, should never even come up in this conversation about God's orchestration of the events of our life.

God *sends* everything

He doesn't just *allow* it; He sends it.

God orchestrates good events and "bad" events (we call them bad, He doesn't) in our life in order to bring every foreknown son and daughter of God to the acceptance of the eternal salvation of Christ—this is the *predestination* described in the book of Romans—and the sanctifying walk with Jesus.

It is an incredibly complex work of perfect relational choreography—the complexity of which only God is capable of even acknowledging and fully understanding, let alone creating!

As seemingly random as a billion human beings all bouncing off of each other's free will decisions seems to be, it is anything but that.

In this life in this world, we are not a randomly careening pinball bouncing off of other randomly careening pinballs, but rather characters in an infinitely complex, perfectly planned, and gloriously orchestrated drama with a cast of fellow actors that numbers in the billions.

This, as impossible as it seems, is a paltry demonstration of the magnificence of God and the infinite expanse of His mind.

God has orchestrated every situation that comes into our life—whether seemingly totally random or seemingly totally predictable—by wielding (like a sculptor's tool) the seemingly random free will decisions of the people in our life, first to save and then to sanctify us—with the ultimate goal of nothing less than eternally molding us into the likeness of His Son Jesus.

Copyright 2013 Michael K. Pasque

All of the free will choices at each of the trillions of decision-points that God places in the lives of countless human beings are all like a Master Sculptor's tools in the hands of the Orchestrator of our life.

Interweaving the thousands of free will decisions of every one of us together with the thousands of free will decisions of all of the people that God brings into our lives results in such an incredibly complex tapestry of life events that we are utterly incapable of imagining it—it is infinite and its understanding is clearly beyond the capabilities of our minds.

Others in our world may appear to be the immediately responsible and direct mediators of both the good and the *bad* that comes our way in every moment of our life.

Further, the true *secondary* mediators of God's influence in our life are not just the individuals that we encounter in this life—but also Satan and his minions.

The influence of the spiritual *otherworld* that parallels our "real" world is Biblically supported and most certainly profound.

Our naïve ignorance of this fact—of the impact of the spiritual otherworld upon our daily lives—surely will be one of the most profound of surprises in the revelation that overwhelms us at the moment of our death.

Regardless of the influence of these *real* world or *otherworld* mediators of God's plan for our life, both the good and the *bad* nonetheless come from God.

This logic is utterly inconvenient to the theologies to which most of us cling.

It takes the air right out of the rationalization we use to justify our desire to strike back at the immediate perpetrators of the *bad* in our life.

This attitude is based on a lie and simply cannot be supported from the text of the Bible—it is God who sends both the good and the *bad* into our life.

Copyright 2013 Michael K. Pasque

This is very literally supported by scripture from almost every chapter of the Bible.

Most critically, this is not just some obscure and insignificant theological discussion.

Understanding the true source of everything that affects us in our life very literally changes everything.

No longer can we rationalize hating, scheming against, plotting the demise of, or any other bad thoughts toward anyone in our life.

There can be no justification of mal-thought toward any person that God brings into our life—no matter what great arguments are put forth by Satan as he tries to convince us to seek retribution against those who have harmed us.

The fact remains that God did not just *allow* them to randomly wander into our lives, brimming hate for us—He planned their attack, put it on their heart, and sent them right at us.

> The next day an evil spirit from God came forcefully upon Saul. He was prophesying in his house, while David was playing the harp, as he usually did. Saul had a spear in his hand and he hurled it, saying to himself, "I'll pin David to the wall." But David eluded him twice. (1Samuel 18:10-11)

We simply have no Biblical justification for railing against these individuals— David did not, and neither should we.

There is no point to this sort of activity.

Further still, based upon the truth of the Bible, there is no *logic* to support this sort of activity.

Copyright 2013 Michael K. Pasque

The *visible and apparent* perpetrators of mayhem in our life are in fact not the true source—God is.

God sends strife as a trial, as a test, as discipline, and as a mediator of change in our life—as is clearly outlined in the written word of God.

> *Our fathers disciplined us for a little while as they thought best; but God disciplines us for our good, that we may share in his holiness. (Hebrews 12:10)*

He wants to show us our hearts.

He wants to be the source of the change in our hearts.

The strife, the testing, all has a purpose.

It is all discipline—it serves to turn us back to the correct path, the correct understanding of God, the correct behavior.

> *No discipline seems pleasant at the time, but painful. Later on, however, it produces a harvest of righteousness and peace for those who have been trained by it. (Hebrews 12:11)*

This is what *having Jesus in our heart* is all about.

All of this activity that swirls madly about us is devised, orchestrated, and directly mediated by Jesus—it has a purpose.

God seeks change.

So, just as the Bible clearly teaches, our response to the tough circumstances in our life should not be to strike out at the visible mediators of God's will in our life, but rather to seek that which God is trying to teach us from each incursion.

Copyright 2013 Michael K. Pasque

Even putting theology completely aside and speaking only pragmatically, understanding that these difficult times are sent as discipline (with a very specific purpose in our life) should change the perspective with which we approach these difficult situations.

God is perfectly efficient—His discipline is never without purpose.

The purpose of discipline in our life is God's will and God's will is to make over each of us in the likeness of our perfect life model—His Son Jesus.

And thus Jesus can, without hesitation, tell us to love our enemies.

No matter what we may be led to believe, our enemies are in our life 100% of the time *to do God's will in our life*.

We can love our enemies because, no matter what it feels or looks like on the surface, they represent—they *are*—the grace and goodness of God sent into our life to bring about change.

In the eternal perspective of God—and in the perspective of the sanctified Christian—our enemies are, in fact, correctly perceived to be *good*, not bad.

Can we imagine how profoundly our lives would change if we were to fully accept that idea as fact?

We would walk boldly in the love of God *toward* our enemies—instead of running away.

We would not fear encounters with them, but rather lovingly anticipate the growth that they represent in our life.

As hard as this is to imagine, it is Biblically supported fact.

The people we hate the most are precisely the individuals who will be responsible for implementing the most *good* in our life.

When viewed from eternity, we will see that our characters were permanently changed by the influence of those who we hate the most.

Copyright 2013 Michael K. Pasque

In other words, the people we hate the most are the ones we should love—with the love of Jesus—the most.

These are bold thoughts.

Their consideration and implementation are possible only because Jesus lives in our hearts.

But, the facts remain, our enemies are not the problem.

No matter what logic Satan uses to support this assertion, these people—the direct mediators of mayhem in our life—are not the problem.

God is also not the problem.

Our nefarious, rebellious, sinful human nature is the problem and our enemies are sent into our life to implement change in our flawed nature.

And God's plan for our life is the solution to our problem—and our enemies are clearly part of that plan.

God wants to use every single set of circumstances, every single environment, every single interaction, and every single relationship in every moment of our life to move us toward the *knowledge* of God—the perfection that will be ours in His Son Jesus.

So yes, Jesus tells us to love our enemies.

This requires that we trust Him.

Every enemy who is sent into battle against us is a test to see if we will trust Jesus.

Every enemy is a test to see if we will surrender the sovereign dominion of our heart to the King of kings.

Every enemy therefore obviously must have a purpose in our life.

Every enemy is sent to move us one step closer to the goal of our life—being made into the likeness of the One who is the perfect human model of the perfect eternal life companion of the Father.

Copyright 2013 Michael K. Pasque

Yes, Jesus tells us always to forgive—this also requires that we trust Him.

Every circumstance in which we are harmed and must then forgive is sent directly into our life with Divine and omniscient forethought and wisdom—with its end being to the glory of God.

For in every circumstance where Jesus requests that we forgive, we must trust Him to deliver us from the harm that this forgiveness might bring—or at least to support us under the load of that harm.

Every circumstance where forgiveness is so necessary and the harm that has been done—and may be done again—is so egregious, is a test sent into our life by God *with our eternal good as its only motivation.*

Keep me as the apple of your eye. (Psalm 17:8a)

Our unforgiveness is, once again, based upon the fact that we hold that person, that mediator of harm in our life, responsible for the pain that he or she seems to bring—but it is God Who sends the pain.

In God's (and eventually our) eternal perspective, the harm and the pain are not bad; they are pure goodness from the heart of God.

We will look back from eternity upon the worst days of our life and see them as they really are—the very best days of our life.

And yes, Jesus says to not judge one another.

This also requires that we trust God.

This also has a purpose.

This temptation to judge another person has been sent to ultimately move us one step closer to resembling Jesus.

It requires that we know the blackness of our own hearts and the depth of the grace and forgiveness that we find (for our own sin) in the cross of Christ.

Copyright 2013 Michael K. Pasque

And thus we know that it is only *logical* to love, forgive, and refuse to judge our neighbor—"Cast all your anxiety on him because he cares for you," (1 Peter 5:7)—for all of the anxiety-provoking circumstances were sent into our life by God anyway.

No matter the details of the difficult circumstances in which we find ourselves embroiled, we can know in our hearts that God sent them to us with perfect thought, perfect wisdom, perfect goodness—and perfect love.

We can love always—just as Jesus requests of us—because we know that God has sent every individual that we encounter into our life for His perfect purpose— our eternal perfection as princes and princesses of the eternal kingdom of God.

> *As for God, his way is perfect; the word of the LORD is flawless.*
> *(Psalm 18:30a)*

The knowledge that every circumstance that we encounter in our life—every one of them—comes from the loving heart of God, truly does change everything.

Copyright 2013 Michael K. Pasque

Day 14

From Where Did Our Sinful Nature Come?
Creation Purpose Versus Sinful Nature

Much can be known about the nature of God.

One of the primary insights into the nature of God is found in the nature of the individuals with whom God wishes to spend eternity in loving fellowship.

We know these individuals—they are we *who believe*.

The fact that the description of the perfect individuals with whom God wishes to spend eternity is found in the description of the individuals in the body of Christ, reveals much about God.

First things first: God is God—He can have anything He wants.

God *will* spend eternity with precisely the individuals with whom He desires to spend eternity.

God, by definition, always gets what He wants and what He wants in eternity is very literally the definition of eternal perfection.

Therefore it naturally follows that the very natures, personalities, wills, emotions, spiritual makeup, and bodies with which God endows us (the body of *believers*) clearly demonstrate precisely what He desires in eternal sons and daughters—that which He desires in eternal fellowship.

So what are the attributes of the individuals with whom God wishes to spend eternity?

Since *free will* is necessary in order to truly love—and voluntary, subservient, sacrificial, and unconditional *love* is the foundation of our eternal fellowship with the three Persons of the Trinity—God gave us precisely that, *free will*.

Copyright 2013 Michael K. Pasque

Unfortunately, that is not all that God gave us.

Along with our free will, God knowingly, with the infinite wisdom, knowledge and foresight that is inherent to all of His decisions, endowed us—with His infinitely perfect eternity in mind—with a nature that is inherently rebellious toward our Creator.

> All of us also lived among them at one time, gratifying the cravings of our **sinful nature** and following **its** desires and thoughts. Like the rest, we were **by nature** objects of **wrath**. (Ephesians 2:3; emphasis added)

Since God is the sole source of all that has been created, He obviously not only knew of our rebellious nature from the very beginning, but He created it.

Further still, He also planned every detail of the creation *for it* from the very beginning—and He even told us such:

> And the LORD God commanded the man, "You are free to eat from any tree in the garden; but you must not eat from the tree of the knowledge of good and evil, for **when [not "if"]** you eat of it you will surely die." (Genesis 2:16-17; emphasis/editorial added)

> **Every** inclination of man's heart is **evil**. (Genesis 8:21; emphasis added)

In the light of God's perfect, bright-light holiness, this rebellion that naturally springs from the heart of man toward God is distinctly defined as pure darkness—defined as precisely that which God calls sin.

Copyright 2013 Michael K. Pasque

God's perfect, infinite holiness will not allow Him to have eternal loving fellowship with the darkness of sinful rebellion and His similarly perfect, infinite justice will not allow sin to exist unchecked, unpunished.

This is because pure bright white holiness and the darkest blackness of rebellious sin *cannot exist in subservient, sacrificially loving fellowship together.*

You are not a God who takes pleasure in evil; with you the wicked cannot dwell. The arrogant cannot stand in your presence; you hate all who do wrong. (Psalm 5:4-5)

> By the very nature of the loving fellowship of the three Persons of the Triune Godhead, that loving fellowship—which is the whole of our eternity with God— cannot exist in eternity with individuals defiled by sinful rebellion against the holiness of that very fellowship.

Praise God for His holiness and His justice—we would not want to live an eternity with a God who did not have them as inherent, perfect, and infinite attributes.

The infinitely perfect nature of God's holiness mandates a black and white, all-or-nothing attitude toward sin, which is therefore also inherent to His nature.

Obviously, this is a problem.

Our heart's one true desire precisely matches that for which we were created in the first place (our creation purpose): to experience loving fellowship with God for eternity as His children.

*What a man desires is **unfailing** love (Proverbs 19:22a; emphasis added)*

Copyright 2013 Michael K. Pasque

But when the time had fully come, God sent his Son, born of a woman, born under law, to redeem those under law, that we might receive the full rights of sons. Because you are sons, God sent the Spirit of his Son into our hearts, the Spirit who calls out, "Abba, Father." So you are no longer a slave, but a son; and since you are a son, God has made you also an heir. (Galatians 4:4-7)

God, in His infinite wisdom, made fulfillment of the purpose of our creation to be precisely the same as our deepest true-heart desire—they are inherently and inseparably tied together.

Our rebellious, sinful nature therefore wrecks everything by denying us the eternal loving fellowship with God that is in fact the exclusive inborn, unchangeable, and eternal purpose of our creation and deepest desire of our magnificent God-ordained hearts.

And yet, we can know—precisely by the perfection of God—that sin would not be a part of the creation if it were not necessary for God's perfect eternity.

Sin in this world is necessary for the end-result, the eternal result, the final product of the creation for which the creation came about in the first place: the perfect eternal children of the eternal kingdom of God.

From this we can know for sure that the sinful nature of man was not only necessary, but also critical to the perfection of every man and woman who would spend eternity as a prince or princess of the eternal kingdom of God.

And from the fact that an individual who overcame his or her sinful nature (by the grace of God as manifest in the cross of Jesus Christ) is precisely the infinitely

Copyright 2013 Michael K. Pasque

perfect person with whom God wants to spend eternity, we can know just a little bit more about our Creator.

How did our sinful nature help prepare us for our eternity?

Why was it critical to our candidacy for an eternity of fellowship with God that we overcome a sinful nature?

What is it about God that makes Him want to spend eternity only with humans who have and overcome a sinful nature?

These questions are not just theological debate topics.

Their answers render pragmatic life perspectives.

And they supply knowledge not only about this life we lead as Christians, but also about our eternity.

Copyright 2013 Michael K. Pasque

Day 15

Did God Really Give Us Our Sinful Nature?
Naturally Nefarious

Understanding the concept of the mandatory perfection of God and its impact on our existence and eternal destiny is obviously critical to a working theology for the practical Christian.

God created everything that has been created.

Since God is infinitely perfect by nature, everything He does is perfect.

God is utterly incapable of creating anything less than perfection.

In His perfectly efficient creation of the creation in which we exist, God, therefore, has not created anything that did not need to be created for the eternal perfection of the creation.

Similarly, in His perfectly efficient creation of the creation in which we exist, everything that needed to be created has in fact been created.

Our rebellious sinful nature is obviously an intrinsic part of God's infinitely perfect eternal creation.

God gave us our rebellious sinful nature—we did not create it, just as we did not create ourselves—and it is a perfect part of God's perfect creation.

> Why, O LORD, do you make us wander from your ways and harden our hearts so we do not revere you? (Isaiah 63:17a)

God knew that Adam would sin even before He created him.

Copyright 2013 Michael K. Pasque

Our sinful nature is not something that we came up with independent of God, our Creator.

Our rebellious, sinful nature, therefore, is *not our fault* and it is *not a mistake*.

For God has bound all men over to disobedience so that he may have mercy on them all. (Romans 11:32)

God, being perfect, has a perfect purpose behind everything that He does.

God, therefore, had a purpose in everything that has been created.

In fact, since God's creation is perfect and our sinful, rebellious nature is part of that creation, it is not just something that God added as "filler" to keep us busy.

We can be assured that our sinful, rebellious nature is an intrinsic and vital part of that perfect creation—and the perfect eternity that is the largest part and point of that creation.

The facts are obvious: something about our sinful nature was critical to the utter perfection of God's creation.

Our rebellious, sinful nature therefore not only wrecks everything, but also must be critical in making us perfect eternal children of God—or things would not have happened the way they have happened.

This means that 10,000 years from now, no matter what we may think of our lives right now, God will look back on them (figuratively speaking, for He exists outside of time) and He will call them perfect—not just *really good*, but perfect (in regard to His good and eternal plan that is based on His eternal desires and will).

Don't believe this is true?

Then think of that imperfection to which your hesitation condemns our perfect God: that He would have to spend eternity with something that isn't perfect.

Copyright 2013 Michael K. Pasque

God forbid.

This means that God—under your plan—will spend eternity wishing that you had not sinned so much or bemoaning that fact that things didn't turn out better or pining away for a second chance so that he wouldn't have to spend eternity with such a bunch of imperfect losers and misfits.

No chance.

God absolutely loves the eternity He has already created because His plan is perfect and His creation is perfect—He has declared them *"good"* (Genesis 1:31)—and He is getting precisely what His heart desires: the right individuals with just the right personal attributes to be His children, the eternal princes and princesses of His eternal kingdom, forever!

So, fine…where does that leave us?

The necessary and logical consequences of this argument reach into every part of our lives as Christians.

As a part of the perfect eternal creation of God, our life—nasty, contemptuous, rebellious, renegade, rogue, filthy garbage and all—is going to end up precisely where God wanted it to end up.

This doesn't mean that your choices are not governed by your free will—they most certainly are.

Every choice you make is yours to make—but even before He created, God already knew which direction you would go at every decision-point in your life—you are part of His eternal creation and He knows every minute detail of it (He did, after all, create it).

And the completion of the rest of the creation—the orchestration of events to take things right where God wanted them to go—was in fact dependent upon each and every one of your free will decisions (more about that later).

Copyright 2013 Michael K. Pasque

This also means that something about our very own personal God-endowed sinful nature was critical to our eternal destiny—critical to that to which our individual eternal hearts, minds, and bodies will be eternally dedicated.

Thus we conclude that somehow our own personal free will tendency toward rebellion against God is critical to the perfection of God's eternity.

In this rebellion is found the hinge-point of our eternity, for it is precisely in the overcoming (only by the grace of the cross of Christ) of that natural inborn tendency toward rebellion that we acknowledge God for who He is and in so doing define the whole of our eternity.

Upon our acceptance of the free gift of eternal salvation that is found in the shed blood of Jesus, God could have—in that instant—suddenly made us into the people with whom He desires eternal fellowship.

But He chose not to!

Something about our actually participating, our *doing it*, our actually *fighting the fight* to overcome that natural tendency toward rebellion makes us creatures with whom God desires eternal loving fellowship.

For some reason, we had to go through the process that is our sanctification— we had to feel it and smell it and hear it and palpably mess it up.

> It is God who arms me with strength and makes my way perfect.
> (2Samuel 22:33)

Thus *our* character attributes tell us much about God, since He obviously considers us (the redeemed, the church of Christ) to be the ideal people with whom to spend eternity.

Copyright 2013 Michael K. Pasque

This is key, because our understanding of the true nature of God is the most important factor that influences the choices we make at the decision-points that God places in our life every day.

God's plan is very specific and is not random—it is perfect.

This means that every part of God's plan, *including every one of the sins that we commit*, is all part of the infinite perfection of God's perfect eternal plan.

> *For **we are God's workmanship**, created in Christ Jesus to do good works, which God prepared in advance for us to do. (Ephesians 2:10; emphasis added)*

We, even in the very depths of our dark rebellion, remain the singular *purpose* of the perfection of God's creation—to the glory of God.

Copyright 2013 Michael K. Pasque

Day 16

Why Did God Give Us Our Sinful Nature? *"Contrast"*

We cannot even begin to comprehend the working of the mind of God.

And yet it is the earthly journey of the children of the kingdom of God to explore God's mind to the fullest limit of that which is provided—by His grace and revelation—specifically for that purpose.

Surely we can know from the logic of the preceding discussion that our nefarious, rebellious nature is critical to our perfection as eternal members of the kingdom of God.

But we want to do more than just logically establish this statement as fact.

We want to know why our nefarious, rebellious nature is critical to our perfection as eternal companions of God.

Specifically, why is a nefarious nature that leaves us bent on rebellion against the righteousness and holiness of our Creator so obviously critical to our perfection as eternal partners sharing in the loving fellowship of the Trinity?

Surely, on this side of eternity, we can never even hope to fully know why a nefarious nature was so obviously critical to the perfection of the sons and daughters of God.

And yet the written Word of God gives us strong hints as to the *why* behind this potentially revealing definer of our eternity.

Thus, our journey to go at least part way in our understanding of the critical necessity of our nefarious and rebellious human nature begins where everything

Copyright 2013 Michael K. Pasque

else in our life begins (and ends)—with the glory of God revealed in the cross of Christ.

Surely the reality of the cross speaks immeasurable volumes to the glory of God.

It is critical that we, as the princes and princesses of the eternal kingdom of God—and destined to share the glorious fellowship of the Trinity—fully comprehend, to the very depths of the capacity of created mankind, the glory of God.

Even Moses openly stated that his heart's desire was to see the fullness of the glory of God.

> And the LORD said to Moses, "I will do the very thing you have asked, because I am pleased with you and I know you by name."

> Then Moses said, "Now show me your glory." (Exodus 33:17-18)

We must know God's Glory.

This fact reverberates through every chapter of the Old Testament.

For it is on the pages of the Bible that we find the revelation of the attributes of God.

God's glory explodes from His every attribute.

God's glory bursts forth from His justice, righteousness, compassion, mercy, holiness, goodness, and love.

And the only way for us to fully know and experience the heights and the depths of the glory found in these attributes is to contrast them against their utter absence.

This is dangerous dark ground we explore.

Copyright 2013 Michael K. Pasque

Nonetheless, we must go further because of a single irrefutable fact: light is not appreciated as light except in the presence of darkness.

The only way to *know* light is to experience darkness.

And the *brightness* and glory of that light cannot be appreciated to its fullest except in the presence of *utter* darkness.

To enter into the eternal fellowship of God, we must *know* Him.

To know Him we must gain an appreciation of the brightness and glory of the bright light of His holiness.

Where do we, the created heirs to the kingdom of God, gain a suitable experience of darkness to provide that critical foil to God's perfect, uncreated, bright light (and thereby allow us to really *know* God)?

There is no doubt that the *perfectly opposite* foil to the bright light glory of God is the black heart of man.

Let there be no question in our minds of the completeness of God's grace in supplying the answer to this foundational question in the very nature of man—which represents nothing less than perfection in its portrayal of utter darkness.

Can we look at the thoughts, words, and deeds of mankind over the history of God's creation and see anything less than the ultimate representation of darkness?

The prince of darkness—himself being the master of darkness—has indwelled the heart of man and perpetrated nothing less than perfection in the display of the fullness of his darkness in the heart of man—that then being fully displayed in the history of mankind.

Indeed, the utter darkness of the nefarious, rebelliously sinful nature of man is the perfect contrast to the very bright light of the righteousness, justice, compassion, mercy, goodness, holiness, and love of God.

Our inherent, God-given, human nature is the precise opposite of God's.

It is the perfect foil.

Copyright 2013 Michael K. Pasque

Thus, only from our God-ordained perspective of utter darkness can the fullness of the glory of God be known.

Our created nature is, like the rest of the creation, perfect.

God in His perfect wisdom knew that we had to be that utter opposite to fully comprehend the grace, mercy, compassion, and love that is found and to be fully explored in our eternity with Him.

To be God's perfect eternal children in fulfilling our eternal destiny of fellowship with the three Persons of the Trinity, we must fully appreciate the glory of God that is found in His most righteous and holy attributes.

This full appreciation was simply not attainable except through the nefarious nature of man.

Many Christians struggle with the whole concept of evil.

We struggle with the obvious fact that God created everything that has been created—including evil—and that with great purpose, wisdom, and forethought.

But we can also know that the perfection of our eternity with Him is dependent upon our full appreciation of the glory found in His righteousness and holiness, and that the full appreciation of this glory is only fully achieved by *contrasting* God's righteousness and holiness with unrighteousness and evil.

We simply cannot appreciate—to the fullest extent possible—the glory of God's righteousness, justice, compassion, mercy, love, holiness, and goodness without the existence in our hearts of the wickedness, injustice, coldness, cruelty, hate, defilement, and badness that so naturally resides there.

In this context and while on this topic, we must also very briefly mention another vexing question that is closely associated with this discussion.

Why did God create people who will ultimately spend eternity in the fiery lake of burning sulfur?

To reach our heart's desire we must love God.

Copyright 2013 Michael K. Pasque

We cannot love Him to the fullest without knowing His glory.

We cannot know the height, width, length, and depth of His glory without living, breathing, touching, speaking with, and interacting with that which is His polar opposite.

Further, to fully know God, we must experience evil not only in ourselves, but also in its *relational* fullness.

This critical relational perspective is vital to the very relational eternity that God has planned for us—the foundation of which will be our fellowship with each other and with the three Persons of the Trinity.

And this relational perspective can only be developed during this earthly life in interpersonal interactions with all varieties of people.

Obviously, evil people are critical to this process if we are to experience relational contrast to the glory of God.

If there was no evil in our hearts and if there were no evil people with whom we could relate, we simply could never come to the fullness of the knowledge of the goodness and glory of God that will usher us into eternity.

If there is no darkness in opposition to God's glory, then there is no contrast to set it off, to explain it, to fully expose its details, to fully reveal the glory of the goodness of God.

Only contrast exposes every nook and cranny of that which must be exposed.

Contrast is the answer.

If there is no darkness, there is no appreciation of light.

And every bit of the inherently sinful nature of man was necessary for the loving fellowship that will be ours.

We are the eternal darlings of God's heart and *fully* knowing Him is the desire of ours.

Copyright 2013 Michael K. Pasque

Day 17

Why Does Evil Even Exist?
Teaching the Knowledge of God

The nature and necessity of evil deserves further exploration.

We were created with purpose.

This purpose extends far outside of the boundaries of this world and this life.

Our creation purpose is to spend eternity as sons and daughters of God in eternal and loving fellowship with the three Persons of the Trinity (and with each other).

> *For while we are in this tent, we groan and are burdened, because we do not wish to be unclothed but to be clothed with our heavenly dwelling, so that what is mortal may be* **swallowed up by life**. *Now it is God who has made us* **for this very purpose** *and has given us the Spirit as a deposit, guaranteeing what is to come. (2Corinthians 5:4-5; emphasis added)*

> *Everyone who believes that Jesus is the Christ is born of God, and everyone who loves the father loves his child as well. (1John 5:1; emphasis added)*

Copyright 2013 Michael K. Pasque

You are all sons of God through faith in Christ Jesus, for all of you who were baptized into Christ have clothed yourselves with Christ. (Galatians 3: 26-27)

The core desire of our deepest heart springs from our creation purpose: to subserviently and sacrificially love God for eternity.

And he died for all, that those who live should no longer live for themselves but for him who died for them and was raised again. (2Corinthians 5:15)

We cannot subserviently, sacrificially love God (and therefore we cannot spend eternity in loving fellowship with Him) unless we *know* Him.

In fact, Jesus addressed precisely this when describing the importance of *knowing* God.

He stated that *"eternal life"* itself is in fact *defined* as <u>knowing</u> the Father, *"the only true God,"* and His Son Jesus.

*Now this is **eternal life**: that they may **know** you, the only true God, and Jesus Christ, whom you have sent. (John 17:3; emphasis added)*

The Garden of Eden is perfect, no doubt.

Nonetheless, at least in part due precisely to this perfection, the state of man in the Garden of Eden was anything but perfect.

Before the fall, man simply could not have *known*, could not have had experiential *knowledge* of, many of the most important core attributes of God.

Copyright 2013 Michael K. Pasque

In other words, in Eden before the fall, man simply did not—could not—*know* God.

Thus, the condition of man in Eden in regard to obtaining his creation purpose and fulfilling his deepest heart desire was not complete and therefore not good.

God is perfect, infinite, and bright white pure in all of His attributes like holiness, righteousness, faithfulness, justice, omniscience, omnipotence, and love.

This is the message we have heard from him and declare to you: God is light; in him there is no darkness at all. (1John 1:5)

It is the perfect purity and infinite depth of each of God's attributes that make it impossible for us to fully understand them and appreciate them to their fullest— thereby making us less than perfect partners for an eternity of fellowship with God.

In other words, the infinite bright whiteness of His attributes keeps us from appreciating their detailed intricacy without the revealing addition of *contrast*.

Thus, it is the infinitely perfect nature of each of God's attributes that makes trying to know them like trying to discern the attributes of pure white objects in a pure white room—the depth, the fullness of the shape, and the richness of the design of the objects in the room simply cannot be appreciated without the definition provided by contrast and shadows.

*Even in the case of lifeless things that make sounds, such as the flute or harp, how will anyone know **what tune is being played** unless there is a **distinction** in the notes? (1Corinthians 14:7; emphasis added)*

Copyright 2013 Michael K. Pasque

Contrast and shadows in a bright white room can only occur by the addition of darkness—the opposite of white.

Thus, in order for us to *see*, we need darkness.

Thus, for mankind to come to even a basic knowledge of the attributes of God—and certainly a knowledge upon which an eternal loving fellowship could be based—man had to be given darkness: man had to be given knowledge of that which God *is not* in order to *know* what God is.

In order to love God with the richness and intensity that is worthy of God, this knowledge of God (derived from knowledge of what He is not), must be mind-transformational, soul-captivating, deep-heart, physically palpable, and spring from our innermost being.

Thus, to obtain a knowledge of the attributes of God that would generate the depth of subservient, sacrificial love that alone allows the deep heart fellowship that is worthy of an eternity as a child of God, man could not be simply *given* a book to read or instruction in a classroom.

Man could not be simply *told* of the darkness that gives contrast to the attributes of God.

Man had to *experience* darkness.

Man had to *live* darkness.

Man had to *be* darkness.

Man had to *confront* darkness.

Man, through the cross of Christ, had to *overcome* darkness.

Man had to experience in the very deep reaches of his heart the very depths of darkness so that he could differentiate, know, and *fully* appreciate the brightness of the infinitely pure white light of God.

Copyright 2013 Michael K. Pasque

Every son and daughter of God who would spend eternity in loving fellowship with the three Persons of the Trinity needed to live and breath darkness—they had to *be* the darkness.

Only a full knowledge of the darkness that is as deep as the light is bright could truly illuminate the attributes of God and serve as a foundation for a love for God that is worthy of an eternity in the fellowship of the Trinity.

In order to gain that full knowledge of the darkness, it was not good enough that we should just see the antithesis of God on display—instead, every son and daughter of God had to become, to embody, to know within themselves, to have their heart ruled by the fullness of the darkness that is the contrast to God.

To know God's love, righteousness, justice, compassion, mercy, faithfulness, and forgiveness, every son and daughter of God had to mentally, spiritually, emotionally, and physically *embody* hate, sinful rebellion, unrighteousness, self-righteousness, injustice, cruelty, unfaithfulness, and unforgiveness.

And we had to witness, feel, hear, smell, and touch His omnipotent power.

Thus, God gave man his sinful nature.

Once again:

Why, O LORD, do you make us wander from your ways and harden our hearts so we do not revere you? (Isaiah 63:17a)

And that is why evil exists in the creation.

And that is why evil people are allowed to continue to exist and flourish in this world.

And that is why we must continue on in our sanctification even after we accept the redemption offered by belief in the shed blood of Jesus Christ.

And this is what the parable of the yeast was really all about:

Copyright 2013 Michael K. Pasque

He told them still another parable: "The kingdom of heaven is like yeast that a woman took and mixed into a large amount of flour until it worked all through the dough." (Matthew 13:33)

Just like the bread, which cannot be the best it can be without the yeast to make it rise, in our life we need that which the yeast represents: evil and sin.

Without the presence of evil in our hearts, without embodying sin, we could never become perfect, we could never become all that we needed to be as adopted children of God enjoying the eternal fellowship of the Trinity forever.

In other words, we had to become *like* God in our knowledge of both good *and evil* in order to be able to fellowship with God for eternity.

*And the LORD God said, "The man has now become **like one of us**, knowing good and evil. He must not be allowed to reach out his hand and take also from the tree of life and eat, and live forever." (Genesis 3:22; emphasis added)*

This acquisition of that knowledge of both good and evil—in its most profound and deepest state—was the whole purpose of *the fall* of mankind.

Yes, *the fall* had a purpose in God's creation—or it simply would not have occurred.

As we have stated, God's creation is infinitely perfect in every detail—nothing occurs that does not need to occur to obtain that perfection.

Besides, without the fall and the flourishing of evil in the hearts of men, how could we have ever had the setting, the backdrop in which we could see the magnificence of God's personality played out?

Copyright 2013 Michael K. Pasque

After all, He is not a machine, a program, or a *force*.

He is a *Person* with a magnificent, unique, relational personality.

How could we have known His personable nature and His flair for the dramatic and adventurous?

How could we have known His quirky taunting—and His desire to *pick a fight* with the evil of self-righteousness—without the fall of mankind?

We had to meet Him in an environment that was rife with danger and battle and intrigue and difficulty and distress—and astonishing rescue!

If we are going to spend eternity with Him, we must first be able to appreciate Him and that can only come with a knowledge of His personality that can only be gained outside of the Garden of Eden.

The solution was simple.

God designed a creation full of quirky, unique, sometimes-bizarre circumstances that would draw out—would fully display—the truly unique personality of our wonderful God.

This includes not only His encouraging, compassionate, empathetic, and extraordinarily loving nature, but also the occasional quirky taunting, kidding, and sarcasm.

The facts are clear.

To fellowship with God for eternity, we had to *know* evil.

We had to see it, encounter it, endure it, and be it.

We had to confront it and, *through the cross of Christ*, we had to defeat it.

We had to have a working knowledge of not only good, but also evil—because we really could not know *good* without knowing evil.

They come together as a set—one is not knowable without the other.

That is why God refers to the missing ingredient above as *"the knowledge of good and evil."*

Copyright 2013 Michael K. Pasque

> Bottom line: to achieve our creation purpose and obtain our deepest heart desire—to spend eternity in loving fellowship with each other and with the three Persons of the Trinity—we needed contrast to the *good* of God; we had to become *"like"* the Trinity in acquiring *"the knowledge of good and evil."*

Before Eden was ever created, God planned the *fall* of man that would take place there.

The *fall* of man in the Garden of Eden was an irreplaceable, mandatory component of God's plan for the eternal fellowship of the Triune Godhead because the eternal sons and daughters of the eternal kingdom of God could not enter into eternal loving fellowship with the three Persons of the Trinity without it.

After all, who can truly love someone that they do not know?

Copyright 2013 Michael K. Pasque

Day 18

If God Did Not Create It, Then From Where Did All This Evil Come?
The "Creation" Of Evil

We have established the critical necessity of darkness, of contrast.

So, from where does this darkness—this evil—come?

Most refuse to believe that God had anything to do with *creating* evil.

Some say that evil is purely the creation of man or of Satan or that it is somehow *the absence* of God (Who is, of course, purely good).

First of all, one cannot attribute the creation of evil to man or to Satan, because the Bible clearly states that *"without him nothing was made that has been made,"* (meaning that God, through Jesus, created everything that has been created).

In other words, man and Satan have created precisely *nothing*.

> *In the beginning was the Word, and the Word was with God, and the Word was God. He was with God in the beginning. Through him all things were made; without him nothing was made that has been made. (John 1:1-3)*

Further, since we have established from the Bible that God created everything that has been created, if you contend that evil was not created by God, then you are saying that evil is *uncreated*.

We also know that nothing fits that very holy word *Uncreated* except God.

Copyright 2013 Michael K. Pasque

For if there was anything or anyone not created and therefore uniquely outside of God, then by definition, it or they are, in fact, *God*. (See *Knowledge of the Holy* by A.W. Tozer)

In other words, if you say that God did not create evil and that evil is, therefore, uncreated (see scripture above), then it must follow that evil is therefore outside of God.

And if you are saying that evil is both uncreated and outside of God, then you are assigning evil *God* status.

There cannot be two separate *uncreated* (and therefore *God*) entities existing simultaneously. (Once again, see *Knowledge of the Holy* by A.W. Tozer)

There can only be one conclusion.

Evil is not outside of God, is not *uncreated*, and is not God; therefore, *evil is created*.

Since God, through Jesus Christ, created everything that has been created, then God created evil.

God created evil.

I form the light and create darkness, I bring prosperity and create disaster; I, the LORD, do all these things. (Isaiah 45:7)

Many would argue that this simply cannot be true.

After all, "God is good—all the time."

Nonetheless, the Bible is clear in telling us that we were created with an evil, rebellious sinful nature.

Who created us?

We did not.

Who gave us our sinful nature?

Copyright 2013 Michael K. Pasque

We did not.

God created us.

God created us with a sinful nature.

God created evil.

So, we are back to our original problem:

If God created evil, why did a *good* God create evil?

This singular question is the foundational objection behind much that troubles believers, adamant non-believers, and seekers alike.

It is the foundation for such questions as:

Why does a "good" God let evil exist?

Why does God allow such "bad" things to happen to "good" people?

Who created bad people?

What happens to bad people?

Do bad people have a choice as to whether they are bad or good?

Were people really created whose only purpose was to be bad?

If, as the Bible says, faith is a gift from God and faith is required for salvation and eternal life comes only from this faith, then are the people to whom God does not give faith created for the sole purpose of burning in hell forever?

Did God really create individuals just to burn in hell forever?

Why did God give man a nature that has a clear proclivity toward rebellion and sin?

If everything in my life is by the careful planning of God, why is it so important to my perfection in the image of Jesus and my eternity that I not only experience so much darkness in my life, but that I also actually generate so much darkness (sin) in my life?

Did the devil really plant the bad people?

Are bad people really sons of the devil?

Copyright 2013 Michael K. Pasque

In other words, were bad people bad from the very beginning with no real hope of any other outcome than that which is reserved for bad people?

Finally, why are the weeds (the bad people) allowed to grow with the grain (the good people) until harvest time?

I purposely saved this last question until last because in this discussion, it is a pivotal question.

Jesus tells us the answer to this last question in a parable.

If the weeds are pulled up—in other words, if the evil people in our life are taken out—then some of the grain may be pulled up also.

In other words, the full maturation and ultimate safe harvest of the ripened grain is dependent upon leaving the weeds in place.

And so it is in our life.

We can be assured that the completion of our salvation and sanctification (i.e. our ripening into that which God planned for us) is dependent upon those weeds being present in our life.

The weeds are necessary.

They are there for a purpose.

They are there to complete our being made into the likeness of the perfect first fruits of the harvest: Jesus.

So, let's get more specific.

How do the weeds—the evil people in our life—contribute to our sanctification, to our understanding of God, to the knowledge that is necessary for our transformation into the likeness of Jesus?

The answer to this question is amply elucidated by a simple illustration.

Imagine that all that existed around us was the bright white light of God's infinitely pure righteousness.

Let's extend the analogy.

Copyright 2013 Michael K. Pasque

Instead of using bright white light as a descriptor of one of God's attributes (in this case, His righteousness), let's take it a step further and actually *substitute*—for the sake of illustration—white light for God's righteousness.

In this extension of the analogy, all that exists around us is the purest, infinitely bright white light.

In other words, imagine that there is no darkness—none whatsoever.

There is no night, no blackness, no contrast—just bright white light.

This means that not only is there no darkness, but there are no slightly differing shades of white—for, after all, differing shades of white are made by adding light touches of darkness.

Thus, there aren't even any shadows.

Imagine only the bright white light representing God's infinitely pure righteousness.

What do you see?

This is a frightening thought for sure.

For in this purely white world that is devoid of any darkness whatsoever, we see nothing.

There is no contrast, so there is no differentiation.

We are blind.

Utterly blind.

Even though we are surrounded by the infinite fullness of utterly perfect righteousness, we are blind—we cannot even see the righteousness *because we have nothing to contrast it against.*

So, we *see* nothing.

Just like we cannot visually separate the objects in our perfectly bright white world from each other, we cannot discern the defining characteristics of the attributes of God.

Copyright 2013 Michael K. Pasque

Without *contrast*, there is no visual discernment—no vision.

Without differentiation of some kind between the various objects or individuals in your bright white immediate environment, there is no differentiating between them.

We are motionless because we are blind.

We cannot move toward God because we cannot seem Him.

Contrast is needed.

Contrast is what differentiates between objects and individuals.

And in the world of bright white, contrast can only be added by the addition of black.

So, in this imaginary pure bright white world of God's righteousness, there is no knowledge of the defining characteristics of the objects and individuals in the surrounding environment—in other words, *there is no knowledge of the attributes or characteristics of God Himself.*

For in a creation that is filled only with the infinitely pure bright whiteness of God's righteousness, we could not even see the bright whiteness of God's righteousness.

We would be totally blind.

God would be hidden from us.

The defining characteristics of God's attributes would be hidden from us.

In fact, by the isolated presence of only bright white, we do not even appreciate the bright white.

It is just background for us.

It is all that we see, so we see nothing.

In this bright white world, God is utterly invisible to us.

Copyright 2013 Michael K. Pasque

So, that which we were created to appreciate, fellowship with, and subserviently love for eternity does not—as far as we are concerned (since we cannot detect it)—even exist.

If our creation purpose is to spend eternity as children of the eternal kingdom of God, then we must be able to participate by subservient sacrificial love in fellowship with the Trinity.

To have fellowship with the Trinity—and the Bible stresses this repeatedly—we must *know* God.

And to know God we must be enabled (by this physical life that we live) to interact with, walk with, obey, serve, and love God—none of which is possible without knowing Him, what He is like—His attributes—and Who He is.

We have to be able to *see* God in the bright whiteness of His purity.

Thus, the only way to *see* God—to physically experience God—is to palpably and *physically experience that which He is not:* we need contrast.

> To obtain our creation purpose and deep heart desire, we desperately need to not just see, but to physically and palpably and audibly and visually *become* the contrast to God's infinitely perfect bright white righteousness.

God had to create contrast.

God had to create darkness.

He reveals the deep things of darkness and brings deep shadows into the light. (Job 12:22)

God had to create the opposite of His bright white righteousness.

God had to create evil.

Copyright 2013 Michael K. Pasque

God needed to set apart that which is of God from that which is not of God so that we could know and experience and appreciate…God.

This is why we could not just be created into heaven or be transported straight to heaven after accepting the gift of salvation offered by Jesus—but instead must live this physical life and experience that which we all experience.

> Dear friends, do not be surprised at the painful trial you are suffering, **as though something strange were happening to you**. (1Peter 4:12; emphasis added)

> No temptation has seized you **except what is common to man**. And God is faithful; he will not let you be tempted beyond what you can bear. But when you are tempted, he will also provide a way out so that you can stand up under it. (1Corinthians 10:13; emphasis added)

But the analogy goes further.

For our world does not just exist simply with infinitely pure bright white being contrasted by infinite darkness.

Our world is not just black and white.

Instead, in order to best display and teach us about the defining characteristics of His attributes, God judiciously and carefully and with infinite wisdom introduced *shades of gray*.

Shades of gray are shades of contrast.

Shades of gray are mixtures of pure white and pure darkness.

Shades of contrast tell us something more about God.

They tell us that God's righteousness is not just *typed* or described by *white*.

Copyright 2013 Michael K. Pasque

As we mentioned already, there are many shades of white.

There is worldly *good* (white) and there is the goodness of God (bright white).

And what the many shades of white give us is not only contrast between the objects, individuals, and deeds in our environment, but also between the work of man and the work and essence of God.

For God is the absolute absence of any darkness.

> *This is the message we have heard from him and declare to you: God is light; in him **there is no darkness** at all. (1John 1:5; emphasis added)*

The infinitely pure bright white of God's righteousness contrasts starkly— infinitely—with even the brightest white of which mankind's very best efforts are capable.

Those very best efforts of mankind are seen as *"filthy rags" (Isaiah 64:6)* when compared to work of God.

These are opposed to the bright white linen garments we are given to wear in heaven.

> *Let us rejoice and be glad and give him glory! For the wedding of the Lamb has come, and his bride has made herself ready. Fine linen, bright and clean, was given her to wear." (Fine linen stands for the righteous acts of the saints.) (Revelation 19:7-8)*

No righteousness even attainable by man can do anything except sharply contrast the infinite purity of the whiteness of God's righteousness.

Copyright 2013 Michael K. Pasque

Only clothed in the bright white righteousness of Jesus Christ do we attain sanctification stature as the bride of Christ.

Thus, not only is darkness necessary to help us separate, define, and acknowledge the attributes of God, but the shades of darkness allow us to fully appreciate not just the whiteness of God's righteousness, but the extreme *fullness* of the infinitely pure bright whiteness of God.

So, not only is darkness necessary, but so also are shades of gray necessary, to contrast, and therefore allow us to see and appreciate to its fullest, the righteousness—and all of the other defining attributes—of God.

So, yes, the creation of evil was necessary.

And yes, the creation of those who would choose eternal darkness over eternal light was necessary to contrast and *set apart* or *make holy* the eternal children of God.

We, by the grace of God, are different and the only way that we can see this God-given, God-ordained difference is to contrast ourselves against the absence of that which is *God's righteousness given as grace to the unworthy*.

So not only is evil allowed to exist in the world, and not only are there evil people in the world *"like brute beasts, creatures of instinct, born only to be caught and destroyed, and like beasts they too will perish" (2Peter 2:12)*, but they (like the weeds in the parable at the beginning of this chapter) are allowed to continue to influence our lives—to supply that vital contrast to God's righteous attributes—so that we can fully know and feel and palpably experience God's righteousness to its brightest and whitest extent during our life—and all of this by the grace of God and in preparation for our eternity.

The evil people who populate our lives serve another similar purpose.

They teach us of another of God's attributes: His power.

By their evil nature, they oppose God and they oppose us.

Copyright 2013 Michael K. Pasque

Rescues are often needed.

That was what the book of Exodus was all about: a rescue!

And the solution was the power of God.

> *But I have raised you up for this very purpose, that I might show you my power and that my name might be proclaimed in all the earth. (Exodus 9:16)*

This is also what the Gospel of Jesus Christ is all about: the demonstration of God's attributes.

The Gospel story teaches us not only of the compassion, grace, mercy, and love of God, but also of His power.

So, God puts up with these evil weeds so that the fullness of the harvest can be realized—so that sons and daughters of God can know to its fullest extent, His *"power"* **and** *"the riches of his glory."*

> *What if God, choosing to **show** his **wrath** and **make** his **power known**, **bore with great patience the objects of his wrath**—prepared for destruction? What if he did this to **make** the riches of his **glory known** to the objects of his mercy, whom he prepared in advance for glory—even us, whom he also called, not only from the Jews but also from the Gentiles? (Romans 9:22-24; emphasis added)*

In other words, God endures the presence of evil so that the future children of the eternal kingdom of God can know *"his glory."*

The definition of *"his glory"* is critical to our understanding of the necessity of evil in the creation.

Copyright 2013 Michael K. Pasque

God's "glory" defies definition.

It cannot be fully defined in a manner that we could ever understand.

Nevertheless, for our purposes, its definition is only adequately defined by the inclusion of all of God's known attributes.

Together, these attributes—most of which are preceded by the words *infinitely perfect*—make up the knowable inherent nature of God from which springs that magnificence referred to here as *"his glory."*

Thus, without God's endurance of the presence of evil, we could not know, to their knowable extent, the fullness of each of God's attributes.

We will review many of these known attributes in light of the presence of evil because the written Word of God uses many—such as His power, wrath, righteousness, justice, and love—as examples in explaining the necessity of the presence of evil, the fall of man, and the creation of those who would never see heaven.

After all, how would we have ever known of God's righteousness and *"wrath"* and infinite *"power"* if not for the presence of *"the objects of his wrath"*?

The case for our need to experience (and thereby *know*) the power of God can be expanded even further than this.

Understanding God's power is not just part of the post-salvation sanctification process of turning us into the likeness of God's Son Jesus, but it is an essential component of the process of our very salvation itself.

I pray also that the eyes of your heart may be enlightened in order that you may know the hope to which he has called you, the riches of his glorious inheritance in the saints, and his incomparably great power for us who believe. That power is like the working of his mighty strength, which he exerted in Christ when he raised him from

Copyright 2013 Michael K. Pasque

the dead and seated him at his right hand in the heavenly realms, far
above all rule and authority, power and dominion, and every title that
can be given, not only in the present age but also in the one to come.
(Ephesians 1:18-21; emphasis added)

We are not just tested daily in our knowledge of God's power; it is also on the *final exam.*

We are told that the essence of our salvation is in the acknowledgement that God has the power to do exactly what He says He will do.

To be saved, we must accept as fact that He who we are trusting for our eternal salvation actually has the power to carry it off.

Yet he did not waver through unbelief regarding the promise of God,
but was strengthened in his faith and gave glory to God, being fully
*persuaded that God had **power** to do what he had promised. **This** is*
why "it was credited to him as righteousness." (Romans 4:20-22;
emphasis added)

It would be illogical to place our faith in someone for something as vital as our eternal salvation without a firm belief that such a task was not only their will, but also within their power.

For not only is it taught to us on a daily basis, but so also is it essential for our eternity.

How would we have ever known of *"the riches"* of God's *"glory"* and *"mercy"* if not for the contrast supplied by the visible lives and final disposition of *"the objects of his wrath"*?

Copyright 2013 Michael K. Pasque

> Righteousness has no meaning without the existence of evil and heaven has no meaning without the existence of hell and the work of God has no meaning without the contrast of the utterly futile works of man.

Further, mercy, compassion, and love have no meaning without the existence of judgment, punishment, and wrath.

At the very least, the *richness* of heaven is not appreciated to the same degree that it would be appreciated without the definition of the *heinousness* of hell.

And, yes, because God's creation is wonderfully physical and appreciated only with a full set of senses, it was necessary for the perfection of the sons and daughters of God and therefore for the perfection of God's eternity—that we be endowed with a sinful, rebellious nature that seeks to actually *physically experience* that which is in full opposition, full *contrast* to God.

For only in the *fleshing out* of our experience of that which so darkly contrasts against the bright whiteness of God do we really gain a palpable, tangible knowledge of God's attributes that will allow us to *see* Him in His fullest in eternity's light and to appreciate Him to the fullest in our eternity of fellowship with Him.

We had to become that unrighteousness that is the polar opposite of the righteousness of God

> *But if **our unrighteousness brings out God's righteousness more clearly**, what shall we say? That God is unjust in bringing his wrath on us? (I am using a human argument.) (Romans 3:5; emphasis added)*

Copyright 2013 Michael K. Pasque

To experience our creation purpose and obtain the God-ordained deep desires of our heart, we had to *be* precisely that which God is not.

We had to feel and smell and hear and touch and *be* the evil darkness that wells up inside of us from our sinful nature so that we could know exactly what God is not.

To do this, we had to travel, very literally, to that edge of obliteration.

How else could we be redeemed?

We had to squarely face our eternal destruction.

How else could we be rescued?

We had to know the depth of our sickening filthiness.

How else could we know the height, width, and depth of God's righteousness?

We had to become darkness rescued by the bright white light of God.

> *Because I have sinned against him, I will bear the LORD's wrath, until he pleads my case and establishes my right. He will bring me out into the light; I will see his righteousness. (Micah 7:9)*

And in knowing the *rescuer's heart* of God we also come to know that which we never could have known except by wandering aimlessly to the brink of destruction: the compassion, mercy, and subservient, sacrificial love of God.

Adam could not have known the depth of God's compassion, mercy and love in the Garden of Eden.

Surely he knew that God loved him.

But there was no way to demonstrate the magnitude of that love or the extremes of the compassion and mercy that are the byproduct of that love without the contrast of evil, without becoming darkness.

Copyright 2013 Michael K. Pasque

God needed to stage the most hopeless of circumstances so that He could show the true depth of His love.

To do this, He was willing to get into the trenches with us to fight the fight that had to be fought on our behalf.

He was willing to truly experience infinite suffering in order to emblazon the impression of His love eternally on our hearts.

He staged nothing less than the most desperate rescue in the most hopeless of circumstances that could be imagined by the infinite, all-powerful, all-knowing, all-wise mind of God: He would die in our place to guarantee our freedom to join Him in the eternal kingdom of God.

> *But God **demonstrates his own love for us** in this: While we were still sinners, Christ died for us. (Romans 5:8; emphasis added)*

How else could we be made perfect and given bright white robes to wear?

How could we know the redeeming *rescuer's heart* of our loving God without the entrance of sin into the Garden of Eden?

In knowing what God is not, we know what God is.

For He is *all else* that He is not.

And now we know what God is not.

We have experienced it to its very deepest mire and slime.

And only in the very depths of our own personal darkness can we know the fullness of the bright white attributes of God that strike deepest in the heart of man.

Only in the darkness of our utter lack of faithfulness can we know the richness of God's faithfulness.

Copyright 2013 Michael K. Pasque

And only in living life in our sinful nature can we know the fullness of the compassionate, merciful, subservient, sacrificial love that is manifest in the grace of the blood of Christ that saves us.

How could Adam and Eve in the Garden of Eden have possibly known of the compassionate, merciful, subservient, sacrificial love of God without the cross of Christ?

> *This is how we know what love is:* Jesus Christ laid down his life for *us. And we ought to lay down our lives for our brothers. (1John 3:16; emphasis added)*

We had to be created with a sinful nature to get the end result that God wanted from His creation (the reason that He created in the first place): to create the children of God who have experienced at every level a *knowledge* of God that thereby enables the deep, rich fellowship of subservient, sacrificial love that characterizes the fellowship in the eternal dance of the three Persons of the Triune Godhead.

And in this same act of salvation on the cross of Christ we live in the midst of the palpable reality of God's *righteousness* and *justice—attributes that remained hidden in Eden.*

Our evil is palpable, tangible contrast to God's infinitely perfect, pure white righteousness.

And that perfect righteousness of God demands justice.

That very same justice is being played out before us in the necessity of the incarnation and death of God's Son—all so that we might live.

How could we have known of God's justice in Eden?

Copyright 2013 Michael K. Pasque

How could we have known of God's justice without our fall?

> God presented him as a sacrifice of atonement, through faith in his
> blood. He did this to **demonstrate his justice**, because in his
> forbearance he had left the sins committed beforehand unpunished—
> he did it to **demonstrate his justice** at the present time, so as to be just
> and the one who justifies those who have faith in Jesus. (Romans
> 3:25-26; emphasis added)

We certainly could not really know the infinite perfection of God's justice
without the very real presence of Hell.

> The LORD is slow to anger and great in power; **the LORD will not
> leave the guilty unpunished.** His way is in the whirlwind and the
> storm, and clouds are the dust of his feet. (Nahum 1:3; emphasis
> added)

How could we have ever known in the Garden of Eden that God was in fact the
center, the seat, the all-encompassing source of *truth* without our embodiment of
falsehood.

> Someone might argue, "If **my falsehood enhances God's truthfulness
> and so increases his glory**, why am I still condemned as a sinner?"
> (Romans 3:7; emphasis added)

Further still, without our fall, God's *wrath*—and in that wrath a true *fear* of
God—could never have been known.

Copyright 2013 Michael K. Pasque

An oracle is within my heart concerning the sinfulness of the wicked: **There is no fear of God** *before his eyes. (Psalm 36:1; emphasis added)*

Without witnessing His perfectly, infinitely righteous response to evil, to rebellious sin, how could we have known the attributes of God that were only demonstrated outside of Eden?

Where in Eden before the fall did God ever have an opportunity to demonstrate His attributes of *jealousy*, *wrath*, *vengeance*, and *anger*?

These most difficult of God's known attributes are, nonetheless, still attributes of God—and in this fact, they are every bit as important as the attributes to which we so readily cling (God's compassion, mercy, kindness, goodness, and love).

The LORD is a jealous and avenging God; the LORD takes vengeance and is filled with wrath. The LORD takes vengeance on his foes and maintains his wrath against his enemies. The LORD is slow to anger and great in power; the LORD will not leave the guilty unpunished. His way is in the whirlwind and the storm, and clouds are the dust of his feet. He rebukes the sea and dries it up; he makes all the rivers run dry. Bashan and Carmel wither and the blossoms of Lebanon fade. The mountains quake before him and the hills melt away. The earth trembles at his presence, the world and all who live in it. Who can withstand his indignation? Who can endure his fierce anger? His wrath is poured out like fire; the rocks are shattered before him. (Nahum 1:2-6)

Copyright 2013 Michael K. Pasque

And only against the dark contrast of the heart, the mind, the thoughts, the words, the actions, the hate, and the eternal destiny of those who will not believe—who were created as *"brute beasts...born only to be caught and destroyed"*—is the fullness of the compassionate mercy, love, and grace of God palpably experienced by the eternal children of God.

And without our God-given nefarious, rebellious sinful nature, there can be simply no understanding of God's *mercy*.

> *For God has bound all men over to disobedience* **so that he may have mercy on them all**. *(Romans 11:32; emphasis added)*

Our knowledge of the fullness of God's *mercy* demanded that we not only become unmerciful, but in that unmerciful state also become hopelessly dependent upon the mercy of God.

> *Who is a God like you, who pardons sin and forgives the transgression of the remnant of his inheritance? You do not stay angry forever but delight to show mercy. You will again have compassion on us; you will tread our sins underfoot and hurl all our iniquities into the depths of the sea. (Micah 7:18-19)*

Without our sinful nature, we would not have heard, seen, touched, smelled— we would never have *known*—the mercy of God.

We can rest assured that in that absence of experiential knowledge, something about us would not have been perfect for the eternity that God has planned for us.

Copyright 2013 Michael K. Pasque

In that experience is the fullness of the knowledge of God that will make our eternity as heirs of the kingdom of God perfect and that makes all of this life of ours not only necessary but infinitely spectacular.

Finally, we must remember that our goal in this life is to be made into the likeness of Jesus, the Son of God.

How can we know where we are headed if we do not know the attributes of Jesus?

How can we seek to emulate these attributes if we do not know them, if we have never experienced them?

Adam didn't know them.

He couldn't have.

So, God's plan is becoming clearer.

We needed to know God and there is no way to know the attributes of He who we would be modeled after—Jesus—without living in the depths of the *contrast* that makes them so very visual, so very audible, so very palpable.

There was nothing complete or perfect about Adam and Eve's knowledge of God in Garden of Eden.

In other words, there was simply no chance that Adam and Eve could know the fullness of God's attributes without *"the knowledge of good and evil."*

> *The LORD God took the man and put him in the Garden of Eden to work it and take care of it. And the LORD God commanded the man, "You are free to eat from any tree in the garden; but you must not eat from the tree of **the knowledge of good and evil**, for when you eat of it you will surely die." (Genesis 2:15-17; emphasis added)*

Only in eating the fruit, did Adam and Eve came to *know* what God is *not*.

Copyright 2013 Michael K. Pasque

And only by knowing what God is not were they enabled to truly know God.

The eating of that low hanging fruit, indeed, indirectly offered a pathway to the wisdom of the full knowledge of God that is so critical to our eternity as members of the fellowship of the kingdom of God.

Surely Eve sinned, but she wasn't wrong in her statements regarding the fruit.

The fruit was indeed *"desirable for gaining wisdom"* — just not in the manner in which she probably expected.

> When the woman saw that the fruit of the tree was good for food and pleasing to the eye, and also **desirable for gaining wisdom**, she took some and ate it. She also gave some to her husband, who was with her, and he ate it. *(Genesis 3:6; emphasis added)*

Adam and Eve could not just hear about what God is not, they had to *embody* it.

> And the LORD God said, "The man has now become **like one of us,** knowing good and evil. He must not be allowed to reach out his hand and take also from the tree of life and eat, and live forever." *(Genesis 3:22; emphasis added)*

We needed that *fall* to complete us for our role in God's eternity.

We had to become what Jesus was not so that we could be made into His likeness.

In other words, we could not spend eternity in fellowship with God without that very same knowledge of good and evil whose acquisition made it impossible for us to join the loving fellowship with the three Persons of the Triune Godhead.

Copyright 2013 Michael K. Pasque

The very thing that made us eligible also disqualified us.

We needed to be rescued from a status that would prohibit us from entering into the loving fellowship for which we were created.

We were in need of a rescue—and this is the Gospel of Jesus Christ.

Thus, evil was always *in* the plan.

God created evil as an intrinsic part of the creation.

Evil is not just an intrinsic part; it is a critical part of the creation.

Without evil, the creation would have been incomplete—and most importantly, the purpose of the creation would have been impossible to achieve: that purpose being the creation and sanctification of the eternal sons and daughters of God who will enter into the eternal fellowship of the three Persons of the Triune God as princes and princesses of the eternal kingdom of God.

The entirety of this process that we call *our life* on this earth has a purpose.

That purpose is to prepare us in a palpable and meaningful manner for our eternity.

That purpose is to prepare us to achieve our creation purpose—to spend eternity in loving fellowship with each other as part of the sacrificially subservient loving fellowship of the Triune Godhead.

For in this process of *our life* is contained our salvation and our sanctification.

*From one man he made every nation of men, that they should inhabit the whole earth; and **he determined** the times set for them and the exact places where they should live. God did this **so that men would seek him and perhaps reach out for him and find him**, though he is not far from each one of us. (Acts 17: 26-27; emphasis added)*

Copyright 2013 Michael K. Pasque

And in that sanctification is found the testing, training, and transformation that are our pathway to godliness.

And that godliness is an utterly radical change from our human perspective to that eternal perspective of God.

And that attainment of godliness is what prepares us for the true *life* to come:

> *For physical training is of some value, but* **godliness has value** *for all things, holding promise for both the present life and* **the life to come**. *(1Timothy 4:8; emphasis added)*

Thus, when we stand back and look objectively at the plan of God, which necessarily includes those two entities that we call *good* and *evil*, it becomes readily apparent that both are necessary to get us where we need to go.

In the attainment of our creation purpose, that which we call *evil* is every bit as necessary, every bit as vital, every bit as critical as that which we call *good*.

We could not achieve our creation purpose, satisfy our deep heart desire, or fulfill the will of God without that which we call *evil*.

It therefore becomes obvious to even the most stubborn of us that when we look back upon our life from eternity—with the eternal perspective of God—it will be obvious that that which we now call *evil* is in fact every bit as deserving of the classification *good*.

In summary:

Only in showing us the utter depths of evil, death, and destruction could God show us the true heights of His glorious attributes.

But it is even better than that.

He did not just *show* us the depths of evil, death, and destruction.

Copyright 2013 Michael K. Pasque

Instead, God actually let us *interact with* and *become* the very depths of evil, death, and destruction—all to ultimately become the true heights of God's glory as we take our position—by the grace of the cross of Christ—as true adopted brothers and sisters of Jesus, and therefore *heirs* to the eternal kingdom of God.

So, did God create *evil*?

Absolutely.

That being said, this statement deserves qualification.

If that which we call *evil* was created to show us what God is by showing us what God is not, then is this so-called *evil* really *bad*?

Certainly, when the presence of evil in the world is viewed from God's eternal perspective (with which we are being endowed in the process of our God-directed sanctification), it's role as an essential component of the process of attaining God's perfect eternity would certainly qualify it as *good*.

Certainly the clarification of the answer to the question regarding the true *source* of the creation of evil is founded in the definition of *good* and *bad*.

Beyond any doubt, the definition of *good* when viewed from a worldly perspective is a polar opposite to its definition when viewed from God's eternal perspective.

The same holds true for the definition of *bad*.

Did God *really* create evil people just to be evil and to go to their eternal destruction?

The Bible tells us the answer to that question.

What if God, choosing to show his wrath and make his power known, bore with great patience the objects of his wrath—prepared for destruction? What if he did this to make the riches of his glory known

Copyright 2013 Michael K. Pasque

to the objects of his mercy, whom he prepared in advance for glory— even us, whom he also called, not only from the Jews but also from the Gentiles? (Romans 9:22-24)

Adam and Eve never knew *"the riches of [God's] glory."*

How could they?

They never experienced the prosperity of evil in the Garden of Eden.

They never knew God's mercy.

How could they?

We get to see evil individuals prosper and have them directly impact our lives.

They are indeed prepared for destruction and yet are a vital part of the preparation of the children of the eternal kingdom of God.

He lets them provide maximal contrast to *set off*, to define, to display, to illuminate the bright whiteness of His eternal glory.

That bright whiteness—to which we would otherwise be blind—is in fact the righteousness, power, justice, wrath, mercy, compassion, and love of our God and we must not just *know* this, we must experience it!

We had to actually become *"the objects of [God's] mercy, whom he prepared in advance for glory"* in order to know *"the riches of his glory."*

We had to experience evil in its fullest form, we had to become ultimate evil, in order to *know* the fullness of God's mercy, compassion, righteousness, justice, love, wrath, and judgment to an infinite extent.

Does God let bad things happen to good people?

It's even worse than that—God planned, orchestrated, and carried out those *bad* things!

Bad things happen to each and every one of the children of God.

Copyright 2013 Michael K. Pasque

No one can be spared because their impact is essential to all.

We have to experience the ultimate bad in order to *know* the ultimate good of God.

And in this is our *reward*.

The rewards of the saints that are spoken of so often in the Bible have to do precisely with this.

The depth of the bad that we experience reflects directly upon the heights of the knowledge of the glory of God that we acquire—and this for all eternity.

And, the more we *know* God in this manner, the better our eternity.

The more that we *get* this in this life, the more that we will do precisely what the Bible tells us to do: the more we will be enabled to praise God with true hope emanating from a joyous heart while all the while submerged in the most desperate and horrible times of our life.

Wow.

What power.

What righteousness.

What justice.

What grace.

What love.

What compassion.

What mercy.

What a plan.

What a God.

Copyright 2013 Michael K. Pasque

Day 19

Did God Really Create Some People Just To Burn In Hell Forever?
The Fate And Purpose Of Those Who Refuse To Believe

Answering tough questions like this is where our understanding of God's sovereignty and God's purpose in His creation really take hold.

At first glance, these may seem to be only the topics of theological discussions of remote application or interest to our life.

But it is God who poses these questions in the minds and hearts of us all—and that for a purpose, His purpose.

Once again, we must take, as the foundation of this discussion, the fact that the creation has a primary purpose: to create, identify, rescue, prepare, and perfect the sons and daughters of God who will spend eternity in fellowship with the three Persons of the Triune Godhead as princes and princesses of the eternal kingdom of God.

God will have that which He desires.

He has a plan to obtain His purpose in the creation.

Once again, His plan is, like Him, infinitely perfect in every detail.

Therefore, God will have, in eternity, the exact perfect individuals with whom He desires to spend the rest of eternity in loving fellowship.

Copyright 2013 Michael K. Pasque

Many are the plans in a man's heart, but it is the LORD's purpose that prevails. (Proverbs 19:21)

The creation has been ordered perfectly to obtain this goal.

The Creator is perfectly efficient, perfectly wise, and all knowing.

Thus, we can know that the creation of those who would never believe in the saving shed blood of the sacrifice of Jesus Christ on the cross of Calvary was no mistake.

We can be assured that, somehow, their creation was absolutely necessary for the perfection of God's infinitely perfect eternity.

As we have discussed, in eternity God will not be forever sitting there on the throne of heaven upset about the way that everything turned out.

No chance.

He will get precisely what He desires.

He is God.

So, since unbelievers do in fact exist—as testified to by the written word of God and by our real-life experience—then we can know that they are a critically necessary part of God' perfectly efficient eternal plan—or they would in fact not exist.

Further, once again based upon the perfect efficiency of God, we can logically assume that you and I and all of the others who will inhabit God's perfect eternity would not have reached that necessary perfection as eternal children of God without these unbelievers existing among us and interacting with us.

This line of logic makes it seem as if all unbelievers were created for one purpose and we were created for another—and in fact, that is precisely what the written Word of God tells us.

Copyright 2013 Michael K. Pasque

Does not the potter have the right to make out of the same lump of clay some pottery for noble purposes and some for common use? (Romans 9:21)

If this is true, then it seems as if we really have no say in our eternal destination.

What then shall we say? Is God unjust? Not at all! For he says to Moses, "I will have mercy on whom I have mercy, and I will have compassion on whom I have compassion." It does not, therefore, depend on man's desire or effort, but on God's mercy. (Romans 9:14-16)

These passages from the book of Romans are critical.

They draw our attention to the fact of God's sovereignty.

How do they do this?

The author of Romans has just told us that our salvation basically has nothing to do with our behavior, but rather God's election.

*Not only that, but Rebekah's children had one and the same father, our father Isaac. Yet, **before** the twins were born or **had done anything good or bad**—in order that God's purpose in **election** might stand: not by works but by him who calls—she was told, "The older will serve the younger." (Romans 9:10-12; emphasis added)*

From this we can know that it is God's *"purpose in election"* that determines who spends eternity in heaven and who spends eternity in hell.

Copyright 2013 Michael K. Pasque

Our natural response to this is exactly as Paul points out.

He asks why they would be punished when it is God's determination: *"What then shall we say? Is God unjust?"*

But the critical revelation follows when Paul answers the question he has just posed: *"Is God unjust?"*

As noted in the Romans 9:14-16 above, his answer to this is very simply to refer to the sovereignty of God: *Not at all! For he says to Moses, "I will have mercy on whom I have mercy, and I will have compassion on whom I have compassion."*

That sovereignty is again echoed several verses later in Romans 9:21 (shown above) when Paul compares God to a potter who makes pots out of clay.

The bottom line is clear.

Just as the Potter is sovereign over the type of pot made with the clay, so also is God the sovereign Creator of everything that has been created.

As the Sovereign Creator of everything, by definition, God defines the words *unjust* and *unfair*.

The Bible repeatedly tells us *"God is just"* (2Thessalonians 1:6).

Thus justice is one of the attributes of God in which—once again, *by definition*—He represents infinite perfection.

God is infinitely perfectly just.

In other words, as the infinitely, perfectly just Sovereign Creator of everything that has been created, *logically* God *alone* defines those words.

And anything that He does must, by definition, be fair and just.

This is huge, because it means that we can know—beyond any shadow of a doubt—that the creation of individuals for the sole purpose of representing evil in our lives ultimately culminating in their eternal destruction is fair and just.

God alone defines fairness and justice.

Copyright 2013 Michael K. Pasque

These passages also point out that God's mercy is the key here and His sovereignty rules its administration.

Thus, the creation of those who would never place their faith in Christ serves God's sovereign purpose and is administered by His mercy.

From this we can deduce that it is obviously critical to our preparation for our eternity that we, God's eternal children, must understand His righteousness and justice.

He doesn't want us to have merely a passing, learned-in-a-classroom head-knowledge of His attributes.

God wants us to obtain by our life experience a physical, tangible, palpable, visual, auditory, and even olfactory knowledge of the righteousness and justice of God.

God wants to add warm flesh to the boney skeleton of the hard facts of his righteousness and justice.

The ministration of this knowledge is so important to God that it required the pouring of His incarnate Son's lifeblood upon the stone roadways of ancient Judea.

And this knowledge requires that His eternal children actually *see* the manifestations of His righteousness and justice displayed as holy wrath and awesome power.

What if God, choosing to show his wrath and make his power known, bore with great patience the objects of his wrath—prepared for destruction? (Romans 9:22)

Copyright 2013 Michael K. Pasque

Somehow, the believer's perfection in eternity as a prince or princess of the kingdom of God would not be truly perfect without seeing, knowing, and experiencing the wrath and power of God in action.

I am sure that in this life we will not fully understand why this is true.

But, we are told in no uncertain terms that the creation of the *unbeliever* is necessary and vital.

Further, we are given hints as to why it is so critical to our perfection.

First of all it allows us to somehow appreciate to a larger degree the *"riches"* of God's *"glory"* as we *"the objects of His mercy"* come to fully understand the truly infinite depth of the mercy that we have received in the shed blood of God's Son, Jesus.

What if he did this to make the riches of his glory known to the objects of his mercy, whom he prepared in advance for glory—even us, whom he also called, not only from the Jews but also from the Gentiles? (Romans 9:23-24)

We can thus be assured that we cannot fully appreciate, understand, and experience the fullness of God's mercy without seeing those who will not experience it because of their unwillingness to accept it.

For the Scripture says to Pharaoh: "I raised you up for this very purpose, that I might display my power in you and that my name might be proclaimed in all the earth." (Romans 9:17)

Copyright 2013 Michael K. Pasque

As hard as it is for us to understand and accept, most assuredly the unbelievers—and their eternal destiny—are vitally important to our perfection and our appreciation of our roles as eternal children of God.

And the toughest of all lessons that we must learn centers on God's grace and compassionate mercy—neither of which can really be understood and appreciated in their fullness without defining precisely what the absence of that grace and mercy looks like in real life.

It is hard to believe that those unbelievers around us were specifically created as everyday tools in the hand of God and are used by Him every minute of every day to bring our appreciation of our position in the incredible grace, love, and mercy of God to the fullness required to make us perfect companions of God for eternity.

But believe it we must.

*This is especially true of those who follow the corrupt desire of the sinful nature and despise authority. Bold and arrogant, these men are not afraid to slander celestial beings; yet even angels, although they are stronger and more powerful, do not bring slanderous accusations against such beings in the presence of the Lord. But these men blaspheme in matters they do not understand. They are like brute beasts, creatures of instinct, **born only to be caught and destroyed, and like beasts they too will perish**. (2Peter 2:10-12; emphasis added)*

For this is precisely that which the written Word of God teaches us.

Copyright 2013 Michael K. Pasque

For the Scripture says to Pharaoh: "I raised you up for this very purpose, that I might display my power in you and that my name might be proclaimed in all the earth." (Romans 9:17)

What if God, choosing to show his wrath and make his power known, bore with great patience the objects of his wrath—prepared for destruction? (Romans 9:22)

And yet, somehow, despite the plan of God that has been perfectly laid out since before an atom was created, practically speaking, every person—right this minute—has the opportunity to just say, "Yes!" and step forever into the eternal kingdom of God.

It is amazing that in that single instant of belief, they are transformed from pottery *"for common use"* as a tool in the hand of God to *"pottery for noble purposes"* whose eternal perfection is in fact the very object of God's use of the common pottery that they *were* a moment before...

May we all honor the purpose of the unbelievers around us by meditating upon and fully appreciating—and purposing our steps upon—the fullness of the power and glory of God that is found in His infinite *mercy* of which we are the eternal, only, exclusive, and all-encompassing recipients.

We must ponder with grateful hearts what this life we are leading would be without any knowledge of the unbelievers.

Could we ever understand the fullness of God's mercy without them?

Would we ever have a contrast to measure the mercy of God against?

Could we even imagine a state of *non-grace* from God with which to contrast that which we have in Jesus Christ if there were no people who refused God's grace?

Copyright 2013 Michael K. Pasque

Would it be *grace* if everyone accepted it?

In other words, would it be *grace* if it were mandatory for everyone?

Indeed, it does not take us long to arrive at the truth: our tangible understanding of God's compassionate, merciful grace is utterly dependent upon the presence of the unbeliever.

Light is fully appreciated as light only because of the existence of darkness—the absence of light.

Likewise, could we ever appreciate the fullness of that which we have been given, of that which by God's grace we *are*, of that which by God's mercy we will be in eternity, without the eternally hopeless plight of the mercy-refusing unbeliever to contrast it against.

Tool for noble purposes or common tool, God's mercy or God's wrath, light or darkness—and amazingly all are encompassed in our freedom to choose and all are utterly available, right this moment, for every one of us.

And it is with awe that we thus see the purpose of this life we live.

For if the purpose of the creation was to identify the sons and daughters of God who will spend eternity as heirs to the kingdom of God, then the purpose of this life is to prepare us for that eternity.

And what preparation is necessary?

We need to, in every respect, *know* this spectacular God with whom we are to spend eternity.

And how could we *know* God without knowing the fullness of His incredible attributes?

And what could be more important than a full appreciation of the compassionate mercy of the God with whom we eternally inhabit the kingdom of God?

Copyright 2013 Michael K. Pasque

And just as His compassionate mercy is *fleshed out* in the working practical knowledge of daily experiencing those who would refuse this compassionate mercy, so also do the other attributes of God become *real* in the exercise of our life.

For instance, we can simply never understand the justice of God without seeing to what lengths He would go to satisfy it on our behalf.

We would never know the fullness of His subservient, sacrificial love—the *currency* of eternity—without acknowledging that which God subserviently and sacrificially surrendered for us in the sacrifice of His only Son Jesus to satisfy the demands of a perfectly just God.

In that singular act, the Trinity showed us what an eternity as a child of God is all about.

Each of the Persons of the Trinity individually showed us what we needed to know to become an heir to the kingdom and to manifest that which has been given to us.

Only in this act of obedient sacrificial servitude do we see that obedience to God's will is in fact *love* for God.

Love for God cannot exist without unrelenting obedience to His will.

And in our humbled acceptance of the free gift of eternal life that is found only in Jesus, we demonstrate the capacity for this same subservient, sacrificial love to which we have been called as heirs to the kingdom of God's eternal love.

This sole trait—this capacity—is that which separates those who would believe (the children of God) from those would not believe (the children of the devil).

We never would have known this fullness of God's love for us without witnessing the height, width, and depth of the gap that He would traverse to complete our rescue.

Copyright 2013 Michael K. Pasque

As we have discussed, many have preached the perfection of life in Eden before the fall.

I'm not buying it.

There was nothing perfect in Eden regarding our knowledge of our eternal King.

Our knowledge of his attributes needed to become real and palpable and tangible and authentic and practical and it needed to have skin and make its home amongst us.

The *fall* had to happen.

It was our only way to know of the fullness of the attributes of God.

And that is why the Bible tells us that angels desire to look into that which we, Christ's church, Christ's bride, through Christ have obtained.

It was revealed to them that they were not serving themselves but you, when they spoke of the things that have now been told you by those who have preached the gospel to you by the Holy Spirit sent from heaven. Even angels long to look into these things. (1Peter 1:12)

The angels are curious, because they had never before seen it.

And thus we see precisely why evil, injustice, hate, immorality, and unfaithfulness must continue to exist in our life.

All of these are the darkness against which the bright white light of the righteousness, love, and faithfulness of God is contrast and seen in the fullness of its luminescence.

And that is why those who would never accept the life-giving grace found in the shed blood of Jesus had to be created, had to live their full lives among us, and must spend a physically, emotionally, and spiritually palpable eternity in hell.

Copyright 2013 Michael K. Pasque

Does this mean necessarily that God specifically created individuals with the express and only purpose of being consigned to the fires of hell for eternity?

Not necessarily.

I don't know how God threw 70 trillion, trillion, trillion stars into the sky.

But in know that He did.

I also know that from its first page to its last, the Bible suggests that we act independently in our choice of whether to entrust our life to God or not and in so doing independently determine our eternity.

This understanding weighs against the very clear all-encompassing knowledge of the sovereignty of God in determining absolutely everything that occurs in the creation—a fact also relayed on every page of the Bible.

And it weighs against our God-ordained understanding that tells us that we are not responsible for where and when and to whom we are born, nor to our early upbringing, nor the countless thousands of people with whom we interact all of our lives—and very clearly these powerful factors strongly influence this so-called *independent* decision regarding God, that which so directly determines our eternity.

So, rather than directly, upfront, and unabashedly doing that which we cannot imagine a God of His obvious compassionate mercy doing, did God (by creating those who would believe and spend eternity with God and those who would not believe and be consigned to the fires of hell) instead somehow create all of us with precisely the same tendency to choose Him and then just wind up the world and let it play out with a predetermined percentage going to heaven and to hell?

In other words, did God create in each of us a *tendency* toward choosing God that is *precisely the same* in each of us—for only then would it be *fair*—and then just let it play out as it would?

I doubt it.

Copyright 2013 Michael K. Pasque

But it is not out of the realm of the capability of God.

We have no possibility of comprehending the thoughts or full capabilities of an infinitely omnipotent God.

> *"Where were you when I laid the earth's foundation? Tell me, if you understand. Who marked off its dimensions? Surely you know! Who stretched a measuring line across it? On what were its footings set, or who laid its cornerstone—while the morning stars sang together and all the angels shouted for joy? (Job 38:4-7)*

> *"I know that you can do all things; no plan of yours can be thwarted. [You asked,] 'Who is this that obscures my counsel without knowledge?' Surely I spoke of things I did not understand, things too wonderful for me to know. (Job 42:2-3)*

Either way, we are just mincing words when we claim that God indirectly determines the number of believers and unbelievers by setting a percentage, but does not directly determine which persons, but only what percentage, would choose Him and be saved.

One way or the other, individuals are created to spend eternity in hell—the only difference is that in one case they are a priori designated and in the other they are determined by the circumstances God sets.

To me, they are the same.

Either way, God is creating some individuals with an unimaginably horrible eternal destination.

Copyright 2013 Michael K. Pasque

And the unimaginably horrible nature of their fate must reciprocate in extraordinarily wonderful eternal benefit it provides for those called by God to be sons and daughters of His eternal kingdom.

And in no uncertain terms, those who will choose to not believe in Jesus, the only Son of God, continue to provide, and for all eternity will be, the contrast against which we measure the compassionate and merciful grace of God—the fullness of which is unknowable without them.

Infinitely and perfectly spectacular is the only phrase to describe the majesty of God and the wisdom of His perfect plan.

Peter, an apostle of Jesus Christ, To God's elect, strangers in the world, scattered throughout Pontus, Galatia, Cappadocia, Asia and Bithynia, who have been chosen according to the foreknowledge of God the Father, through the sanctifying work of the Spirit, for obedience to Jesus Christ and sprinkling by his blood: Grace and peace be yours in abundance. (1Peter 1:1-2)

Copyright 2013 Michael K. Pasque

Day 20

Do I Really Deserve To Burn In Hell Forever Just For Stealing A Paperclip?
God's Justice And The Cross Of Jesus Christ

Each and every one of God's revealed attributes exist in unity and are indivisible in the nature of God.

Understanding each and every one of God's attributes is of critical importance to our understanding of the nature of God.

Perhaps the most intriguing of all of God's attributes is His infinitely perfect justice.

God's justice is intriguing because of its profound impact upon any discussion of our eternal destiny.

As we have discussed, our eternity revolves singularly around the crucifixion and resurrection of Jesus Christ.

God's justice explains so much of that which is so hard to explain about this pivotal moment in all of creation history (in all of eternity).

It is in its revelation about the nature of the crucifixion and resurrection of Jesus Christ that God's justice both poses and solves *the problem* in His creation.

As discussed, that problem is that the very nature—our nefarious tendency toward rebellion against the holiness of God—that somehow makes us potentially perfect as eternal heirs to the kingdom of God, simultaneously disqualifies us.

God's justice poses the problem because in His infinitely perfect justice, evil must have consequence—wrong must be righted, sin must be atoned for.

Copyright 2013 Michael K. Pasque

God can't *just forgive* us—after all, even we would not want to spend eternity anywhere other than a kingdom where justice is palpably real and infinitely *perfect*.

But God's justice does more than just tell us that sin must be atoned for, it also tells us the price of atonement—for in infinitely perfect justice, the atonement must be precisely equal to the offense.

So God's justice tells us not only that something must be paid for our evil rebellion against His holiness, but also precisely what must be paid.

That payment, that punishment is *death*.

If you are like me, you may struggle with this a bit.

The Bible clearly tells us that even the tiniest of sins—like stealing a scrap of bread, for instance—disqualifies us from even standing in the presence of God, let alone spending eternity with Him as co-heirs to His kingdom!

> O LORD, God of Israel, you are righteous! We are left this day as a remnant. Here we are before you in our guilt, though because of it not one of us can stand in your presence." *(Ezra 9:15)*

The perfect holiness of the loving fellowship of the Triune Godhead—to which we have been invited—cannot exist between God and the *defiled*.

For absolute, infinitely perfect subservient sacrificial love cannot exist between two parties unless both are infinite in their faithfulness.

A rebellious sinful nature results in rebellious sin, which is the ultimate demonstration of unfaithfulness.

Therefore, infinite faithfulness cannot exist in the rebellious sinful heart without the presence of the Purveyor of faithfulness, Jesus Christ, resident within.

Copyright 2013 Michael K. Pasque

And even the theft of a scrap of bread represents heinous rebellion against God and therefore defiles us—for even in that tiny act of rebellion have we scorned and devalued the perfect holy righteousness of God in the ultimate act of unfaithfulness.

We have not only refused to bow before, but have in fact *confronted* the unapproachable.

We have rebelled against a perfect Father.

We have contested perfect wisdom.

We have raised ourselves above our Creator.

And still, the severity of the associated punishment is so hard for us to understand.

After all, even the most self-righteous among us would never demand the forfeiture of life in return for the theft of a scrap of bread!

We, in our human wisdom, only execute people who have committed crimes that are on the order of murder itself.

So, how does an infinitely, perfectly just God demand death for even our small offenses?

The classic response centers on the infinite glory of the perfect holiness of God.

Most certainly this is the foundational theology supporting the necessity of death as atonement for our sin.

Every account that is given in the Bible of a mortal man standing in the presence of God is not subtle in reminding us that we are created and He is the Uncreated God—entirely *set apart*, entirely different than us.

He is, in every sense of the word, unapproachable.

Surely if each of us were to stand in the presence of God for even a single second, the deepest dark blackness of the rebellion that is inherent to even the

Copyright 2013 Michael K. Pasque

theft of a scrap of bread would be starkly apparent to even the most blind among us.

But there is more.

The infinitely perfect justice of God has much more to teach us regarding the specifics of the atonement for our sin.

The word of God tells us that the best way to define the gravity of any sin is *not* by somehow inventing and applying metrics to measure its severity—metrics like: "What is the value of that which has been stolen?" or "Who got hurt?" or "How badly is he hurt?" or any other metric of the gravity of the sin.

Instead, God measures the gravity of any particular sin by *that which is forfeited because of the sin.*

In other words, in regard to any and all sins—big or small—the price to be paid back is exactly the same, regardless of its *size*—because all result in the forfeiture of *life*.

In eternal terms, you don't have to pay back a scrap of bread for the theft of a scrap of bread.

Rather, since even the tiniest sin—even the theft of a piece of bread—defiles our holiness, our standing in God's presence, then that which is lost as a consequence of such sin is not measured in bread, but rather in terms of, very literally, the whole goal of our creation: eternal life.

That which is lost because of the theft of a scrap of bread is the God-ordained righteousness and holiness that God originally gave us in the Garden of Eden, where Adam and Eve walked in the very presence of God.

That which is lost is our deepest heart desire, the very purpose of our creation.

This deep heart desire and purpose is to love God eternally as heirs to the loving fellowship of the Triune Godhead—and this is *life*.

Copyright 2013 Michael K. Pasque

So, that which is lost by the theft of a scrap of bread is perfect, eternal life (which is defined as acquiring the deepest desire of our heart and attaining the purpose of our creation, to love God as a member of the eternal fellowship of the Trinity).

> Thus, since perfect, eternal life is given up—and the payment for the sin that results in loss must equal that which is lost—then perfect eternal life must be paid in atonement.

Wow.

Do we even have the capacity to really *get* the gravity of our situation?

If we had to rely upon our own efforts to fix this situation, then this leaves us utterly and hopelessly lost without possibility of recovery—because of our sin, we are eternal toast.

We have no way to pay the price of a perfect life because we, by definition, have proven ourselves incapable of living a perfect holy life.

And thus we get back—as we always do—to the cross of Jesus Christ.

No human being who has ever lived (or will ever live) has (or can) lead the perfect human life that is required in atonement for that which we have lost by our rebellion—only the perfect 100% human, 100% Son of God, Jesus, could do that which had to be done.

But, this is where it really gets scary.

We need to understand the fullness of the fact that Jesus led a perfect life.

The completely emptied 100% human Son of God gave Himself over to the perfect guidance of the Holy Spirit and carried out that which we could not—the perfect life that was required to substitute in atonement for the perfect life that we have gave up in our rebellion.

We don't even know what perfect life looks like.

Copyright 2013 Michael K. Pasque

Our lives are not even close.

But, the life that Jesus led was right in step with the will of God and the direction of the Holy Spirit.

We cannot, in the blindness of our sin, even understand the possibility of this.

But what we can know is that perfect life is precisely that for which we were created.

We can know that perfect life is precisely that which we gave up in our sinful rebellion against the will of God.

We can also know that perfect life is that which, by the grace of God, lies in our eternal future.

In other words, we will mirror the perfect life of Jesus in eternity.

There will be no stepping outside of the direction of the Holy Spirit.

There will be no stepping outside of the will of God for our life.

There will be no rebellion.

It will be magnificent.

And will be perfect and it will be pure joy because it is precisely that for which our heart was created.

We will face all of the challenges, adventures, passions, and glorious revelation of the life God has planned for us in eternity with our eyes riveted squarely on Jesus, with our feet traveling squarely in the footsteps of the will of God for our eternity—and it will be grand—it will be perfect, eternal life!

Thus it is that which is lost as a result of our sin that therefore determines the gravity of the sin and therefore the valuation of that which must be paid in atonement.

Okay, we have thus defined the need for the perfect Jesus to lead a perfect life to become the perfect sacrificial lamb that is worthy of the price that must be paid.

But there is more.

For the life that is lost is not just perfect, it is eternal.

A perfect, eternal life lost (because of our sin) = a perfect, eternal life must be paid.

We must understand this.

It was not just *life* as we define it here on earth in human terms that was lost by our sin.

It was *eternal* life.

Eternal life.

That is what was lost and that is what must be given in atonement.

This means that at the crucifixion the 100% human Jesus gave up more than just the life of His air-breathing, food-eating human body.

He also sacrificed—in the most incredible demonstration of subservient, sacrificial love that has ever occurred—precisely that *life* that is lost by our sin.

In other words, Jesus had to sacrifice for a timeless moment the eternal love of the Father in the midst of the loving fellowship of the Trinity (for that is what is lost to us because of our sin) in order to justly atone for our sin.

We have no idea what this means.

There is simply no possibility that we, created and unholy man, can understand the infinitely perfect fullness of the loss that Jesus suffered on the cross.

We have no mental, spiritual, or emotional capacity—in this life—to understand this.

This is the scary part that I referred to earlier.

All true Christians try as hard as possible to understand what occurred on the cross of Christ 2000 years ago.

But, we just don't get it.

I am convinced that we can't—until we step into eternity.

Copyright 2013 Michael K. Pasque

That is why the Holy Spirit, in the written Word of God, always describes the crucifixion in terms that are bigger than we can understand—He always ascribes more to the cross of Christ than we can even imagine.

Read the descriptions.

There is so much going on there.

The facts are clear.

Jesus has lived glorious *life* with the other Members of the Triune Godhead for a timeless period that we naively call *eternity*.

He had never experienced—in all eternity—*life* without the Father and the Holy Spirit.

But that is precisely what He experienced in that timeless moment between the moment of His death and the moment when the Father restored the humbly subservient Jesus (who had emptied Himself to become lowly man) back to true, perfect, eternal *life*.

We struggle with understanding the real difference between the death of the human body and the death of the soul.

God knew we would struggle with understanding this, so He describes these two *deaths* separately in the Bible—there is the *first death* (death of the human body) and the *second death* (being cast away from the presence of God and into the burning lake of fire).

That which we absolutely must grasp is that Jesus did not just suffer the first death—the death of His very human body—for us.

Truly, He did suffer the first death and it was absolutely heinous in its every human detail and can never be minimized and never described in terms that are luminous and heinous enough to do it justice.

Copyright 2013 Michael K. Pasque

But the full price for our eternal redemption would not have been paid if Jesus had not also suffered the second death—for that is what is sacrificed in our sinful rebellion against God and that is what must be redeemed.

The perfect eternal life that is given to those who trust in Jesus and thereby become heirs to the eternal kingdom of God—*that* is what is lost.

Since this eternal, perfect life is what is lost because of sin, its loss by Jesus (the second death) is the only atonement that could redeem the lost sons and daughters of God.

It is precisely also from this second death that God resurrected Jesus.

This changes everything.

This means that in His substitutional and atoning death for us, Jesus—for the first and only time in timeless eternity—was separated from the life that is found in the joyous, glorious loving fellowship of the three Persons of the Triune Godhead.

> He said: "In my distress I called to the LORD, and he answered me. From **the depths of the grave** I called for help, and you listened to my cry. You hurled me **into the deep**, into the very heart of the seas, and the currents swirled about me; all your waves and breakers swept over me. **I said, 'I have been banished from your sight**; yet I will look again toward your holy temple.' (Jonah 2:2-4; emphasis added)

The implications are not subtle.

This makes the death of Christ on the cross the single most cataclysmic event of not just the creation—*but of all eternity.*

What?

Copyright 2013 Michael K. Pasque

Are you saying that Jesus, the eternal Son of God and eternal member of the Triune Godhead gave up perfect eternal life with the Father in the fellowship of the Trinity?

No doubt.

The revelation found in the written Word of God is clear in this regard.

In the timeless instant in eternity represented by His death on the cross of Calvary, Jesus went to the precise place where those who shun God for their whole life (in the unrepentant hatred that characterizes the unsaved) are destined to spend eternity—this is the place where evil will be confined for eternity.

Jesus went to the lake of fire for us—out of the Presence that He had enjoyed for all eternity—and all motivated by the subservient, sacrificial love that is the currency of the eternal fellowship of God—and all so that we, the redeemed, would not have to spend a single moment of our eternity out of the loving presence of God.

And this makes that moment of the cross of Calvary a disruption in eternity of very literally infinite and cataclysmic magnitude.

We don't have a clue.

We just don't get this.

We can't.

We, the created, unholy, unrighteous, can have no idea of the gravity of that timeless moment in eternity—literally.

A full understanding is impossible for us as we are now—because we have simply not experienced an eternity with the Father and the Holy Spirit as Jesus has.

And all of this makes the restoration of everything by the resurrection of the slain Messiah the focal point of all joy, compassion, mercy, and subservient, sacrificial love *for all eternity*.

Copyright 2013 Michael K. Pasque

The resurrection of Jesus Christ is everything.

To die with Jesus and to be resurrected into eternal perfect life is the destiny of the saved and it is *everything*—there being nothing of even trivial significance found outside of it.

Further still, the disruption (in eternity) that took place in the moment of the death of our Savior, by its infinite magnitude, truly defines our worth, our value as the redeemed, the bride of Christ.

The Members of the Triune Godhead very literally sacrificed everything for us—all for the subservient, sacrificial love that is the foundation of their eternal loving fellowship, the keynote of our life, and most definitely that which defines our eternity with God.

There is nothing halfway about Jesus, the Spirit, or the Father.

They went for the whole show.

To think upon the event of the crucifixion of Jesus Christ with the attitude that it really didn't cost God anything (after all *He is God*) is, therefore, the most heinous of heresy.

In that moment of the crucifixion and resurrection of Jesus Christ, God defined our sin as infinite, His loss on our behalf as infinite, His atonement for us as infinite, our worth as infinite, His willingness to do anything for us as infinite, His compassion as infinite, His mercy as infinite, His justice as infinite, His holiness as infinite, and His love for us as infinite.

Further, by sacrificing the loving fellowship of the Trinity, that which He had enjoyed for eternity, Jesus rendered in fact the very perfect—and infinite—demonstration of the higher calling, the foundation of that fellowship—subservient, sacrificial love.

And this is why we get everything with Jesus and nothing without Him.

Copyright 2013 Michael K. Pasque

The purpose of our creation and the deepest single desire of our hearts are rescued, redeemed, and eternally sated exclusively and wholly by our Redeemer, Jesus Christ, on the cross of Calvary.

Copyright 2013 Michael K. Pasque

Day 21

Is My Salvation Really My Decision?
Yes! And No. Taking The Sovereignty Of God One Step Further

The creation and continuing existence of seventy trillion, trillion, trillion stars is a staggering reality when the presence of a Creator God is contemplated.

The extraordinary complexity of DNA and the genetic code and their implementation in the continuing re-creation of life is astounding.

And yet what in God's creation can top the dichotomy of realities that face mankind every single moment of his humble existence?

We know that there is nothing outside of God.

There is nothing outside of the mind of God.

If there were anything outside of the mind and will and providence of God, then that *anything* would be God.

Similarly, there is no thought, no matter how unique, that was thought first by a man before God thought it.

There is no activity, no matter how unique, that was performed by man without the prior knowledge and ascent of God.

Man has created nothing—not even his thoughts or actions.

And yet to us an entirely different reality is apparent.

And our reality is just as *real* to us as the reality of God's omniscience.

For to us our new thoughts every day were unknown the day before and are in fact *new* to us today.

Copyright 2013 Michael K. Pasque

They are as uniquely *ours* as they could possibly be.

And they matter.

Our thoughts direct our life.

They direct our actions, they reveal our hearts—they are uniquely *ours*.

And yet the dichotomy of realities prevails: every one of our unique thoughts is a creation of God.

God thought of our thoughts, orchestrated the milieu in which they would occur, and created every single one of them.

We have created nothing that has been created.

But it just doesn't seem that way to us—for to us our reality is *real* and our thoughts remain uniquely *ours* and, we believe, uniquely under our control.

Amazing.

Further still, God, of course, did not just have dominion over our thoughts.

He in fact planned the subatomic course of every subatomic particle in the universe and He planned it for every moment of time that has been created—and that for eternity.

And yet everything in our world seems so random.

And so much in our immediate environment seems so totally under our control—*our* dominion, not God's.

And yet God has already created the entirety of the creation—including the time in which we live—for all time is a part of that creation (the creation does not exist in time, time exists in the creation).

Further still, He planned and orchestrated and implemented every event of every moment of that creation to occur precisely as He wants it to occur for all of created time.

The creation is complete.

God rested on the seventh day because all of His work was finished.

Copyright 2013 Michael K. Pasque

All of eternity has already been completely created in its entirety and that, all to the minute detail of God's infinitely perfectly detailed plan.

The actions and events of every microsecond for all eternity will all happen exactly as God has planned it.

And yet we are told on nearly every page of the Bible that our choices at each of the decision-points that God places in our life all *really* matter.

We have been told that our decision in regard to Jesus determines our eternity.

And yet we have also been told—on those same pages—that the determination of our faith, which determines our salvation, is by God alone.

For it is by grace you have been saved, through faith—and this not from yourselves, it is the gift of God—not by works, so that no one can boast. (Ephesians 2:8-9)

We are told that God has, in His sovereignty, chosen those who will spend eternity with Him.

And yet each one of us, right this minute, has the utter and complete ability and power to determine our eternity—the dichotomy of the two realities could not be more profound than in this.

God will have it in eternity exactly as He has precisely planned it—and yet we in our very real reality have utter and complete control with the power to change our fate in a moment with a single thought.

The Word of God and our real world experience both attest to the reality of our power to change our moment, our life, and our eternity.

And yet both realities encompassed in the preceding two statements are indeed real.

Amazing creation!

Copyright 2013 Michael K. Pasque

Every one of our decisions is ours.

Every one of our decisions matters.

Every one of our decisions impacts our future, our eternity.

Every one of our decisions, to some variable degree, changes the course of our life, our eternity.

We have complete control over every one of our decisions—by definition, or it would not really be a decision.

We are, and will be, held responsible for every one of our decisions.

The consequences of those decisions will be absolutely palpable and *real* in every sense of the word.

And yet God knew, orchestrated, implemented, and created every situation in which we find ourselves—and every one of our responses to these situations.

In other words, God orchestrated the decision-point and actually planned our response to it.

And yet to us, our decisions are very much truly and uniquely *our* decisions.

We are right here in this very real reality making very real decisions that really will determine our future—and yet God planned them all.

After all, what factors are at play in the making of our free will decisions?

Our personalities, our sense of justice, our moral strength, our likes, our dislikes, our sense of right and wrong, our moral tendencies, our genetic makeup, our recent and past experiences and relationships—all of those things that make us "us," those things that we claim as *self*, those things that govern our free will decisions *were in fact all given to us by God.*

Can you name one of those factors that we actually determined?

The answer is most certainly *no*.

After all, who determined our genetic makeup, our race, the year when we were born, the place where we were born, the family into which we were born, the

Copyright 2013 Michael K. Pasque

ethnic, racial, and cultural milieu into which we were born, the relationships that we have experienced, our mothers, our fathers, our siblings, our friends, our relatives, our education, the traumatic and the joyful episodes of our life—and all of the other things that make us, "us"?

> And he is not served by human hands, as if he needed anything, because *he himself* gives *all men* life and breath and *everything else.* From one man he made every nation of men, that they should inhabit the whole earth; and *he determined the times set for them and the exact places where they should live.* (Acts 17:25-26; emphasis added)

I am still *me* and you are still *you*, but it is clear that God has made us everything that we are.

> For I am the least of the apostles and do not even deserve to be called an apostle, because I persecuted the church of God. But *by the grace of God I am what I am,* and his grace to me was not without effect. No, I worked harder than all of them—yet not I, but the grace of God that was with me. (1Corinthians 15:9-10; emphasis added)

There is not a thing that we *are* that God has not determined.

> For it is by grace you have been saved, through faith—and this not from yourselves, it is the gift of God—not by works, so that no one can boast. For *we are God's workmanship,* created in Christ Jesus to do

Copyright 2013 Michael K. Pasque

good works, which God prepared in advance for us to do. (Ephesians
2:8-10 [emphasis added])

God made us precisely who we are and that makeup is all part of God's plan for our life and for His entire creation.

There is no part of us that was made up independent of God or independent of God's eternal plan.

LORD, you have assigned me my portion and my cup; *you have made my lot secure. (Psalm 16:5; emphasis added)*

It is readily apparent that God will indeed have precisely the eternity that He desires.

This eternity—despite the very *free* will that we have been given—is entirely under the control of God, such that we cannot mess it up.

God not only controls all of the events, relationships, challenges, trials, and joys of our every single day, but He has also controlled that which actually determines our free will choices in the circumstances and relationships that He orchestrates into our life.

And yet I am still *me* and you are still *you* and we have the ability to do whatever we want to do right this minute—and all by God's orchestration.

God will have His perfect eternity and you and I will be individuals with free wills driven by our personal attributes and characteristics all of which were given to us by God.

And we will romp through the adventures, joys, passions, and experiences of our eternity with Jesus—and all as if we never perpetrated a single crime against the holiness of God.

Copyright 2013 Michael K. Pasque

Some of us will spend eternity in heaven with God.

Some of us will spend eternity in hell away from God.

And God has planned it all.

And yet, at this very moment you and I have complete power over where we spend eternity.

It *really* is our choice.

Right this minute it *is* our choice.

And thus exists the dichotomy of two very real and very different *realities*: the reality of the sovereignty of God and the reality of our God ordained free will.

Surely, we exist in the midst of a truly spectacular creation.

Copyright 2013 Michael K. Pasque

Day 22

The Bad Stuff Really Seems Bad—Are You Sure It All Really Came From God?
Developing An Eternal Perspective

There is an amazing enigma that courses all through the pages of the written Word of God from page one of Genesis to the last words of the Book of Revelation.

It is the source of a great deal of tension.

This tension swells deep in the hearts of non-believers and believers alike.

The tension is between two clearly stated facts that are undeniably supported by the written Word of God.

To develop an eternal perspective specifically regarding the *bad* stuff that occurs in our life, we must first, once again, restate the facts regarding the perfect sovereignty of God and His gift of a likewise perfect free will in the decisions with which He challenges us.

The first fact is that God is sovereign over *everything*.

Everything.

The first lines of the Gospel of John clearly tell us that everything that has been created was created by and is sustained by God through the Person of Jesus Christ.

We know that this includes the entirety of the creation and that time exists in the creation—so it includes all people and all things for all time and eternity.

This is not just a theological discussion.

It has huge practical consequences in every moment of every day of our life.

Copyright 2013 Michael K. Pasque

It tells us that nothing that happens to us is random.

It tells us that everything that we are and have and achieve and become and do is, in fact, only by the hand of God.

It tells us that despite the fact that it may look like our neighbor just perpetrated a heinous offense against us, it was an offense that was sent into our life by none other than God Himself.

It tells us that despite the fact that the car accident that just injured a family member seems to be an utterly random act, God in fact sent it into our life.

It tells us that as tragic as the loss of a child is, it is part of God's plan for *all* of the involved lives.

Most disturbingly, it also tells us that God created two sets of human beings to occupy His creation.

It tells us that there are children of God and children of the devil.

Then he left the crowd and went into the house. His disciples came to him and said, "Explain to us the parable of the weeds in the field."

He answered, "The one who sowed the good seed is the Son of Man. The field is the world, and the good seed stands for the sons of the kingdom. **The weeds are the sons of the evil one,** *and* **the enemy who sows them is the devil.** *The harvest is the end of the age, and the harvesters are angels. (Matthew 13:36-39; emphasis added)*

This is how we know who **the children of God** *are and who the* **children of the devil** *are: Anyone who does not do what is right is not a child of God; nor is anyone who does not love his brother. (1 John 3:10; emphasis added)*

Copyright 2013 Michael K. Pasque

God created one group of individuals to become children of God in the eternal kingdom of God and another group of individuals who were created only to be destroyed in the eternal fires of hell itself.

> *But these men blaspheme in matters they do not understand. They are like brute beasts, creatures of instinct, born **only** to be caught and destroyed, and like beasts they too will perish. (2Peter 2:12; emphasis added)*

And yet there is a problem.

It has to do with another fact that is also stated on nearly every page of the Bible.

For the written Word of God also tells us that it is *our choice* regarding into which group of individuals we fall.

The Bible tells us that not only is our eternal fate 100% in our hands, but so also is the choice at every one of the thousands and thousands of decision-points that God orchestrates into the days of our life.

And in fact, practically speaking, we know this to be true.

So despite the fact that God created the reader of these words and determined every single moment of his or her eternity, right this moment, if that reader is not a *believer* who is saved by the grace found only in the shed blood of God's only Son, Jesus, he or she can—right this moment—acquire that salvation by believing.

Right this minute, if you are not a believer, you can make the choice to believe and place your eternal fate in the hands of your Savior, Jesus.

Copyright 2013 Michael K. Pasque

Or, you can choose, once again—for you have already denied Him a thousand times—to put off this decision as if one of the possible choices regarding Jesus was to ignore Him (which it is not).

And yet, God already knew your response—from before time began.

And He already knew mine.

And, further still, God actually already made that choice for you—from before time began—because He created every single part of you, your knowledge, your personality, your emotions, and every single moment of your life.

And yet still—right this minute—the choice is totally, 100% yours!

And in this lies immeasurable tension and wonder.

It is the primal enigma of my life—and of yours, too.

But the ramifications of this enigmatic problem are even further illuminated in the words of the Bible.

This problem, in fact, touches every part of our life.

There are many examples in the Bible, but perhaps none is as undeniable as that described regarding Babylon.

For clearly God states that He uses Babylon as an instrument to shape Israel.

When the sin of Israel grows to such a point that it seems to suggest that it has no boundary, God summons Babylon.

When Babylon attacked Judah, I am sure that the people of Israel saw it just like we see any really *bad* thing that happens to us.

I am sure that life was just going along normally when all of the sudden along comes a big bully to pick a fight with them.

I am sure that to most of them this seemed just like any other random event in the world, since the Babylonians, just like the Israelites, after all, also had free will to do whatever they wanted to do.

Copyright 2013 Michael K. Pasque

But the prophets of Israel clearly delivered the truth of this situation to all of those Israelites who would listen.

They were not subtle in pointing out the clear and heinous sin of Israel.

They were also not subtle in clearly delivering God's message that repentance and a return to the Lord were the only solution.

These prophets clearly described the punishment from the hand of God that would befall the nation of Israel if they did not change their ways.

Israel ignored their prophets.

And so, God brought Babylon against them.

Babylon was clearly an instrument in the hand of God used for His clear purpose.

His purpose was to *discipline* Israel.

Discipline is not just punishment—it has a purpose.

The purpose was to get the people of Israel to acknowledge their sin, turn from their sinful ways, and return to worshipping the one true God.

So, we see God's sovereignty in full swing here as He brought Babylon against Israel for His Divine purpose.

God didn't just *allow* it.

He orchestrated it.

And yet to the Babylonians, the decision to attack Israel was a clear and objectively defined free will *choice*.

The Babylonian King, Nebuchadnezzar, in the moment of His decision to attack Judah, clearly recognized and exercised his free will choice in this decision-point in his life: simply stated, he could attack or not attack.

It was his choice.

And yet the course of history had been clearly laid out by its Creator to occur in precisely such a manner.

Copyright 2013 Michael K. Pasque

In other words, God had brought the peoples of Babylon together, formed a nation out of them, empowered them mightily, and turned their eyes toward the conquest of Israel.

God brought the Babylonians against Israel.

He even told them He was going to do it over a hundred years before He did it, just so they—and we—would know beyond any shadow of any doubt that He was, in fact, sovereign over the entirety of His creation.

And yet, the choice to attack Israel was—at the moment it was made—entirely Nebuchadnezzar's: attacking Israel represented a carefully orchestrated choice at the *decision-point* placed into the life of the king of Babylon by the providence of God.

Nebuchadnezzar made the decision to wage unmerciful and devastating war against Israel with the direct result of that decision being the slaughter of countless thousands of the men, women, and children of Israel.

And God held him responsible for that choice at that decision-point just like He holds us responsible for every choice we make at every decision-point that He orchestrates into the moments of our every day.

I was angry with my people and desecrated my inheritance; I gave them into your hand, and you showed them no mercy. Even on the aged you laid a very heavy yoke.

You said, 'I will continue forever—the eternal queen!' But you did not consider these things or reflect on what might happen.

"Now then, listen, you wanton creature, lounging in your security and saying to yourself, 'I am, and there is none besides me. I will never be

Copyright 2013 Michael K. Pasque

a widow or suffer the loss of children.' Both of these will overtake you in a moment, on a single day: loss of children and widowhood. They will come upon you in full measure, in spite of your many sorceries and all your potent spells.

You have trusted in your wickedness and have said, 'No one sees me.' Your wisdom and knowledge mislead you when you say to yourself, 'I am, and there is none besides me.' Disaster will come upon you, and you will not know how to conjure it away. A calamity will fall upon you that you cannot ward off with a ransom; a catastrophe you cannot foresee will suddenly come upon you. (Isaiah 47:6-11)

And so God states in the written Word of God that He held Babylon directly responsible for the very choice that He, in fact, had orchestrated in the history of the nation of Israel for His specific purpose.

If that doesn't jack with our minds, then we are not listening!

This is the very perfection of *tension*!

Babylon was a tool whose free will choice was used by God in orchestrating His perfect will into the history of Israel.

His purpose, His will, will stand.

I make known the end from the beginning, from ancient times, what is still to come. I say: My purpose will stand, and I will do all that I please. (Isaiah 46:10)

Is this a purposeless theological discussion?

It is anything but that.

Copyright 2013 Michael K. Pasque

For clearly we can see that Babylon represents all evil and all perpetrators of evil in our life and in our world—most specifically Satan.

So, did God create *evil*?

Did God bring evil against Israel?

How can this be?

God is good.

All the time.

But God clearly created Satan—and all that He has done and ever will do.

Does that mean that God is evil?

Of course it does not.

The solution to this question requires that we understand God's eternal perspective.

We live and think in a worldly now perspective.

We see something like the destruction of Jerusalem and the slaughter of countless thousands of men, women, and children as *evil* because in our worldly perspective we, of course, cannot define it any other way.

But God sees things in an eternal perspective.

The eternity He has planned for us will be perfect.

He is God, its Creator, and is, Himself, perfect—and so (by definition) anything He creates must also be infinitely perfect (or He, Himself, would, in fact, not be perfect!).

That which logically follows from this statement truly changes everything.

When we look back on these events from eternity—and, thus, ourselves have (and view things from) an eternal perspective—we will see all that we called *bad* and *evil* as having been *perfect* for the accomplishment of everything that was critical to the perfection of the eternal plan of God.

Copyright 2013 Michael K. Pasque

And, in that perfection, all that we currently (in our worldly perspective) have labeled as *bad* and *evil* will be defined as the very great goodness of God.

And yet God still holds Babylon responsible.

Just like God holds Satan responsible for his actions, God also holds Babylon (and all of us) responsible for evil thoughts, words, and deeds.

Those of us who are under the grace that is found in the work of Jesus on the cross of Calvary hold a very special position in this regard.

For in those incredible events of the death and resurrection of the Son of God, Jesus bore our sins for us.

He, in fact, accepted all of the responsibility for our evil thoughts, words, and deeds.

And we are no longer held responsible because Jesus accepted the righteous and most severe punishment for our sins.

How incredible this is!

For it is clear in the written words of the Bible, God holds Babylon responsible for the very actions that He, God, in fact orchestrated in their lives.

He is the Potter and we are the clay.

Some clay is formed for exceptional purpose and some for common.

God is the Sovereign Potter who determines all.

And yet He holds Babylon responsible, for in that moment of their choice, Babylon—Satan—chose to destroy Jerusalem.

And God holds them responsible for that choice.

And so, God punished Babylon and will punish all whose sins are not covered by the shed blood of Jesus.

So, yes, God has created some people to burn in hell forever.

He tells us that clearly in indisputable terms in the Bible:

Copyright 2013 Michael K. Pasque

But these men blaspheme in matters they do not understand. They are like brute beasts, creatures of instinct, born only to be caught and destroyed, and like beasts they too will perish. (2Peter 2:12; emphasis added)

This seems so unfair to us—that God would create beings only to eternally burn in hell.

God anticipated our feelings in this regard and answered them through the Apostle Paul.

He answers this by telling us, once again, that He is God and we are not.

He is the Potter and we are the clay.

Just as a lump of clay cannot challenge the plan of the potter who forms it into whatever type of pot he chooses, so also can finite, imperfect, created man not challenge the infinite perfection of the Uncreated God.

It is not as though God's word had failed. For not all who are descended from Israel are Israel. Nor because they are his descendants are they all Abraham's children. On the contrary, "It is through Isaac that your offspring will be reckoned." In other words, it is not the natural children who are God's children, but it is the children of the promise who are regarded as Abraham's offspring. For this was how the promise was stated: "At the appointed time I will return, and Sarah will have a son." Not only that, but Rebekah's children had one and the same father, our father Isaac. Yet, before the twins were born or had done anything good or bad—in order that God's purpose in election might stand: not by works but by him who calls—she was told, "The older will serve the younger."

Copyright 2013 Michael K. Pasque

Just as it is written: "Jacob I loved, but Esau I hated." What then shall we say? Is God unjust? Not at all! For he says to Moses, "I will have mercy on whom I have mercy, and I will have compassion on whom I have compassion." It does not, therefore, depend on man's desire or effort, but on God's mercy. For the Scripture says to Pharaoh: "I raised you up for this very purpose, that I might display my power in you and that my name might be proclaimed in all the earth." Therefore God has mercy on whom he wants to have mercy, and he hardens whom he wants to harden.

One of you will say to me: "Then why does God still blame us? For who resists his will?" But who are you, O man, to talk back to God? "Shall what is formed say to him who formed it, 'Why did you make me like this?'" Does not the potter have the right to make out of the same lump of clay some pottery for noble purposes and some for common use? (Romans 9:6-21)

Surely God has created those who are destined to burn in hell forever.

But, as we have discussed, they are critically necessary for the perfection of the eternal sons and daughters of God.

For without their existence—their use as tools by the creator—the perfection of the knowledge of God in the hearts of the children of God would not have been perfect.

Specifically, Paul continues on, we would never have know the fullness of His wrath and power—nor would we have known the riches of the glory of the mercy of God:

Copyright 2013 Michael K. Pasque

> *What if God, choosing to show his wrath and make his power known, bore with great patience the objects of his wrath—prepared for destruction? What if he did this to make the riches of his glory known to the objects of his mercy, whom he prepared in advance for glory—even us, whom he also called, not only from the Jews but also from the Gentiles? (Romans 9:22-24; emphasis added)*

Without these men and women who by their own free will choice choose to turn their backs on the mercy of God and ignore the specter of his wrath and power, our knowledge of God in eternity would have been incomplete.

We could not have known God's *power* in Eden.

The room was pure bright white.

There was no contrast.

There was nothing for God to wield His awesome power against.

We needed the darkness.

We needed the knowledge of good and evil.

We needed contrast to see the nuances of His power.

We needed to physically embody the darkness to actually experience His power first hand.

We needed to be that against which His power was to be wielded.

And we need to be that which was saved only by the extremes of His power.

> *Yet he did not waver through unbelief regarding the promise of God, but was strengthened in his faith and gave glory to God, being fully persuaded that God had power to do what he had promised. (Romans 4:20-21)*

Copyright 2013 Michael K. Pasque

Only in our palpable rescue by the Almighty, All-powerful God is our sanctification—our worthiness to spend eternity as heirs to the Kingdom of God—made complete.

And, that, all in the *power* of the cross of Christ.

The eternity that God has planned for us would not have been perfect.

Without the perfect knowledge of God that is provided by this magnificent plan—of which the *"brute beasts"* are an irreplaceable, critical part—we, the eternal children of God would simply be incapable of the subservient, sacrificial love that is the critical song that drives the eternal dance of the Trinity.

We would be incapable of achieving our creation purpose and sating the deepest desire of our heart to join the fellowship of the three Persons of the Triune Godhead in subserviently, sacrificial love.

We proclaim to you what we have seen and heard, so that you also may have fellowship with us. And our fellowship is with the Father and with his Son, Jesus Christ. (1John 1:3)

Thus, these individuals who are born with a destiny of destruction are given for us, for our salvation, for our sanctification.

This is further illustrated for us in the book of the prophet Isaiah, as God explains to Israel that He will give the Egyptians to Babylon in order to spare Israel.

For I am the LORD, your God, the Holy One of Israel, your Savior; I give Egypt for your ransom, Cush and Seba in your stead. (Isaiah 43:3; emphasis added)

Copyright 2013 Michael K. Pasque

This is what the LORD says: "The products of Egypt and the merchandise of Cush, and those tall Sabeans—they will come over to you and will be yours; they will trudge behind you, coming over to you in chains. They will bow down before you and plead with you, saying, 'Surely God is with you, and there is no other; there is no other god.'" (Isaiah 45:14)

Thus the Egyptians are given over to utter destruction by the Babylonians in exchange for the redemption of Israel to illustrate the mechanism and fate and necessity of the creation of those who would be used by God to orchestrate the achievement of the creation purpose of the saints of God.

Just like God created Pharaoh to show His glory to the Israelites, so also did Babylon—and all of those who turn their backs on God's gracious offer—serve to show us the justice, grace, mercy, compassion, wrath, glory, and love of God.

Without knowledge of these vital attributes of God, how could we *know* God?

Without *knowing* God, how could we serve as worthy partners in the eternal dance of loving fellowship to which He has invited us?

Without the *evil* people and the *bad* things that they do to us, how could we, therefore, attain our creation purpose and sate the deep desire of our heart to spend eternity in loving fellowship with God?

In other words, God's perfect eternity—our perfect eternity—would not be complete without the presence of these individuals in our lives.

And thus *evil* men and women, destined (like Satan) for the eternal fire of hell, and all of the evil that they perpetrate against us were not only created by God, but also purposefully allowed to coexist with us—and even to prosper in our very sight.

Copyright 2013 Michael K. Pasque

As we have discussed, the parable of the weeds clearly tells us that God purposefully allows them to continue to exist in our lives because their removal would result in the imperfection of the final harvest.

"The owner's servants came to him and said, 'Sir, didn't you sow good seed in your field? Where then did the weeds come from?'

" 'An enemy did this,' he replied.

"The servants asked him, 'Do you want us to go and pull them up?'

*" 'No,' he answered, 'because **while you are pulling the weeds, you may root up the wheat with them. Let both grow together until the harvest.** At that time I will tell the harvesters: First collect the weeds and tie them in bundles to be burned; then gather the wheat and bring it into my barn.'" (Matthew 13:27-30; emphasis added)*

Again, the *evil* people need to exist in our lives in order to orchestrate our salvation and perfect our sanctification.

God's perfect result in our lives, and thus God's infinitely perfect eternity, would not be achieved without the continued existence in our lives of those who are destined for destruction.

And thus the enigma—and its tension in our life—fills the words of Holy Scripture and fills our life.

We will never understand it like God understands it.

We simply do not have that capacity.

Copyright 2013 Michael K. Pasque

But of this we can be certain: the tension is holy tension and was placed into our lives and illuminated in the written Word of God for God's divine eternal purpose.

And much can therefore be known of its impact in our daily life—and in our eternity.

Copyright 2013 Michael K. Pasque

Day 23

What Do You Have That Wasn't Given To You?
Understanding The Full Impact Of Grace In Our Daily Lives

Grace.

Grace may be the only real lesson that we have to learn in life.

We like to think that it was our act of placing our faith in Jesus that has saved us.

This is true.

But the Bible teaches us that even that act of placing our faith in Jesus is a gift from God.

> *For it is by grace you have been saved,* **through faith—and this not from yourselves, it is the gift of God**—*not by works, so that no one can boast. For we are God's* **workmanship**, *created in Christ Jesus to do good works, which God prepared in advance for us to do.* (Ephesians 2:8-10; emphasis added)

This becomes *logical* to us when we remember that everything that has been given to us is from God.

Everything that we are, everything that we have, everything that we know, everything that we can do, every gift that we get—all of these are from God.

Copyright 2013 Michael K. Pasque

> Yet, O LORD, you are our Father. We are the clay, you are the potter; we are all **the work of your hand**. *(Isaiah 64:8; emphasis added)*

> For we are **God's workmanship**, created in Christ Jesus to do good works, which God prepared in advance for us to do. *(Ephesians 2:10; emphasis added)*

Grace.

Everything is a gift.

Our parents, our siblings, our upbringing, our education, our physical gifts, our mental gifts, our personality strengths—all are inborn attributes given to us from God and *none* resulted from *our* effort.

It is God who determines every single detail of our physical, inter-relational, and spiritual environment from the moment of our birth until our death.

Since our mental, physical, relational, spiritual, and personality-related inborn attributes and the physical, family, social, and relational-related environment in which they have matured are the only two things that go into determining whether we ever have a chance to say, "Yes!" to Jesus and, in fact, whether we do precisely that when offered the chance, are all determined by God, it is *logically* deduced that, in fact, *God determines whether we are saved or not.*

So, we don't have to believe that God determines who is saved and who is not just because it is a fundamental teaching of the Bible:

> And we know that in all things God works for the good of those who love him, who have been called according to his purpose. For those God **foreknew** he also **predestined** to be conformed to the likeness of his Son, that he might be the firstborn among many brothers. And

Copyright 2013 Michael K. Pasque

*those he predestined, he also **called**; those he called, he also **justified**; those he justified, he also **glorified**. (Romans 8:28-30; emphasis added)*

Instead, it can be logically deduced.

Thus, the cold, hard reality of the fact that we have *nothing* to do with our salvation is supported by the Bible *and* supported by logic—but, that is not all.

The entirety of the New Testament, from the teachings of Jesus to their prophetic expansion by the epistle writers, describes a way of life that is 180 degrees opposite of what the world tells us is *reality*.

God's desired way of life can only come from our adoption of a new perspective.

We are not to judge each other.

We are not to be arrogant.

We are not to boast.

We are not to raise ourselves above our fellow man.

We are not to raise our interests above those of our fellow man.

We are to love every single individual that God brings into our lives.

We are to serve every individual that we meet.

We are to lower ourselves below every individual we meet.

We are to lower our desires below those of every other individual we meet.

In other words, we are to do the impossible task of subserviently, sacrificially loving every individual that God brings into our lives.

Impossible.

Impossible unless you adopt the perspective that the written Word of God tells us that we are to adopt.

Copyright 2013 Michael K. Pasque

That new and radical perspective is one that recognizes that *everything* that we have is a gift from God.

This includes our salvation.

This includes our sanctification.

Most of us like to believe that we are responsible for the *act* of insuring our salvation.

We take credit for the *act* of *believing* in the holy Name of Jesus.

We believe that we are solely responsible for the "Yes!" answer that we give to the most important question of any person's life: "Will you bend the knee to Jesus and make Him the Sovereign King of your heart and your life?"

And yet, how readily we believe that the *act* of saying *yes* is based wholly in *our* logic, *our* reasoning, *our* wisdom, and *our* faith.

We only said yes because we are logical, wise, and full of reasoning and faith.

In other words, we readily take full credit for our *yes* answer.

We take credit for doing that final thing that was necessary for our salvation.

In other words, we are, by our logic, clearly stating that it was Jesus *plus something* for our salvation.

It was Jesus *plus* our saying *yes* that were required for our salvation.

In other words, the death of Christ, the Son of God, on the cross of Calvary *was not enough in and of itself—it required something more*—it required us to say *yes*.

And thank goodness that we were able to supply that something more by saying *yes* to the question—because we would not have been saved otherwise.

In other words, if we had not been able to muster the courage, reasoning, logic, wisdom, love, and faith to say *yes*, God would have been denied His perfect eternity.

We came to Jesus' rescue right at the very last moment!

Copyright 2013 Michael K. Pasque

How lucky He is!

Pure heresy.

All are utter and damnable lies.

The facts are these.

It is Jesus plus *nothing* for our salvation.

It is Jesus plus *nothing* for our sanctification.

It is Jesus plus *nothing* for the entirety of our righteousness.

We add *nothing* to this.

The facts are clear.

The Bible is clear.

Before time began, God determined who was going to be a child of God and who was going to be a child of the devil.

Both were equally critical to the plan, because the former could not be the former without the latter.

In other words, as we have discussed in depth elsewhere, the *contrast* supplied by *evil* was needed to illuminate the attributes of God and bring us to a full understanding that would allow full participation in the loving fellowship of His eternal kingdom.

Further, we must realize that the only way that we can have the proper perspective to allow and empower the behavior that Jesus and the writers of the epistles describe is if we understand that surely we *will*, in fact, spend eternity in heaven—but that we had *nothing* to do with it.

Only in that perspective are we able to see that in regard to *every* other human being that we will encounter in our lives, nothing could be truer than the statement, "There, but for the grace of God, go I."

Only with this perspective are we empowered to *never* raise ourselves above another human being—*even the unsaved*.

Copyright 2013 Michael K. Pasque

Only this perspective allows us to subserviently, sacrificially love *every* individual that we encounter in our life.

Only this perspective reminds us that we have, just like the Bible tells us, *nothing* to boast about.

> *But God chose the foolish things of the world to shame the wise; God chose the weak things of the world to shame the strong. He chose the lowly things of this world and the despised things—and the things that are not—to nullify the things that are, so that no one may boast before him. It is because of him that you are in Christ Jesus, who has become for us wisdom from God—that is, our righteousness, holiness and redemption. Therefore, as it is written: "Let him who boasts boast in the Lord." (1 Corinthians 1:27-31)*

Only this perspective allows us to never raise ourselves above another individual.

Only this perspective allows us to never raise our interests above those of the people that we encounter.

Only this perspective allows us to fully realize that we have no justification to *ever* place ourselves in a position to judge another human being.

Only this perspective makes the otherwise unfathomable requests of Jesus in the Sermon on the Mount a reality in our life.

Only this perspective allows us to praise God every minute of our life for all that He has given us.

"There, but for the grace of God, go I."

Grace, the only lesson we have to learn in this life.

Copyright 2013 Michael K. Pasque

Day 24

Beauty Fascinates Us—What Does It Have To Do With God?
Beauty: The Magnificence And Glory Of God...Utterly Without Purpose

Beauty is the most intriguing attribute of God.

Beauty is magnificent, but not because it needs to be.

There is no utility in the magnificence of beauty.

The magnificence of beauty provides no answer to any question.

Beauty is magnificent because it cannot help itself.

Beauty is enthralling, but not because of what it can do.

Beauty is captivating, but not for a purpose.

Beauty solves no problem.

Beauty is inherent in God, but not for a reason.

Beauty is all of these things just *because*—and it is glorious in its magnificence.

All beauty is glorious because all beauty is *of* God and He is glorious.

All beauty is *of* the glory of God.

Beauty is a consequence, an inherent effect, and an expected and natural product of the *glory* of God.

Beauty is indeed glory by its very nature.

Beauty is fueled by, inherent to, and a natural result of the glory of God.

God did not come up with beauty because He needed it.

Copyright 2013 Michael K. Pasque

Beauty was not created; it just *is* as a natural consequence of God inhabiting the creation.

Beauty had to happen.

It was inevitable because of the inherent glory of God.

In our world, when the glory of the not-of-this-world *Uncreated* interfaces, intersects with the creation, the result is beauty.

Thus, wherever we see beauty in the creation, it is because we are looking at an intersection point between the glory of the Uncreated Creator and His creation.

Our world is 4-dimensional.

The glory of God is infinitely dimensional.

When God's infinite dimensions intersect with our 4 dimensions, at that point is His glory manifest as beauty.

This is God's glory—the thrill of looking into the eyes of Jesus not because He, in His strength, is our Savior or because of what He has already done for us or because of what He will still do for us, but instead, just because He is by His glorious nature *beautiful*.

And beautiful *feels good* to our eyes because God feels good to our hearts.

We are irresistibly drawn to the beauty of God—but not for what it can do for us.

We are drawn to God because our hearts seek our Creator.

We are drawn to God because our hearts seek His beauty.

We may think we are drawn to God for any number of reasons—and yet, His beauty is always there.

God's beauty has no function.

God's beauty has no purpose.

God is not beautiful so as to draw us to Him; He is just beautiful.

Copyright 2013 Michael K. Pasque

He is beautiful whether we are there or not.

God was beautiful before we existed.

God's beauty has no reason.

God's beauty is inherent in Him.

God's beauty in and of itself solves no problem, and yet the cry of our deep heart is for nothing less.

God's beauty is just the very essence of His utter magnificence and glory on display, as it must—by its very nature and His very nature—be displayed.

It is a natural outpouring of His Essence.

In this respect, God's beauty is like His love—He cannot help but express it. Just as He is a slave to His loving heart, His beauty explodes forth from His essence because He simply cannot help Himself.

God's beauty cannot help but be enthralling to humankind because we are made in His image and therefore have *His* beauty in our heart and as an intrinsic part of every fiber of our being.

The imprint, the reflection of God's beauty brilliantly blasts forth from our heart.

For surely our hearts are the *primary* intersection points between the glory of the Uncreated and His creation.

The personal impact of God's beauty on each of us has nothing to do with salvation or sanctification or service or obedience, but rather it just captivates our heart—by its inherent nature—by His glory.

We see hints of God's beauty—specifically of the beauty of Jesus—in stunning sunsets, in the cascading slopes and crevices of the Rocky Mountains, in a summer storm in the Grand Canyon, in the color array of the wildflowers that adorn every pasture—and in the faces and form of women.

Copyright 2013 Michael K. Pasque

Women were chosen to most magnificently embody the beauty of God. Jesus is *"strength and beauty."*

> *Splendor and majesty are before him;* **strength and beauty** *are in his sanctuary. (Psalm 96:6 [ESV]; emphasis added)*

And women are the God-ordained primary focus of the fullest expression of God's beauty.

The creation was not complete until the creation of woman from man ushered in the fullest expression of God's beauty.

Woman's creation was left to the final step and was the crowning moment of the entire creation because God's beauty is the very elite essence of His existence and His Presence.

Men naturally—by their relative void of beauty (also God-ordained) in their hearts—seek beauty in the faces and form of women, women being the most resplendent reflection of God's beauty that God has placed before us on this magnificently beautiful earth.

We can know and recognize the reflection of God's beauty because truly beautiful things in God's creation *captivate* us.

We know they are *of* His beauty because the things that captivate us—like a stunning sunset that takes our breath away or the face and form of our beloved—have absolutely no pragmatic purpose in our lives.

We are very pragmatic by nature.

And yet the very non-pragmatic beauty that surrounds us in our lives draws us to it—like moths to a flame—by some intrinsic, deep-seated and irresistible desire.

Copyright 2013 Michael K. Pasque

Despite its utter lack of utility, this desire of ours for *functionless* beauty is the most incredibly powerful and motivating desire in our life.

This is because it is solely and exclusively *of* God.

There is no beauty outside of God.

This desire for God's beauty is so powerful that it can make us do crazy things.

It obscures vision and confounds logic and singularly focuses our attention like blinders on a draw horse.

And yet this beauty that draws our hearts with such immeasurable power has no pragmatic purpose; it just simply fills an otherwise unknown, indescribable, undetectable, and non-existent void in our hearts—yet that is enough.

That is enough to keep us running after it every moment of all of the days of our life.

It is man's deep heart desire for the beauty of God that drives him to its earthly substitute—it drives him to strive to conquer and hold captive the beauty of woman.

The quest for beauty on earth has led every man (save Jesus) to do crazy things in his life.

Men do crazy things in seeking the beauty inherent to women.

And, of course, it is woman's deep heart desire to be that expression of beauty in a man's life.

Need I say anything about a woman's quest to *be* beautiful?

Women spend billions every year on cosmetics, clothes, jewelry, and plastic surgery.

Needless to say, our world-centered attempts to fulfill our desire to pursue beauty (men) or to embody *beauty-pursued* (women) can lead to much sin in our life.

Copyright 2013 Michael K. Pasque

And yet in every case the beauty that we seek—both men and women—is a mere surrogate, a powerless, hollow, substitution for the beauty of Jesus.

Much of sexual sin—for both genders—has to do with this substitution.

For instance, the most common relational activities and the repetitive behavior of men readily reveal that it is not so much about sexual gratification as it is about hunting, pursuing, capturing, and possessing beauty.

Instead of seeking to possess the beauty of God, some men substitute the culmination of the hunt, the surrogate sexual *possession* of the beauty of women.

For women it is not so much about sexual gratification as it is about embodying beauty by becoming a surrogate sexual substitute—*beauty-pursued*—for that great motivator of mankind (the beauty of God).

When women succeed in being the substitute for the beauty of God in a man's life, it culminates in their giving (sexually) their beauty to the man.

In other words, women allow men to *possess* their beauty by giving themselves sexually to men.

It is in the act of allowing themselves to be possessed that women seek to confirm their worth by confirming to themselves that they are *beautiful*—that they embody the beauty that man desires and pursues to possess, that they embody the beauty of God.

And it is in sexually possessing the beauty of women that men seek to confirm their *strength* by obtaining by pursuit that which they substitute for the real desire of their heart (the beauty of God).

Thus, sexuality becomes a metric by which women measure their beauty and men measure their strength.

Woman: beauty, compassion, mercy.

Man: strength, leadership, warrior.

Copyright 2013 Michael K. Pasque

> Only together do man and woman reflect the fullness of the glory of attributes of Jesus.

God obviously takes the expression of His beauty to each of us very seriously.

In fact, beauty is very personal.

There are probably very few things in this life that are more personal to each of us than our perception of beauty.

The definition of precisely *what* is beautiful seems very unique and personal to each one of us—such that we even claim the *definition* of what is beautiful (to us) as our *exclusive* jurisdiction.

We all believe in our hearts that *we* define what is beautiful to us.

But we need to think about this.

When did we ever sit down and decide that the stimulation of our optic nerves by the light rays reflected from the shapes and colors that adorn the beautiful flowers of this earth would light up our heart?

And when did we decide which shapes and colors would not?

When did we sit down and decide which particular curves of a woman's face would be beautiful to us—and which ones would not?

When did we sit down and decide what musical chord progressions would be beautiful to our ears—and which ones would not?

When did we sit down and decide that the bright reds, pinks, oranges, and yellows of a summer sunset would be *beautiful*, but the brown color of horse manure would not?

On careful introspection, the answers to these questions are clear in their implication: we in fact never sat down and, after consciously and volitionally evaluating all of the literally infinite number of alternatives, decided which things would be beautiful to us.

Copyright 2013 Michael K. Pasque

We never did this.

It simply never happened.

> Despite what we think, we do not define what is beautiful to us.
>
> We very literally have nothing to do with the declaration and definition of beauty in our life—*this is in God's dominion alone.*

We each surely do have a different perception of what we call beautiful, but this is not because we came up with—in our divine wisdom—our own personal definition of beauty.

> Instead, God wrote a very personal definition of beauty on each of our hearts—it encompasses some of the beauty that everyone sees, but also includes a personal glimpse of His beauty that He does not share with anyone else.

This revelation of a special part of God's beauty to each of us is His personal loving and unique gift to each of us.

This gift from God allows us to perceive something as beautiful in our environment because it reflects that special unique and personal glimpse of God's beauty that not everyone else—maybe not *anyone* else—has written on their heart like it is written on ours.

And thus not everyone agrees with our definition regarding that which should be called *beautiful*.

In fact, the knowledge of God's beauty is one of the defining characteristics of our individual uniqueness.

In other words, God has made His beauty unique to each of us.

All beautiful things are uniquely beautiful—beautiful in a unique manner—to each one of us.

Even those things that appeal to *many* still appeal individually to us in a manner that is personally unique to our hearts.

Copyright 2013 Michael K. Pasque

Indeed, most of us have had the baffling experience of observing the rest of the world simply pass aimlessly by things that our heart considers to be beautiful to a near staggering proportion.

If indeed, the very *definition* of beauty that God has written on each of our hearts is unique to our heart, then each of us cannot help but also perceive the beauty of Jesus in a different and unique way.

Jesus takes great delight in our uniquely unique view of His beauty.

He has parceled out portions of it to each of us—different portions in different amounts to differing degrees at different times—all unique to each of us.

The uniqueness of that view of the manifestation of His inherent beauty is His gift to us and is what—at the bottom line—makes our relationship with the God and Creator of the Universe so very personal.

All beauty in our life is a reflection of Jesus.

There can be no beauty outside of Jesus—if there could be, He would not be God.

Since beauty is the essence of God's glory, any beauty that resides outside of God would necessarily detract from the glory of God—which simply cannot happen.

Our hearts define beauty for us.

God wrote that definition of beauty on our hearts.

Only Jesus can fit that definition, since our hearts are attracted to beauty and our hearts can only be attracted to their Creator.

If there was any beauty outside of Jesus, then there would be something else written in the Most Holy Place of our heart other than the Name of Jesus.

Which is certainly not the case.

Think about this.

It can be no other way.

Copyright 2013 Michael K. Pasque

Beauty by its inherent nature has an almost magical draw upon our hearts.

Could there be anything outside of Jesus that has a genuine draw on our hearts?

It cannot happen.

He is our Creator.

Logically, everything must go back to our Creator.

And if the logic is not enough to persuade us, the Bible says precisely this.

One thing I ask of the LORD, this is what I seek: that I may dwell in the house of the LORD all the days of my life, to gaze upon the beauty of the LORD and to seek him in his temple. (Psalm 27:4)

When a sunset or the face of our beloved reflects Jesus' inherent glory, it is recognized by our hearts and by our minds as beautiful.

This is why some things that have no practical, functional, objective, or common sense attraction still manage to captivate our hearts—because they reflect His beauty and therefore His glory.

Thus it changes everything to the commonsense-oriented man when he realizes that the quirky beauty that he sees—that makes no sense at all—*really is* only and absolutely *of* Jesus Christ.

Indeed it changes everything when we realize that even quirky beauty—every bit of it in the world—must be *of* Jesus.

Thus the beauty of Jesus, as reflected by any number of things and individuals in our world, is to be starkly contrasted against the strength and leadership of Jesus that is similarly reflected by things and individuals in our world.

Strength and leadership—as opposed to beauty—literally define *pragmatic*.

Copyright 2013 Michael K. Pasque

Beauty on the other hand is 180 degrees in the opposite direction, having no *pragmatic* sense about it whatsoever.

Strength and leadership are literally brimming with purpose and functionality.

Beauty has none.

Strength and leadership solve problems, overcome obstacles, and conquer kingdoms.

Beauty causes problems, is an obstacle, and conquers men's hearts.

When men step forward in *strength* to lead (by serving!), we see the magnificence of the glory of Jesus in the fullness of the subservient, sacrificial love that He modeled on the cross of Calvary—and we stand in awe.

And in everything *beautiful* we see a tiny portion of the glory of Jesus—and it takes our breath away and captivates our heart.

Thus, we can know that this is why things that don't *look* anything like Jesus (like the face and form of our beautiful wife, snow-capped silver mountains, or a magnificent red-hewn sunset) still reflect as beauty the very essence of the glory of Jesus—that part of Jesus that serves no purpose except the radiance of His glory.

God's beauty is as fundamental a part of His nature as any of His other attributes.

Despite the fact that God's beauty is all around us, we only see a mere reflection of God's beauty now.

The fullness of God's beauty—as much as we think we know about it now—can only be defined in the *presence* of God and will remain unknown to us until we stand before Him.

This is good.

Copyright 2013 Michael K. Pasque

In our current state, the full, unrestrained impact of God's beauty would overwhelm us.

All that we call *beautiful* in this life is *of* God and represents a brief fluttering of a window into the real beauty that will be defined for each of us only in the presence of God.

Beauty in this world is appealing to us because all that is beautiful is by its very nature *of* this *presence* of God and our heart's deep heart desire is *for* this presence of God.

In the depths of our heart we desire to love God in subservient, sacrificial fellowship.

He made us in His image and He put this desire there.

We have nothing to say about the presence of this desire—except that we can ignore it, cover it up, and substitute for it if we so desire.

But, our efforts do not change the fact that the desire is still there.

We desire to love God and, as a result, we desire to be in the presence of God.

We cannot help but desire beauty because the desire for beauty is a manifestation of the desire for God that is written on our hearts—and God is beauty.

When we see beauty, we see a part, a glimpse, an enticing portion of the manifestation of God.

When we are in the presence of beauty, we are in the presence of God.

Although none of God's great attributes—sovereignty, omniscience, omnipotence, justice, compassion, mercy, and love, to name a few—overrides the others in importance, His beauty is the only one that exists only for itself.

God's beauty exists only of itself and for itself—it is the expression of God's glory that is independent of all of His other attributes and yet encompasses and emanates from all of them.

Copyright 2013 Michael K. Pasque

In God's sovereignty, He is beautiful.

In God's infinite justice, He is beautiful.

In His infinite power, He is beautiful.

In His omniscience, He is beautiful.

In His infinite compassion, mercy, and love, His beauty is simply mind-boggling.

In each of these attributes, God reveals His glory.

God's beauty serves no other purpose except to be a manifestation of His glory—and it is that glory that draws us to Him like moths to a flame.

Our individual, unique definition of beauty—whether it be expressed in colors, shapes, smells, chords, or touch—is a personal gift to us from Jesus Himself, and much about our Savior can be known from savoring it.

Copyright 2013 Michael K. Pasque

Day 25

How Do God's Sovereignty And Our Free Will Allow For The Presence Of God's Grace In Our Daily Lives?
Grace, Decision-Points, And The GPS Analogy

When we love God, we simultaneously fulfill not only the purpose of our life, but also the deepest eternal desire of our heart.

Jesus became incarnate man to tell us how to do this, how to love God.

Jesus told us that we love Him when we love the individuals that He sends into our life.

> *If you obey my commands, you will remain in my love, just as I have obeyed my Father's commands and remain in his love. I have told you this so that my joy may be in you and that your joy may be complete. My command is this: Love each other as I have loved you. (John 15:10-12)*

As simple as these words may seem, it is easy to become confused in their application to our life—especially when we are confronted by the sheer complexity of the interpersonal relationships in which we are all involved.

The best way to apply God's truth to our often overwhelmingly complicated life is to go back to the basics—back to a framework that encompasses that which

Copyright 2013 Michael K. Pasque

is really going on—especially in regard to relationships with the individuals that God sends into our life.

This framework allows a uniformly similar, standardized, and godly approach—that is founded in the Word of God—to be applied to the many and widely differing variations in the situations, scenarios, and interpersonal relationships that we encounter in our day-to-day life.

Let's define the basic foundational components of this framework with which we can approach the many relational decision-points that God orchestrates into our daily life:

God is primarily relational being three Persons, one God.

Thus, the majority of the major decision-point circumstances that we confront in our life (that God carefully and wisely planned out for us before time began) involve our relational interaction with at least one other human being.

These are precisely the individuals—those that populate our daily life—whom God has commanded us to love.

Since the meat of our life is therefore primarily *relational*, the framework with which we approach our God-orchestrated decision-points must be primarily grounded in interpersonal encounters and must have the potential to modify the perspective with which we approach every moment of our relational life.

Our lives exist primarily as a near-continuous string of consecutive God-orchestrated decision-points that occur in all of the events, circumstances, interactions, challenges, and situations of our daily life.

God has carefully crafted each of these events and each of their respective decision-points with the express purpose of testing our hearts.

Copyright 2013 Michael K. Pasque

> The summation of our lives can literally be found in the choices that we make at each of the decision-points that God has strung together for us during the days of our life.

God tests our hearts in each set of circumstances to show *us* our true heart (He, of course, already knows our true heart).

God has no need to examine men further, that they should come before him for judgment. (Job 34:23)

He does this (tests us to show us our true hearts) by asking us to make choices at carefully designed decision-points that are all consistent and uniform in their basic structure.

We should not let the simplicity of the structure of this basic framework fool us—its applicability in fact spans the many widely varying complexities of all of our daily lives.

The structure of these many critical and life-defining decision-points is uniform and simple: each and every God-ordained and God-orchestrated encounter simply and uniformly makes us choose—each and every time—between God and non-God.

Despite God's careful and precise orchestration and control of the circumstances of every one of these events in our life, we are nonetheless utterly free to respond to each individual set of circumstances in any way that we choose.

That being said, we must also acknowledge that the sum of our personality, intelligence, wisdom, past experience, hopes, and dreams (all of which are at the very least partially *God-determined*) cannot help but profoundly influence our decision at each of these God-ordained decision-points.

Copyright 2013 Michael K. Pasque

In addition, God readily acknowledges in His Holy Word that He *changes hearts* in regard to personal decisions—this God-intervention most likely representing a unique combination of the above-described *God-determined* influences.

> *As Saul turned to leave Samuel, God changed Saul's heart, and all these signs were fulfilled that day. (1Samuel 10:9)*

Although each situation that poses a decision-point is unique and specific to God's plan at that precise moment in our life, the choice offered at each of these decision-points is simple, straightforward, and consistent: God or non-God.

The ultimate goal of the plan of God for our life is to take us, in the depth of our God-given, God-celebrated individual uniqueness, and mold us into the likeness of His Son Jesus—while still retaining our very special unique attributes.

There is a reason that being made into the likeness of Jesus is our life goal.

The *only* human who is capable of truly subserviently and sacrificially loving and bringing glory to God—our greatest deep-heart desire for sure—is Jesus.

This fact mandates that if we are to become that which we were destined to become, achieve our creation purpose, and attain that which is our deepest heart desire, our hearts must be indwelled by the Spirit of Jesus and our character must be molded into His.

This is not negotiable; it is fact.

To further explain the uniform structure that God utilizes to achieve His goal of making us into the image of His Son Jesus, we need an illustrative analogy to illuminate the details of the mechanism behind God's plan for our life.

We need to understand how God works these thousands and thousands of decision-points that He places into each person's life into a mechanism to achieve

Copyright 2013 Michael K. Pasque

our life goal, our eternal purpose, and our deep heart desire—to subserviently and sacrificially love God.

One analogy that is particularly applicable and helpful is that of the modern day GPS (global positioning) navigation system.

This analogy takes the simple structure of the decision-point (with its God versus non-God choice) and places it in a very applicable mechanistic model that illuminates the real day-by-day anatomy of our walk with Jesus Christ.

This analogy also helps explain how God can still do what He says He will do in the book of Romans (predestine, call, justify, glorify) in the lives of those that He *"foreknew"* would choose to give Jesus dominion in their hearts, while at the same time allowing us to exercise the *free will* that God has championed as a critical attribute of all eternal children of God.

> *And we know that in all things God works for the good of those who love him, who have been called according to his purpose. For those God foreknew he also predestined to be conformed to the likeness of his Son, that he might be the firstborn among many brothers. And those he predestined, he also called; those he called, he also justified; those he justified, he also glorified. (Romans 8:28-30)*

In other words, this GPS navigation system helps to explain the mechanism by which God's grace is implemented in our life.

It explains how two seemingly tangential forces, God's grace and our free will, can simultaneously coexist, intermingle, and somehow become even more than their sum in the life of a child of God.

Copyright 2013 Michael K. Pasque

It explains how God can take the disaster of our humanly flawed (by our rebellious, sinful nature) free will decisions and turn them into a life destined for the kingdom of God.

The GPS analogy is straightforward:

1) Our life is a long string of decision-points that populate our every day in a linear, sequential fashion.

2) These decision-points are the basic building blocks of our life.

3) Every moment of every day of our life is in some way dependent upon or involved in these decision-points—they (and our responses to them) are the substance of that which we refer to as *our life on earth*.

4) Each decision-point has an identical structure.

5) Each decision-point offers only two choices: God or non-God.

6) To control the destiny of believers while not only allowing, but also championing, their free will, God carefully orchestrates the events of our life not only before but also *subsequent to* each decision-point.

7) This subsequent orchestration of events *after* each decision-point is (just like a GPS system) based upon 1) our *pre* decision-point position on the path toward God's ultimate destination in our life, 2) our free will choice at that decision-point (did we choose God or non-God?) and 3) the ultimate goal or destination of the trip (God's ultimate goal for our life).

8) All the events of our life that follow these decision-points are directed at the single goal of attaining God's goal for our life: changing us into the likeness of Jesus by molding our character to resemble His.

9) So, lets work through an example.

10) Today as we approach a decision-point in our life, we are like a driver in a car approaching a fork or intersection in the road upon

Copyright 2013 Michael K. Pasque

which he is driving on his journey to a specific destination that has been entered into his car's GPS navigation system.

11) The GPS navigation system's voice is like the Holy Spirit in our life and directs the driver to turn onto the road that will most directly get him to the entered destination—just like the Holy Spirit tells us to make the choice at the decision-point that most honors God and therefore takes us most directly toward our life-destination of being made into the likeness of Jesus.

12) If we choose the *God choice* then we are like the driver who chooses the GPS recommended road.

13) When we choose the *God choice*, then we are one step further along God's ideal path for us just like the driver is one step closer to the entered destination—and therefore no recalculation of a new route is necessary.

14) If we choose the *non-God choice* at the God-orchestrated decision-point, then we are just like the driver who believes the GPS is—for any number of reasons—*wrong* and therefore chooses the road not recommended by the GPS navigation system voice.

15) Obviously, for the driver who did not follow the GPS recommendation, a new route to the desired destination must be immediately recalculated by the GPS navigation system based upon where the non-recommended choice took him.

16) And, similarly, when we choose the *non-God choice*, we mandate that God (even before the creation) recalculate our life-solution based upon our *non-God choice*.

17) Thus, God, like the GPS navigation system, allows us our free will choices at each of the decision-points that He places in our life but,

Copyright 2013 Michael K. Pasque

unlike the GPS navigation system, He does not need to immediately recalculate a new path because He knew all about that bad choice before the creation and already made that recalculation in advance.

18) Thus, God has already (before time began) recalculated a new set of decision-points based upon our known bad choice at that decision-point and where it took us—all of which are designed to get us as far down the path toward our goal as we will allow Him.

Just like the GPS navigation system, therefore, before time began God designed our lives to get us as far toward the goal of being made into the likeness of Jesus as our free will choices at each of His carefully orchestrated decision-points would allow.

*In him we were also chosen, having been predestined **according to the plan of him who works out everything in conformity with the purpose of his will**, in order that we, who were the first to hope in Christ, might be for the praise of his glory. (Ephesians 1:11-12; emphasis added)*

We can therefore know that whatever point in our life at which we now find ourselves—the *current* GPS recalculated plan for our life (that was recalculated and put into place at our last non-God choice)—has now at this precise moment in our lives become *God's perfect plan* for the rest of our life.

When we next make another *non-God choice* at one of the thousands of decision-points God has built into our life, then *that* plan will change.

God will have known of our bad choice and will have already recalculated the new *solution* to getting us as close to the destination of being made into the likeness of Jesus as we will let Him.

Copyright 2013 Michael K. Pasque

Obviously, God has orchestrated thousands and thousands of decision-points into every one of our lives, each one requiring us to choose between a God choice and a non-God choice.

If we did not have an inherently sinful nature, we would never make non-God choices—we would never sin and our life would be perfect.

As sons and daughters of Adam, we do have a sinful nature, we do make non-God choices, we do sin, and our life is anything but perfect.

Jesus, being the Son of God and not the son of Adam, did not have a sinful nature and therefore made no non-God choices to the many decision-points that were similarly placed in His life.

Therefore, the life of Jesus Christ followed the precise plan and will of God and was the only perfect life that has ever been lived.

Since Jesus made no non-God choices in the many decision-points that were orchestrated into His life, no pre-creation GPS solution *recalculations* were needed.

The life of the only perfect man, Jesus, therefore made no deviations from the original and most efficient, God-directed path to the perfect final destination.

The perfect final destination of *His* life on earth was the perfectly sinless life that made him the only perfect atoning sacrifice for our sins.

He did that of which we are incapable since we are incapable of making God choices at every decision-point in our life and thus incapable of perfectly modeling the life of Jesus Christ.

But, when we accept the gift of His atoning grace, His perfect life is attributed to us—and our much-less-than-perfect life is attributed to Him in His death on the cross of Calvary.

God's *perfect* plan for our life (a life perfectly modeled after the life of Christ) is therefore in place until our first free will, non-God choice at a decision-point in

Copyright 2013 Michael K. Pasque

our life, which, by definition, deviates us from the original *ideal* life course planned by God.

God therefore already—before time began—recalculated a new *ideal* life course (which best satisfies His loving desire for our eternal good) to follow each of our non-God choices at the decision-points in our life.

In sharp contrast, when we make Godly choices at these decision-points, God's ideal plan for our life—which was originally set in place at our birth and had been recalculated with each non-God choice—remains intact since its last recalculation at our last non-God choice.

Thus, God knew of each non-God decision that we would make and countered it—as best He could (and that, perfectly!)—by recalculating the perfect pathway such that the circumstances that followed our non-God choice would get us as far along toward the goal of this life (to subserviently and sacrificially love God—like Jesus did—by being made into the likeness of Jesus) as we would allow Him—until another recalculation was needed for yet another non-God choice.

These recalculations are the palpable manifestation of God's grace in our life.

The sum total of God's grace in our life comes from His determination of the path of our life that, after our first deviation from it (first non-God choice), is primarily revealed in the recalculations following each non-God choice.

Thus, this GPS analogy renders insight into the mechanism and implementation of God's grace in our life.

It logically follows, therefore, that the nature of each of God's recalculations of our perfect life pathway are based upon only two factors: 1) where we ended up as a result of the non-God choice that necessitated the recalculation (our current position relative to God's last recalculation of the path for our life) and 2) God's ultimate planned destination of the path of our life.

Copyright 2013 Michael K. Pasque

The Bible clearly teaches that we can know that every one of God's recalculations of our life path following every one of our free will choices at the God-ordained decision-points has our eternal wellbeing (founded entirely in God's love for us) as its primary driver.

We can also know by the known attributes of God that our life plan is perfect in regard to the achievement of God's purpose for it—God would have nothing less.

Once again, our primal, eternal, and deep-heart desire is to truly, unconditionally, subserviently, and sacrificially love God—and the only way to do this is to mimic the only man who has ever accomplished this feat, God's Only Son Jesus.

Since God plans every moment of our life based upon our eternal wellbeing, then rather than taking credit for the good things and railing against the bad, we should instead acknowledge all of our circumstances—*good* or *bad*—as God's *perfect* plan to get us where God wants us to go—toward the purpose of this life— being made into the likeness of His Son Jesus.

It is only in this acknowledgment of God's loving will for our lives that we can find true joy in any circumstance that befalls us—for God is not just watching helplessly from the sidelines, He is in tight control of everything that we encounter.

We must remember that our rebellious human nature is an integral part of that which makes us ideal eternal children of God.

God will have perfection in regard to the princes and princesses of His kingdom with whom He will spend eternity and this fact is not negotiable.

He doesn't do anything halfway and He is incapable of doing anything less than perfect.

Copyright 2013 Michael K. Pasque

Our complicated life—complete with the countless recalculations necessitated by our too-numerous-to-count non-God decision-point choices (and which in no way, shape, or form resemble that original "ideal" life pathway that would have resulted from a complete absence of non-God choices)—is nonetheless "ideal" and perfect in light of the rebellious nature that God has given us (and which is somehow critically vital to our eternal worthiness as children of God).

And that is the perfection of the glory of God that is found in His compassionate and merciful grace.

Copyright 2013 Michael K. Pasque

Day 26

Do We Really Control *Anything* In Our Life? *What We Control And What We Only Think We Control*

A Bible-based governance of our life mandates that we understand what we can control in our life and what we cannot.

It is in this discussion that our understanding of the nature and mechanics of the decision-points that God places in our life becomes critical—for it is only in those moments when we actually exert control that we can contribute to God's *"work[ing] out"* of our faith.

> *Therefore, my dear friends, as you have always obeyed—not only in my presence, but now much more in my absence—continue to* **work out** *your salvation with fear and trembling, for* **it is God who works in you** *to will and to act according to his good purpose. (Philippians 2:12-13; emphasis added)*

In creating all that has been created, God not only created every single nano-particle of every atom of every object in the universe, but He also planned and implemented every *moment* of their existence for the duration of the world and for eternity (the creation does not exist in time, time exists in the creation).

It can therefore be concluded that before time began God planned and orchestrated every single event of every single moment of our life on earth (both now and in eternity).

Copyright 2013 Michael K. Pasque

As we outlined in previous chapters, His plan in orchestrating the events of our life is simple: the essence of our life can be defined as, very simply, a temporally consecutive string of *decision-points*.

It is precisely this string of decision-points by which God chooses, confirms, sanctifies, and glorifies each of the eternal sons and daughters of God.

Despite the seemingly infinitely complex nature of our life, it can be assembled in total by the summing of these decision-points, each of which poses only one question with only two possible answers: *God* or *non-God*.

That which is *God* is good and that which is *non-God* is, of course, evil.

God endowed each of us with *free will*, which is simply, and yet completely, defined as the ability to actually freely choose between the God or non-God answers at each of the innumerable decision-points of our life.

It is very important, therefore, to realize that our *control* in our life is not exerted in the circumstances or personal interactions which envelope us—we have no real control over any of them (except for some predictable consequences of our behavior—but even those are never for sure)—but rather is limited only to our *choices* at each of these God-ordained decision-points that result from the circumstances that God orchestrates in our life.

We therefore cannot control *any* of the events and circumstances of our life *except* as each of our choices at each of the decision-points influence the subsequent events of our life that God has planned in response to our choice at each decision-point.

But, it is critical to refocus on the fact that all that we really control is our response to the decision-points—for even when we think the consequences of a particular choice at a decision-point are *predictable*, God can (and does) change them to fit His plan.

Copyright 2013 Michael K. Pasque

Before time began, God foreknew every single choice that we would make by our own free will at each of the countless decision-points that He would place in our life.

Before time began, God also knew every possible decision-point choice by every single other individual who would live before, during, or after our lifetime.

God then, before time began, knew the choices of every person who would ever live in every possible situation and personal interaction between every individual in every possible ordering of events—a very literally infinite number of possibilities—and He chose the perfect combination of timing, people, and situations to achieve His eternal goal perfectly: the precisely perfect sons and daughters of God to spend eternity in loving fellowship with each other and with God.

And this is why the construction of the tapestry of life—of all of the personal interactions between all of the individuals who would ever live on this planet—such that it perfectly achieves the precise and perfect eternal sons and daughters of God (achieves God's perfect eternity) overshadows even the trillions of stars of the cosmos as God's most magnificent creation.

God planned the perfect course of our lives (including the perfect sequence, nature, and order of decision-points) to lead us—those of us who He foreknew would actually accept it—to that decision to accept His invitation to spend eternity in loving fellowship with Him by accepting the salvation from our sins that is offered only by faith in the shed blood of Jesus Christ.

God of course has also already carefully planned the lives of those who He knows will not accept the salvation offered by Jesus Christ to mesh with, compliment, optimize, and stand in stark contrast to the God-ordained glory of the lives of those who will be saved.

Copyright 2013 Michael K. Pasque

O LORD, you have searched me and you know me. You know when I sit and when I rise; you perceive my thoughts from afar. You discern my going out and my lying down; you are familiar with all my ways. Before a word is on my tongue you know it completely, O LORD.

You hem me in—behind and before; you have laid your hand upon me. Such knowledge is too wonderful for me, too lofty for me to attain. (Psalm 139:1-6)

God also planned the perfect post-acceptance, post-salvation sanctification course for every believer's life such that He gets them as far along toward being transformed into the likeness of Jesus as the individual believer will—by his or her decision-point free will choices—allow.

As part of our salvation/sanctification life course, God has also already planned all of the perfect *"good works"* that we will do for the entirety of our life—by which His grace is made palpable in our life and brings glory to His Name by His strength alone.

And God raised us up with Christ and seated us with him in the heavenly realms in Christ Jesus, in order that in the coming ages he might show the incomparable riches of his grace, expressed in his kindness to us in Christ Jesus. For it is by grace you have been saved, through faith—and this not from yourselves, it is the gift of God—not by works, so that no one can boast. For we are God's workmanship, **created in Christ Jesus to do good works, which God prepared in advance for us to do.** *(Ephesians 2:6-10; emphasis added)*

Copyright 2013 Michael K. Pasque

In our salvation statement of faith we proclaim our faith in Jesus Christ and give dominion of our hearts and our lives to Jesus to the glory of God—and it is then in our sanctification and in the good works He planned for us that God actually makes that statement true.

God watches every decision-point that He has placed in our life and waits—from before time began—to intervene on our behalf if we choose God over non-God and thereby empower Him in our life.

> But you, O God, do see trouble and grief; you consider it to take it in hand. The victim commits himself to you; you are the helper of the fatherless. (Psalm 10:14)

Our free will choices at each of the decision-points that God places in our life are determined by those personal attributes that make us, *us*.

These personal attributes define our perspective and include such things as our personality, our work ethic, our perseverance, our level of optimism, our level of energy, our happiness, our sadness, our wickedness, our goodness, our intelligence, our wisdom, our joy, our faith, our mercy, our trust, and our compassion.

> For you created my inmost being; you knit me together in my mother's womb. I praise you because I am fearfully and wonderfully made; your works are wonderful, I know that full well. My frame was not hidden from you when I was made in the secret place. When I was woven together in the depths of the earth, your eyes saw my unformed body. (Psalm 139:13-16a)

Copyright 2013 Michael K. Pasque

All of these attributes are either God-ordained by our personal genetic make-up or God-ordained by the life circumstances and experiences that we have been through to that point in our life—which are, once again, God-ordained.

Think not?

Who gave you your genetic makeup?

Who sequenced the strands of DNA that directed the construction of your body, especially your brain?

Who determined which century and at what hour and minute you would be born?

Who determined who your parents would be and who determined what their attributes would be?

Who determined your siblings, aunts, uncles, cousins, and grandparents?

Who determined your early life experiences?

Who determined which individuals, of what personality makeup, would cross paths with you to this point in your life?

In fact, who determined the precise nature of *all* of your life experiences to date?

Are you going to assign it to the random oscillations of the billions of people in the world?

Are you going to assign it utterly to happenstance?

Are you going to claim it as your own, as if you had anything to do with it?

Are you going to take *any* credit for any of it?

We are so quick to take credit for all or our *hard work*.

And yet even our hard work comes from our work ethic, which is some product of unknown variables—none of which we control—multiplied times the experiences of our early childhood and then again by subsequent experiences.

Copyright 2013 Michael K. Pasque

The hard facts are clear: we have had very little—if anything—to do with our acquisition of any of our many favorable attributes, all for which we are so very quick to take credit.

We make decisions based upon this gigantic conglomerate of DNA, environmental influences, personal experiences, and human physiology/psychology—none of which did we determine.

Of course there is some degree of influence by our past decision-point choices.

Clearly our past choices influenced our current situation and therefore our current decisions—but we had nothing to do with them in the first place.

We, and our decisions, are a product of God's hand in our life.

So what?

Exactly.

No matter who was responsible for giving us our current makeup and our current situation and the circumstances that we currently find ourselves facing each day, *we* still get to make these decisions and they still matter.

This applies to both our salvation and our sanctification.

Clearly if the above discussion applies to those of us who are saved by our belief in Jesus Christ, so also does it apply to those of us who are not.

God, as the Bible repeatedly tells us, made the decision before time began whether you would be saved or not.

And yet, right this moment, that decision is yours to make.

If you have not accepted the salvation found in the forgiveness of your sins offered by the cross of Jesus Christ, you can do it right this minute.

Have you ever wondered why Jesus told the parable of the workers?

Have you ever wondered why someone who dies at the age of 87, two weeks after accepting Christ, gets the same eternity as someone who dies at the age of 87 after 70 years of being a believer?

Copyright 2013 Michael K. Pasque

Maybe it is because when we stand before God stripped of *all of that with which God endowed us*, we will *all* stand devoid of anything—utterly and pervasively equal in every respect.

Just something to think about.

> *At this, Job got up and tore his robe and shaved his head. Then he fell to the ground in worship and said: "Naked I came from my mother's womb, and naked I will depart. The* Lord *gave and the* Lord *has taken away; may the name of the* Lord *be praised." Job 1:20-21*

Thus, only in the understanding of the detailed anatomy, mechanism, and implementation of the decision-points that God places in our life can we appreciate the true nature of the fight in which we find ourselves.

The foundational concept in this regard remains critical: we do not control *anything* in our life except our choices at the decision-points that God places in our life (and thereby, to some limited degree—for God controls everything—the introduction of the consequences of those choices into our life).

Even though the consequences of our choices at the decision-points may be somewhat known and anticipated (and thus even influence our choices), ultimately we do not even control the consequences of our choices that we think we control—only God does, and no matter what we believe to be the consequences, God can do what whatever He wants in response to any choice we make.

Thus, when we view the circumstances in which we find ourselves, we must understand that we have only God or ourselves to blame.

This is critical.

Copyright 2013 Michael K. Pasque

This is where this seemingly theological discussion becomes palpably pragmatic.

The pragmatism is centered in the fact that in every set of circumstances in which we find ourselves, God has placed other individuals.

And it is so incredibly human—as a direct result of our rebellious, sinful nature—to assign the *blame* for those circumstances to those individuals with whom we interact.

Even in those circumstances in which the malady that afflicts us seems directly attributable to the actions of another person, we must realize that it is God who has orchestrated their presence in our life.

In other words, God placed precisely the right person at precisely the right time in our life to inflict this challenge upon us.

We can acknowledge that it is from God and act accordingly to learn and love and bring glory to God, or we can rail against and strike out against those human perpetrators to whom we ascribe responsibility.

Both are choices at this God-ordained decision-point in our life, the former being a *God* choice, the latter being a *non-God* choice.

Living a life in which we believe we are faithfully *doing the work of God*, only to look back and gaze upon the carcasses of our fellow human beings that our actions have left strewn along our pathway to "success," is the ultimate human tragedy.

Copyright 2013 Michael K. Pasque

Day 27

Who Really Controls Your Thoughts?
You Don't Control As Much As You Think

This is where it gets interesting.

We do *not* control the deepest desire of our heart.

God placed it there and it is unchangeable in its purest form.

We do not control *anything* that occurs in our environment outside of our own free will choices.

God orchestrates every single event that fills every single nanosecond of our life.

But wait—it gets even worse.

Not only do we not control our heart's desires or our environmental circumstances, we do not even control our *primary* thoughts!

What?

They are *our* thoughts!

Who else controls them?

How naive we are about this.

We think all of those thoughts that we have in our minds are *our* thoughts, personal and specific and unique to us—all generated, initiated, propagated, and controlled by *us*.

Nothing could be further from the truth.

Copyright 2013 Michael K. Pasque

Let's start with a definition: *primary thoughts* are defined as any thoughts that *pop* into our mind in response to any of the circumstances or events in our life, current or past.

These primary thoughts may be an immediate and obvious direct response to a change in our environment, such as our thought, "She is attractive," when a pretty girl walks by.

These primary thoughts may also be delayed and not obviously related to circumstances in our environment, such as a thought that suddenly enters our mind regarding something that happened to us a day, a week, or even a year earlier—a thought that we may not even recognize as related to any particular relational or environmental event.

This whole concept—that we don't control the thoughts in our own minds—is unsettling to say the least.

After all, most human beings automatically assume that we must be entirely responsible for the thoughts that enter our minds as *primary* responses to the circumstances that occur in our environment since no one else on earth has access to our thoughts—or can even know them if we don't tell them.

Nonetheless—and whether we like it or not—the facts are clear: we do not independently generate the primary thought responses to the circumstances that arise in our surrounding environment.

We do not generate these primary thoughts—they arrive into our minds, into our consciousness, without our prompting.

The very presence of these thoughts and the recognition that we did not volitionally place them there can lead to only one irrefutable conclusion: somebody else not only has access to our minds, but can independently place thoughts there.

Copyright 2013 Michael K. Pasque

If our minds were a computer, we would say that this person or persons probably has not only "read" capabilities, but also "write" capabilities upon the hard drive of our mind.

The full acceptance of this paradigm takes introspection on our part—for we naturally abhor the very thought that somebody else controls anything in our minds.

We inherently and absolutely do not want to believe that this is even possible, let alone true in *every* case for *every* primary thought!

Thus, we need to stop and think about how these primary thoughts actually occur in our minds and from whence they come—these thoughts that seem to just *pop* into our minds.

Although we obviously control at least some of the thoughts in our mind (these are called *secondary thoughts* and we will get to them in a moment), we must recognize and understand that just because a thought occurs in *our* mind—and nobody else in our environment knows this thought—doesn't mean that *we* generated it.

In fact, do this little test: try to think of a primary thought.

Whatever you came up with was in response to my challenge.

The fact is, *you can't do it*—you can only volitionally generate thoughts that are in response to primary thoughts—the primary thoughts themselves *come from somewhere else!*

The question regarding the origin of these primary thoughts is therefore obviously pivotal if we are to try to deal with them.

Let's start from the beginning.

Nothing in the creation occurs outside of God's plan.

The primary thoughts that enter our mind are indeed a part of the creation and therefore known and created by God—for nothing that has been created can fall

Copyright 2013 Michael K. Pasque

outside of God's control (once again, if it were independent of His control, it would be God, not Him).

Therefore, even though Satan and his minions may be the mediators or implementers of God's plan and therefore the direct instillers of the evil primary thoughts in our minds, Satan does not work outside of God's direct control.

Ultimately, therefore, God is the Author and Controller of the primary thoughts of our minds that occur in response to the circumstances of our environment.

Knowledge of God's sovereignty over everything is critical when we consider our response to these thoughts.

Since God places these primary thoughts in our mind, we can make the safe assumption that they are very important—absolutely critical—in the ultimate completion of His plan for our life.

God is perfectly efficient.

Since God places these primary thoughts in our mind, we can also make the safe assumption that each one has a purpose—none are random or unimportant (no matter what source or significance we wish to assign them).

This *purpose* behind each of our primary thoughts is to *test* us, to show us the state of our hearts, to confront us with the key issues that must be addressed, to discipline us, to direct the course of our life, and to—ultimately—mold us into the likeness of God's Son, Jesus.

We must understand that these primary thoughts are the mediators—along with the relational and environmental events that God orchestrates in our life—by which *He precisely directs the course of our life.*

Because He loves us so much, the course of our life is far too important to God for Him to not be directly and palpably involved in every single nanosecond of it!

Copyright 2013 Michael K. Pasque

This critical direction from God must take the form of both good *and evil* thoughts.

Most of these primary thoughts are what God defines in His Holy Word as good or *righteous* and are in fact placed there *directly*, without mediator, by the Holy Spirit of God.

The generation of these good primary thoughts is precisely the mechanism by which God attempts to steer us along the godly path He desires for our life.

The bad news, of course, is that Satan—also not only by God's allowance, but by His direction—also has access and can directly place in our minds primary thoughts that are defined by God's Holy Word as *evil*.

The generation of these primary *evil* thoughts is in fact precisely the mechanism by which Satan and his minions wish to guide us along a path that is 180 degrees opposite of that path that God desires.

Whether we will let the Holy Spirit guide us—and this is the critical decision of every moment of our life—is determined by our *secondary thoughts*—our volitional agreement or disagreement with the primary *righteous* thought that has been put into our mind.

In like fashion, whether we will let Satan and his minions guide us or not is also determined by our *secondary thoughts*—our volitional agreement or disagreement with the primary *evil* thought that has been put into our mind.

As previously mentioned, although we do not control the primary thoughts that occur in our minds as a response to the circumstances in our environment, we do, nonetheless, control the secondary thoughts that occur in response to these primary thoughts.

Copyright 2013 Michael K. Pasque

Day 28

Where Does The Fight For Our Heart Really Take Place?
The Critical Importance Of Our Secondary Thoughts

Why is this discussion of primary and secondary thoughts so important?

Precisely because the interaction between our primary and secondary thoughts is the mechanism by which the entirety of the battle for our eternal hearts—for our very life—is fought.

It is critical that we understand the practical significance of this knowledge, specifically in regard to our goal of goals as believers: walking step by step with Jesus every day.

As discussed, our daily lives are basically a long string of temporally sequential decision-points that the all-wise God has placed in our life with specific design and purpose.

Not one of these decision-points is unimportant, not one can be dismissed—and not one is missing.

Every single one—large or small, critical or mundane—is irreplaceable in regard to the perfect outcome of our life that has been carefully planned to the detail by our Creator God.

In this regard, God's plan for our life is precise: not a single decision-point can be left out and no others need be added.

These decision-points appear to take many different forms in the many different sets of environmental circumstances in which we live our lives.

Copyright 2013 Michael K. Pasque

But, in actuality they boil down to one common final pathway:

These decision-points all take the final form of a primary thought that occurs in response to the particular environmental circumstances in which God has placed us.

In other words, these critical decision-points occur by no other mechanism than that of the instillation of a primary thought into our mind, primarily in response to the God-ordained, God-orchestrated circumstances within which we find ourselves.

The *temporal relationship* between the unique set of environmental circumstances and the occurrence of the primary thought that has come into our minds as a primary response to them is also not under our control.

The timing of the circumstances, events, decision-points, and primary thoughts are exclusively under God's control.

The primary thought may occur as an immediate response to the set of environmental circumstances from which it was generated and be readily perceived as directly related to the circumstances—or it may not.

The primary thought can occur very literally anytime in relation to the circumstances that generated it—waking us up in the middle of the night several days or even several years later.

Either way, all such *primary* thoughts are the *final common pathway* of the wide variety of environmental circumstances that trigger the staging of decision-points in our every day lives.

Once again, these primary thought decision-points have only two choices— *God* or *non-God*—and all are designed and implemented by God to test us.

Copyright 2013 Michael K. Pasque

> Our choices—our decisions—in each of these decision-points are *entirely* manifest by our secondary thoughts—how we *choose* to *think* about these primary thoughts.

We control the entirety of our response to these decision-points by our *secondary* thought response to the primary thoughts that pose the decision-point.

When confronted by a decision-point—i.e. a primary thought—we have only two choices.

We can *agree* with the primary thought—good or bad, God or non-God—and thereby let it influence and determine our further thoughts, words, and actions.

Agreeing with them is, of course, good when the thought is righteous and from the Holy Spirit.

Agreeing with them is, of course, very bad when the thought represents a non-God choice that comes directly from the minions of Satan.

We can also disagree with them—good or bad, God or non-God—and thereby grab them and cast them out of our minds, refusing to let them determine or influence in any way our further thoughts, words, or actions.

Disagreeing with them is obviously bad when they are from the Holy Spirit and good when the thoughts are from Satan.

It is critical to emphasize a key difference between primary thoughts and secondary thoughts:

> These *choices*—these *secondary* thoughts, this agreeing or disagreeing—unlike the primary thoughts to which they occur in response, *are entirely under our control.*

These decision-points—manifest by primary thoughts that occur in response to God ordained life circumstances—are staged by God to make us declare our

Copyright 2013 Michael K. Pasque

hearts and, as discussed, we do not have a choice as to whether or not to respond to these primary thoughts.

Although it is true that we do not have to respond by *action* to every environmental event that challenges us, we do not have a choice in regard to *mandatory* secondary thought responses to our primary thoughts.

It may not be apparent to those in our immediate environment, but we respond in one way another to *every* primary thought with a *secondary thought response*— we cannot help it.

Thus, the primary thoughts that occur in our minds many times each day are the bottom-line decision-points of our life.

They are placed there by God to influence, to guide, to direct the course of our life.

And, indeed, our choices at these decision-points very literally determine the actual day-to-day course of our life.

The entirety of our life course, in fact, can be summed up by the choices—the responses, *the secondary thoughts*—that we make in response to these primary thoughts.

These choices that we make are entirely embodied and encompassed by our *secondary thought* response to the decision-points—there is nothing more to them.

These choices then do indeed direct the words and actions that the world sees as our response.

But, the true battle is not fought over words and actions.

By the time the words are being spoken and the actions are being carried out, the battle is over.

The outcome of the battle may be displayed for all to see in our words and actions, but the battle was 100% fought in our mind.

Copyright 2013 Michael K. Pasque

Thus these secondary thought responses are responsible for generating the actions that are perceived by the individuals around us—the words and deeds that are the overt manifestations of our secondary thought decisions.

Those who live according to the sinful nature have their minds set on what that nature desires; but those who live in accordance with the Spirit have their minds set on what the Spirit desires. (Romans 8:5)

A primary thought, for example, may be seized upon, mulled over, brought up repeatedly, and ultimately form the foundation of the rationale for other evil secondary thoughts—all of which apparently empower Satan to throw more evil primary thoughts into our minds.

And then the multitude of evil primary and secondary thoughts coalesce into the generation of the most dangerous of all secondary thoughts—those that embody scheming and plotting against those individuals whom God has brought into our life.

And directly from the secondary thoughts that scheme and plot against others come evil actions that inflict real damage on our friends, enemies, and acquaintances—all of which (unlike the thought processes that generated them)—are visible to everyone.

The Bible concisely describes this process:

Then, after desire has conceived, it gives birth to sin; and sin, when it is full-grown, gives birth to death. (James 1:15)

Copyright 2013 Michael K. Pasque

To deal with these decision-points effectively and in a godly manner, we must *focus* our attention on the *primary thoughts* themselves and not be distracted by the environmental stimuli and events that generate these thoughts.

This is very difficult for us.

As human beings, we naturally focus most of our attention on the environmental stimuli around us—primarily, of course, on the other people that fill our immediate environment.

Our perception of our environment—especially in regard to the people that God brings into our environment—is important, but it is futile to attempt to implement a remedy in our environment without first dealing with the primary thoughts (that are generated from the environmental stimuli) by first responding with the appropriate secondary thoughts.

As go the secondary thoughts, so go our words and deeds.

> *The entirety—the sum total—of the fight that we fight in this life is found in our choice of secondary thoughts.*

*"I hate divorce," says the LORD God of Israel, "and I hate a man's covering himself with violence as well as with his garment," says the LORD Almighty. So **guard** yourself **in your spirit**, and do not **break faith**. (Malachi 2:16 [emphasis added])*

We can't let the fact that the fight is fought in our minds—and not in the streets—make us mistakenly and naively believe that it is any less *real* and any less tangible and that the consequences are any less palpable in our life.

It is our mind that is the battlefield and the fight is *for our eternal heart*—there can be no more important discussion than this.

Copyright 2013 Michael K. Pasque

Day 29

How Do I Win The Battle For My Heart?
The Summation Of The Battle

In summary, our initial and most critical, life-determining responses to the God-ordained, *primary thought* decision-points that occur many times every day of our life are the generation of secondary thoughts.

Once again, secondary thoughts are defined as *any* thoughts we generate *in response* to primary thoughts.

In contrast to the generation of primary thoughts, which are not under our control, we exercise complete and direct control over our secondary thought response to these primary thoughts.

In other words, our God-ordained *free will* ensures that the generation of the secondary thoughts is completely under our control.

In fact, our God-ordained *free will* operates only in, and finds its *only* real expression in *the generation of secondary thoughts.*

There is no other venue in which the expression of our free will is enabled other than in the generation of our secondary thoughts.

Our secondary thoughts are therefore the exclusive and only palpable mechanism, manifestation, and embodiment of our most treasured gift, our *free will.*

In fact, God has not granted us complete control over anything except our secondary thoughts.

God controls everything else in our world except our secondary thoughts.

Copyright 2013 Michael K. Pasque

Our *actions*, which are manifest as further thoughts, words, or deeds that are then perceived by and act upon the individuals and circumstances in our environment, occur exclusively and only as a *direct* response to our *secondary* thoughts.

The actions that occur as a result of our secondary thoughts are the mechanism by which we *implement* our secondary thoughts in and upon the environment in which we live.

Since our secondary thoughts and their related actions are the <u>only</u> place that we have control over anything in our lives—and since they very literally control the course of our lives—they therefore represent *the* very critical intervention point that is offered to believers upon which they can—through the grace and strength found only in the cross of Christ—uniquely implement heart and soul change in their lives.

This is critical.

The only place that we can implement real change in our life—and that, only through the power of the death and resurrection of Jesus Christ—is in our secondary thoughts.

In order for us to make progress in controlling our words and actions, the process by which we determine what thoughts fill our mind must be an *active* process.

We are in control of our secondary response to our primary thoughts and we must take control of the primary thoughts that enter our minds.

Controlling what we choose to dwell upon and act upon is, therefore, the meat of the battle in which we fight.

We must take control of our secondary thought response to the primary thoughts that are placed in our mind.

Copyright 2013 Michael K. Pasque

*We demolish arguments and every pretension that sets itself up against the knowledge of God, and **we take captive every thought to make it obedient to Christ.** (2Corinthians 10:5; emphasis added)*

To some finite degree, we can therefore control our eternal destiny and our life course based upon the choices that we make in our secondary thoughts.

Although we can control our secondary thoughts and therefore our actions (thought, word, or deed) and we can often at least partially know (from revelation in the word of God and from our life experience) what God's response will be, we utterly do NOT control the consequences of our secondary thought response to the primary thoughts (decision-points) God places in our life—only God does.

Copyright 2013 Michael K. Pasque

Day 30

If They Are Occurring In My Mind, Then Why Aren't These Thoughts Under My Control?
Practical Examples

The importance of understanding our secondary thoughts cannot be overstated.

Mastery of our secondary thoughts is the crucial foundation of our sanctification.

It is always helpful to review practical examples in developing our understanding of the importance of controlling our secondary thoughts.

It is not God's will for our life for us to think hateful secondary thoughts in response to a primary thought placed in our minds regarding another individual— friend or enemy.

In a similar fashion, it is not God's desire that we dwell upon lustful secondary thoughts in response to a primary thought regarding the attractive young woman or man who just walked by us.

Of critical importance in regard to these examples: it is a very short step from either hateful or lustful secondary thoughts to sinful actions that reflect and have been motivated by these sinful secondary thoughts.

> *But I tell you that anyone who looks at a woman lustfully has already committed adultery with her in his heart. (Matthew 5:28)*

We are also clearly outside of the will of God for our life when we generate even more hateful or lustful thoughts by dwelling, ruminating, meditating, or

Copyright 2013 Michael K. Pasque

scheming (more secondary thoughts) in response to our own initial bad secondary thoughts.

Further, our ability to resist the generation of bad actions or more bad secondary thoughts gets weaker and weaker the more our secondary thoughts repeatedly submit to—agree with—an evil primary thought.

In other words, Satan and his minions gain easier, more frequent, more convincing, and more empowered access to our minds every time that we do not resist, but instead agree with, the evil primary thoughts that they have placed in our minds.

In a similar fashion, when we immediately resist evil primary thoughts and deny agreement with the ungodly statements that they make, Satan and his minions have more difficult, less enabled access to our minds.

In other words, if we resist Satan, he will indeed flee.

Submit yourselves, then, to God. Resist the devil, and he will flee from you. (James 4:7)

This battle that takes place in our minds and hearts is really only won by one mechanism: the Christ-empowered instantaneous rejection of evil thoughts that pop into our mind (placed there by Satan) or by the immediate agreement with righteous thoughts that pop into our mind (placed there by the Holy Spirit).

Timing, as always, is critical—the longer we wait to righteously respond to the primary thought, the less likely that our response will be righteous.

The battle is won only by *guarding our hearts* by scrutinizing what secondary thoughts we allow ourselves to think.

Copyright 2013 Michael K. Pasque

Above all else, guard your heart, for it is the wellspring of life.
(Proverbs 4:23)

If we brood, scheme, plot, or ruminate upon evil thoughts, then we have turned over the control of our mind—and our heart—to Satan and his minions...and nefarious activity is not far behind.

Thus, the careful inspection of the newly arrived primary thought must be followed by the immediate rejection of evil primary thoughts and the immediate agreement with righteous primary thoughts.

Copyright 2013 Michael K. Pasque

Day 31

How Important Are My Secondary Thoughts In The Battle For My Sanctification?
The Bottom-Line Of Christian Living

Every choice that we make at every decision-point in the entirety of our life is, in one way or another, a response to a primary thought.

In other words, *primary* thoughts are the sole mechanism by which God places decision-points in our lives.

It is critical to realize that all of these primary thoughts—either directly from the Holy Spirit or indirectly from Satan—ultimately come from God.

Thus, the course of our lives—which is a summation of all of our choices at all of the decision-points in our life—is directed by the primary thoughts that God sends into our life.

The primary thoughts that enter our minds are the mechanism by which God points us in the direction that He wants us to go—they are the mediators of His will and of His grace in our life.

They are the way that He has—with infinite wisdom—determined to direct our life.

This is a sure and palpable manifestation of God's endless grace in our lives.

It is critical that we understand this: the primary thoughts that enter our mind are all clear-cut, unavoidable decision-points and all are from God.

As decision-points, these primary thoughts *demand* a choice on our part—and, by God's plan, we uniformly must respond with secondary thoughts of some kind.

Copyright 2013 Michael K. Pasque

The course of our lives is also influenced by our secondary thought responses to the primary thoughts that God sends into our life.

This is a sure manifestation of the influence of our free will upon our lives.

Once again, we do not have a choice of whether we respond or not—a secondary thought response of some kind is *mandatory* to every primary thought and thus to every decision-point that is represented by that primary thought.

To not respond is to respond—we either agree with the point or we don't.

This is why we *must* be *active* in this process.

Learning to *actively* engage each of the primary thoughts that come into our minds with a godly secondary thought responses is the key to our progress in the sanctification process that God has placed in our life.

We must volitionally grab the good thoughts and agree with them and unhesitatingly act upon them.

In a similar fashion, we must also actively grab the bad thoughts and disagree with them and act immediately in accordance with that disagreement—primarily by casting them from our minds.

> *Love must be sincere. Hate what is evil; cling to what is good.*
> *(Romans 12:9)*

To not *actively* disagree with an evil primary thought by a secondary thought that grabs it and casts it out of our mind and thus out of our heart is, in fact, *to wholeheartedly agree with that evil primary thought.*

To not *actively* agree with a righteous primary thought is indeed to wholeheartedly *disagree* with it.

Copyright 2013 Michael K. Pasque

The lesson here in controlling these thoughts is to *never* be passive, moving to and fro, whichever way the wind blows us.

> *If any of you lacks wisdom, he should ask God, who gives generously to all without finding fault, and it will be given to him. But when he asks,* **he must believe and not doubt**, *because he who doubts is like a wave of the sea, blown and tossed by the wind. That man should not think he will receive anything from the Lord; he is a double-**minded** man, unstable in all he does. (James 1:5-8; emphasis added)*

A passive response to *any* of our primary thoughts is a sure road to disaster.

We must be active in this process or we will, by default, let the evil spiritual otherworld—with which we are at war—totally control our thoughts and thus our actions.

Thus the only way that a believer moves more into the will of God, and thus more toward the goal of being made into the likeness of Jesus, is to (and this only by the grace and the power of the cross of Christ) actively grab and control our secondary thought response to every single primary thought that enters our mind.

This is the most critical part of our sanctification and it is all about *grace*.

When we fail in this process, in the process of actively grabbing these thoughts and thus actively controlling our secondary thought response, our response should not be to *just try harder*.

That will never work.

Instead, our job can be summed up in one action.

We are to repeatedly and continually beseech the Father, in the Name of His Son, Jesus, *to help us*—by the power of the death and resurrection of Jesus Christ—*to actively control our secondary thought response*.

Copyright 2013 Michael K. Pasque

There is no other way.

The written Word of God is clear in this regard.

No other way is mentioned.

It is by the grace of the cross of Christ and nothing else.

It is never by our strength, our resolve, or our willpower.

It is by the grace of the cross of Christ or it is not at all.

These primary thoughts that pose decision-points for us may be loving or hating, generous or coveting, truthful or lying, sated or lustful—any number of options that offer us a choice to approve or disapprove, agree or disagree about something or someone in our environment.

Thus the choice that we have in regard to these primary thoughts is straightforward.

We either agree with the thought or we disagree with the thought.

This agreement or disagreement is the very critical foundation of our secondary thought response to the primary thought.

Upon this nidus of agreement/disagreement is built the crystal of our secondary thought response.

Obviously, the ability to discern which is an evil primary thought and which is a good primary thought is foundational to our success—and this discernment is found almost exclusively in the written Word of God.

After choosing to agree or disagree with the primary thought, our secondary thought response is encompassed in our choice to either seize/dwell upon or ignore/dismiss the primary thought.

Obviously, the response that is supported by the written Word of God is to agree with, seize, and dwell upon righteous (once again, as defined by the Bible) thoughts.

Copyright 2013 Michael K. Pasque

In a similar fashion, evil thoughts are to be met with immediate disagreement and dealt with by their immediate seizure and dismissal—no dwelling on these!

Note that these are all active responses.

These are all volitional responses.

Unlike anything else in our world, *we* completely control these responses.

And they control the course of our day—and thus cumulatively they ultimately control the course of our life.

Most critically, it must be understood that to blithely ignore in utter passivity an evil primary thought is indeed to agree with it.

There is no in-between.

Examples that illustrate this primary/secondary thought mechanism are readily available—everyday—in the life of anyone who is alive and functioning in an environment with other individuals.

For instance, we get to choose our thought response when we suddenly remember how someone has hurt us—this *remembering* of their offense is the primary thought and it is not of our doing.

Our response, on the other hand is all ours—we can either agree or disagree with this thought.

And then we can volitionally choose to dwell on the love for that person that is available in Jesus Christ—just as Jesus told us to—with full faith in the fact that He is in charge.

If we are able to grab that primary thought and respond in this positive manner, we can be assured that Jesus will go before us into any battle that results from our faith and He will be our rear guard.

Or we can choose the *non-God* response to this decision-point and dwell upon thoughts of self-righteous hate and vengeance.

Copyright 2013 Michael K. Pasque

In a similar fashion, when our neighbor drives his Ferrari by our house and the thought that *we deserve to be driving that car more than he does* suddenly pops into our minds as a primary thought (no need to feel guilty here, we are not the source of this thought), our secondary thoughts can agree with this primary thought—and that agreement leads immediately to sin as we then *covet* our neighbor's car.

Or, alternatively, we can disagree with that evil primary thought and instead choose to dwell upon the richness of that which God has already provided in our life.

God puts the primary thoughts into our minds.

And it is entirely in our secondary thought response that we therefore *live* our life.

It is also in this secondary thought response that we live out our *faith*.

It is, therefore, precisely and uniquely and exclusively in our secondary thought response that our true commitment to Jesus is tested.

Our secondary thought responses to the primary thoughts that are placed in our minds thus encompass the whole of what we call *our life*—for they are the only thing that we actually control.

And, in a similar fashion, our secondary thought responses also encompass the whole of our Christian *walk* with our Savior, Jesus.

Satan may be the intermediary of the evil primary thoughts, but, for the most part, they are generated by circumstantial stimuli from the environment around us.

Thus, it is clear that the real fight does not even begin until the primary thought is delivered into our mind.

It is only then that the Holy Spirit and Satan both try to convince us that their respective secondary thought response is the correct one.

Copyright 2013 Michael K. Pasque

The Holy Spirit desires that we immediately disagree with and reject the evil thoughts.

And He wants us to dwell upon the righteous ones.

Satan, in direct contrast, tries to convince us to dwell upon the evil thoughts and ignore the righteous ones.

The primary battlefield of our life therefore is *not* in the *events* around us as we most commonly believe—it is in our thoughts.

> The *entirety* of the *spiritual battle* that is referred to repeatedly in the Bible is fought in our thoughts.

The individuals who inhabit the spiritual *otherworld* that parallels ours clearly have influence over our thoughts—and the battle is all about what we choose to dwell upon in these thoughts.

So, that precarious interface between our world and the spiritual *otherworld* (that is inhabited by angels and demons) is found precisely in this juncture between what God controls and what we control—it is found in the fight to control the *nature* of our *secondary* thoughts.

In other words, even though Satan may be the mediator of your heart attack or your cancer, ultimately he is not the primary source.

Further, even though Satan may be the mediator of the primary thoughts that come along with your heart attack and your cancer, ultimately he is not the primary source of them either.

Further still, even though Satan wants to direct our secondary thought response in regard to our heart attack or cancer by the primary thoughts he gives us in their response, ultimately this is all a test sent from God to show us our hearts.

How are our hearts revealed to us?

Copyright 2013 Michael K. Pasque

When we choose to repeatedly dwell on our sinful secondary thoughts, we further empower Satan in our secondary thoughts and therefore in our life.

When we choose to repeatedly dwell on our sinful secondary thoughts, we are making an active, volitional choice not only to empower Satan, but also to exclude the influence and power of the Holy Spirit.

When we choose to repeatedly agree with and dwell upon the righteous primary thoughts that the Holy Spirit places in our minds, then we enable the power of God's Holy Spirit *in our life*.

Despite the fact that this is all a test from God, Satan still exists and his influence is still critical in our responses.

Despite the fact that God has determined all of this, right this moment, our response is still our response—and we are still held accountable for it.

Despite the fact that this is all a test to show us our true hearts with God's loving plan for our sanctification as the motivation behind it, right this minute Satan is still a very real player with very real influence and with whom we must deal.

> *For our struggle is not against flesh and blood, but against the rulers, against the authorities, against the powers of this dark world and against the spiritual forces of evil in the heavenly realms. (Ephesians 6:12)*

Satan knows that all of the choices that define our lives are made in our secondary thoughts.

Satan knows that they are the only things that we control in our life.

Satan knows that they control our actions—our words and deeds that directly impact those individuals whom God has brought into our life.

Copyright 2013 Michael K. Pasque

Satan knows that the fight for the sovereign dominion of our hearts occurs in our secondary thoughts and therefore that is where he attacks with his only weapon—deception.

Did you ever wonder why Satan is called *the deceiver* and why his primary weapon is described as *deception*?

It is because his real fight with us—the whole of the battle for our hearts—is in our thoughts and in convincing us to respond with sinful secondary thoughts.

Deception—the substitution of a lie for truth—is the most lethal way to adversely influence our secondary thought choice and Satan knows this.

This deception primarily revolves around Satan convincing us that something that is righteous is evil or that something that is evil is righteous.

This is why reading the Bible is so important—it helps us discern what is righteous and what is evil.

Do not conform any longer to the pattern of this world, but be transformed by the renewing of your mind. Then you will be able to test and approve what God's will is—his good, pleasing and perfect will. (Romans 12:2)

The written word of God helps us discern the righteous *godly* choice at each decision-point from the evil *non-godly* choice.

It is quite clear that if the fight is in our mind for control of our thoughts, then Satan's logical weapon of choice is deception.

Satan is a liar and the place that he wields his lies is in trying to convince us that the non-God choice is the *best* choice.

He uses many metrics to characterize *best*, including ease, safety, righteousness, all of which add up to the ultimate composite metric: *logical*.

Copyright 2013 Michael K. Pasque

His lies are his weapons in this fight because changing the perspective or the *logic* with which we make that choice is the target of his weaponry.

The countering force to Satan's influence on our secondary thoughts is, of course, the righteous force that also has access to our minds—the Holy Spirit.

If life is a battle, if we are truly embroiled in a war from the moment of our first breath until our last, if our enemy is really the dark principalities of the spiritual world, if there really is a continual struggle between good and evil in this universe of ours, and if that battle is of monumental importance in our lives, then that fight occurs there in our minds in our secondary thoughts.

The fight occurs there in our secondary thoughts with Satan trying to convince us *that God's heart for us is not good*: that He is not with us, that He does not love us, that He has abandoned us, that He cannot be trusted, that He does not have our eternal wellbeing as His primary motivator, and therefore that His heart is not for us—all lies aimed specifically at the particular decision-point that God has placed in our life at that moment.

These were the original lies with which Satan lured Eve to the fall of mankind—and they are still the lies that Satan tells each of us every day.

The Holy Spirit opposes Satan on every point—trying to influence us toward believing and trusting that God's heart for us is always good—and therefore influencing us to make godly choices at each decision-point.

Let's summarize this whole process:

God controls the course of our life by controlling the decision-points that confront us, which are entirely encompassed and composed by the primary thoughts that come into our minds—all by controlling both the environmental stimuli and the actual formulation of the stimuli-associated primary thoughts.

Copyright 2013 Michael K. Pasque

Our secondary thoughts that we formulate in response to the primary thoughts (that God formulates) are therefore the true meat of the battle—they *are* the trenches in which the fight is fought and the battle is won or lost.

Further still, it logically follows that our secondary thoughts are also therefore where the whole of both our *salvation* and *sanctification* takes place—if we are to make progress in either, it is in our secondary thoughts that progress will or will not be made.

Obviously, that which makes secondary thoughts important in the process of both salvation and sanctification is the fact that our secondary thoughts are, once again, the only part of our life that we actually control.

It is in our secondary thoughts that we accept the salvation offered by the cross of Christ.

It is in our secondary thoughts that we take every step forward that is taken in our life toward our sanctification—toward being made into the likeness of Jesus Christ.

As such, our secondary thoughts are thus the most important part of our life.

All that we are in charge of is our humility—we will either surrender to the will of God by our secondary thoughts or we will abandon humility and seek to maintain total control over our lives, once again by our secondary thoughts.

This cannot be emphasized enough—our secondary thoughts are the key to the entirety of the outcome of our life.

Our whole life—which is a linear string of decision-points in the form of primary thoughts—thus boils down to a battle over the control of our secondary thought responses to those primary thoughts.

This foundational paradigm has profound practical implications for our day-to-day lives.

Copyright 2013 Michael K. Pasque

If *we* are to *intervene* to implement change in our life—to change the course or ultimate outcome of our life—we are wasting our time unless we intervene at the level of our secondary thoughts.

Every single day, we all waste our time 1) trying to control the *circumstances* in which we live and 2) feeling guilty for the primary thoughts that enter our mind—neither of which are under our control and neither of which can *ever* be under our control because both are utterly under God's complete control.

The knowledge of this paradigm in which we live our life has paramount practical application that finds its pinnacle in the realization that the only thing that we need to work on in the post-salvation process of our sanctification is our *secondary thought control.*

Copyright 2013 Michael K. Pasque

Day 32

How Can I Actually Achieve Secondary Thought Control?
How To Respond In Order To Win The Fight

The battle for our secondary thoughts is the whole show.

The whole show.

Secondary thoughts determine the process and progress of our sanctification.

The critical first step toward winning the secondary thought battle of the mind, is to immediately quit beating ourselves up over the heinous primary thoughts that invade the sacred confines of our mind.

Evil primary thoughts that *pop* into our mind *never* represent sin in our life.

Satan wants to make us believe that we are sinning when he throws those evil primary thoughts into our minds.

Placing *guilt* and *shame*, where none is due (in the heart of the believer), is one of Satan's favorite tactics to deceive the believer into thinking that Jesus could not possibly love them or that they really are not saved because they are not worthy.

Satan's persistence in this same tactic allows him to pummel us to the point of just *giving up*.

The facts, however, are clear in this regard.

We have nothing to do with the actual generation of evil primary thoughts into our consciousness—they always seem to just *arrive* there.

This is because, in fact, they are indeed *sent* into our minds.

We are not responsible for, and have no control over, either the good or the bad primary thoughts that pop into in our minds.

Copyright 2013 Michael K. Pasque

The only exception to this rule is the fact that whenever we agree (by way of our secondary thought response) with an evil primary thought, we obviously augment Satan's power over us.

When we agree with him, we give Satan easier access to our minds and make it easier for him to introduce more evil primary thoughts—this is the mechanism of the *spiritual blindness* or the *"hardening of [our] hearts"* that is described in the Bible.

> So I tell you this, and insist on it in the Lord, that you must no longer live as the Gentiles do, in the **futility of their thinking**. They are darkened in their understanding and separated from the life of God because of the ignorance that is in them due to the **hardening** of their hearts. Having lost all sensitivity, they have given themselves over to sensuality so as to indulge in every kind of impurity, with a **continual lust for more**. (Ephesians 4:17-19; emphasis added)

Recognition of our lack of responsibility for primary thought generation allows us to focus on that for which we really *are* responsible.

This focuses the attention of the battle on our very direct responsibility for our secondary thought response to the primary thoughts that are sent into our minds.

Let there be no question about this: in direct contrast to our primary thoughts, the entirety of the responsibility for our secondary thoughts lies on no one else but us.

Thus we have discerned the structure and make up of the battle for control of our heart via control of our mind—and, therefore, the control of our salvation and sanctification.

Let's summarize the *order of battle* and our response to it.

Copyright 2013 Michael K. Pasque

The battle always begins with an attack from outside our mind.

The attack can be from Satan and his minions…or it can be from the Holy Spirit of God.

Although the nature of our response is 100% under our control, the *necessity* of responding is not.

In other words, we have no choice in regard to responding to the primary thought—we *must*, by God's design, *respond*.

One way or another we *always* respond to a primary thought.

So our fight is not over whether or not we will respond, but instead solely over the nature of our response.

We kid ourselves in this regard.

We think that we can avoid the responsibility by simply refusing to respond.

But in this case, as is the case in the question regarding our response to the Person of Jesus Christ, *to not respond is very definitely to respond.*

We always think that no response is precisely that, no response.

In this case, this is never true.

We *must* respond.

There is no choice in regard to whether to respond or not.

A response must be given, one way or the other.

To give no response—to take that gutless way out— is very definitely to give a response.

In other words, to give no response to an evil thought is nothing less than to fully accept, concur with, and condone that evil thought as truth.

Similarly, to give no response to a righteous, godly thought is nothing less than to fully disagree with it, to deny the truth that it conveys.

Copyright 2013 Michael K. Pasque

So, instead of responding to the primary thought by not responding at all (to that which represents a very definite attack), we must counterattack.

We have no choice in this matter.

What does this mean in the daily real life battle of our minds?

In the case of *righteous* primary thoughts from the Holy Spirit, it means that we must, in our secondary thought response, actively dwell upon and agree with the primary thought—we must *"hold on to the good."*

> *Test everything. Hold on to the good. Avoid every kind of evil.*
> *(1Thessalonians 5:21-22)*

In the case of an *evil* primary thought, we must actively disagree and cast the thought from our mind—we must *"avoid every kind of evil"* thought.

This active resistance to evil *cannot be over emphasized.*

This seemingly inconsequential step of resistance has the ability to turn the tide of the most vicious spiritual battle.

Our response is the hinge-point upon which the entirety of the battle for our hearts (that is fought in our minds, in our thoughts) is won or lost.

There is very great power in this resistance.

Indeed, the immeasurably great power of the cross of Christ is manifest in nothing less than resistance to the evil primary thoughts that are placed in our minds by Satan.

The Bible is very clear in this regard.

The importance of our resistance to the entrance of evil thoughts into our minds could not be more emphasized than in the Bible's graphic description of Satan's response to this resistance.

Copyright 2013 Michael K. Pasque

*Submit yourselves, then, to God. **Resist** the devil, and **he will flee from you**. (James 4:7; emphasis added)*

We should ponder this verse in our hearts.

We should remember that we are speaking about the single most powerful created being in the entirety of the creation.

As weak as you or I am in respect to the fearsome might of Lucifer (who was the most luminous guardian cherubim given dominion over the whole earth), we square off with him in battle every single day of our life.

And, amazingly, we have the ability—only by the power of the cross of Christ—to outright defeat him with simple resistance to the evil primary thoughts that he places in our mind.

You and I have the ability to rout the greatest evil warrior in existence.

Further, to not volitionally and actively and purposely counterattack in response to an evil primary thought in fact constitutes utter agreement and opens us immediately to more evil primary thought attacks.

In other words, we further empower the most fearsomely powerful evil angel in all of creation when we do not purposely, with resolve, cast his evil primary thoughts from our mind.

In a similar fashion, to not volitionally and actively and purposely *agree with* a righteous primary thought attack is in fact a secondary thought *counterattack* of *disagreement* and squelches the Holy Spirit by lessening His access to our mind.

This is an awesome struggle that we face every day of our life.

We should not downplay its importance.

Nor should we ignore or decry the very powerful weapons against Satan's assault that are ours only in the knowledge of Jesus Christ.

Copyright 2013 Michael K. Pasque

Day 33

How Can I Discern Righteous From Evil Primary Thoughts?
The Importance Of The Written Word Of God

Job #1 for all of us, therefore, is to respond with 1) negative, disagreeing *secondary* thoughts to evil *primary* thoughts, and 2) positive, affirming *secondary* thoughts to righteous *primary* thoughts.

As big a problem as this can be, there is yet another problem that we must deal with first.

This critical problem is in the accurate identification of the true nature of the primary thoughts that are cast into our minds.

If we don't get this vital first step right, all of the best intentions in the world will not allow our recovery.

If we do not get this first step right, the enemy will already be inside the gates.

This first step involves the *knowledge*, the *wisdom*, and the *discernment* that is spoken of in the Bible.

The Bible also tells us that *we* are held responsible for attaining this knowledge, wisdom, and discernment from the pages of the Bible itself.

How can a young man keep his way pure? By living according to your word. I seek you with all my heart; do not let me stray from your commands. I have hidden your word in my heart that I might not sin against you. (Psalm 119:9-11)

Copyright 2013 Michael K. Pasque

Once again, we must remember that *Satan* means *deceiver*.

Satan tries two distinct ploys in his primary thought attack on our hearts.

First, Satan absolutely will attempt to make us believe that we came up with these primary thoughts.

As we discussed, this then gives him the chance to whisper in our ears that *we* are the guilty ones.

These whispers regarding our guilt, of course, come in the form of more primary thoughts that follow immediately behind the original evil primary thoughts—all empowered by our lack of resistance to the original evil primary thoughts.

Satan immediately follows the instillation of these guilt-declaring primary thoughts with more primary thoughts that tell us that the very presence of these primary thoughts proves that we are worthless sinners, hopelessly despised by God, and not worthy of the salvation that we have attained in the shed blood of Jesus.

Satan's hope is that these seemingly innocuous primary thoughts represent a deceptively nonthreatening first step down a very dark pathway.

Satan's plan is to make us lose all hope and give up on our Savior.

He can then tell us precisely what He told Eve in the Garden of Eden: that God's heart for us is not good and that He has already abandoned us.

He asks in the darkest of primary thoughts, "Where is your God now?"

Satan wants desperately to convince us that God's heart is not good, God does not have our wellbeing at heart, God has already abandoned us, and God will never be there for us.

Satan's hope is that along with all of this will come *condemnation*—with ultimate defeat just a short step away.

Copyright 2013 Michael K. Pasque

Secondly, Satan uses even more deceptive *primary* thoughts to try to make his evil primary thoughts look like righteous primary thoughts.

The discernment of the true evil nature of a primary thought that Satan has disguised as a righteous primary thought is why we *must* read the Bible.

Every day.

This is simply not negotiable.

Any other methodology by which we think we can discern righteous from evil is folly.

The Bible is the only reliable way that we can detect and snare Satan in his deceit.

Jesus holds us responsible for reading and knowing the written Word of God.

We must read the Bible.

Reading the Bible is the single most important contribution that we can make to our sanctification.

We must read the Bible *every* day.

The Bible is always the last word on the true nature (righteous versus evil) of our primary thoughts and from it we can discern several fundamental general differentiators of righteous and evil thoughts.

For example, it becomes readily apparent from reading the Bible that a primary thought that condemns us (as opposed to condemning our actions) is from Satan—always and every time.

Similarly, a primary thought that praises the holy Name of Jesus is always from the Holy Spirit—since Satan cannot bring himself to do this.

Thus, the discernment that is necessary to guide the choice of our secondary thought response to every primary thought of every moment of our every day is found only in the written Word of God.

Copyright 2013 Michael K. Pasque

This is a war.

We need weapons to fight this war.

The written Word of God is our most powerful weapon in the war for our hearts that goes on every moment of every day.

Without it, every day, we are food.

Copyright 2013 Michael K. Pasque

Day 34

What Is The Eternal Impact Of My Response To Primary Thoughts?
Every Primary Thought Is An Opportunity With Eternal Consequences

Let's define sin.

Sin is exclusively and only defined as any secondary thought that 1) agrees with (or ignores) an evil primary thought or 2) disagrees with (or ignores) a righteous thought (the nature of both of these being determined exclusively by the revelation of the Word of God).

It is therefore critical that we focus *all* of our sanctification efforts on exercising control over our secondary thoughts.

Once again, in this life our secondary thoughts are the whole show.

In fact, it is in our secondary thoughts that we respond to the primary thought regarding the primacy of Jesus Christ.

It is in our secondary thoughts that we implement in our life the salvation that is made available to us solely by the work of Jesus Christ on the cross of Calvary.

Thus, it is in our secondary thoughts that we determine our eternity.

In a similar fashion, it is in our secondary thoughts that we determine the outcome of every single God-ordained event of our sanctification—second only to our salvation in its importance in our life.

Our secondary thoughts determine whether each particular sanctification event moves us closer to, or farther away from, the goal of being made into the likeness of Jesus Christ.

Copyright 2013 Michael K. Pasque

And that would be the whole purpose of our life.

So, are our secondary thoughts important?

Only in determining the entirety of the outcome of our life as measured by every meaningful metric.

In our secondary thoughts, we bring either glory or anguish to God.

In fact, our secondary thoughts constitute the *only* mechanism by which we can bring glory to God.

Every opportunity (every primary thought) is, therefore, a chance to bring glory to God that, if passed by, *is lost forever*.

Our secondary thoughts are the only mechanism by which we make a decision for or against God in every one of the thousands of primary thought-based decision-points that God places in our life.

And it is precisely in the *summation* of all of our volitional secondary thoughts that is found the very definition of our life, of our very existence.

These are the output of our efforts in Christ—the gold and silver (or the wood and stubble)—that will be tested by the fiery sword of the Word of God when we finally stand before Jesus.

It is also the summation of all of our volitional secondary thoughts that defines the true nature of our eternity.

Our secondary thoughts are the *only* thing in this life that we control and therefore constitute the defining components of what makes you, *you* and me, *me*.

Our secondary thoughts are very literally *everything*.

They represent the only participation that we have in our reaching our ultimate goal of resembling Jesus (the whole point of our salvation and sanctification process).

Copyright 2013 Michael K. Pasque

In other words, our secondary thoughts ultimately define how much we resemble Jesus.

They define what we actually did with the life and the gifts that were given to us by God.

And only in the resembling of Jesus in the nature of our secondary thoughts do we bring glory to God.

Only in resembling Jesus in the way that we formulate our secondary thoughts do we obey, serve, love, and bring glory to God.

Only in resembling Jesus in the way that we formulate our secondary thoughts do we love one another—as Jesus commands us.

Only in the way that we resemble Jesus in the subservient, sacrificial loving nature of our secondary thoughts do we really love God.

We, therefore, simply cannot over estimate the importance of our secondary thoughts.

We cannot dismiss our deep heart desire to concentrate exclusively on control of our secondary thought responses to our primary thoughts—this is not some ancillary, inconsequential fight, but rather the entirety of the battle and, in fact, the whole war.

Every primary thought is an opportunity eternally lost if we choose to rebel against God in our secondary thought response—and I cannot help but believe that we will at some point regret them all as we look into the eyes of the only One who ever really loved us.

Copyright 2013 Michael K. Pasque

Day 35

What Is The Practical Goal Of The Sanctification Process?
Changing The Focus Of Our Heart

God did not reveal the presence of Satan in His holy written Word so as to allow us to blame everything on him.

God did not tell us about Satan so as to focus all of our attention on fighting this very dark force.

We are told of the nature of Lucifer's fall not to tell us about our spiritual enemy.

We were told about Satan because his story is our story; his rebellious sinful heart is our rebellious sinful heart.

In His description of Satan, God has revealed the dark secret longings of the sinful human nature that resides in the deep reaches of every human heart.

So, many of us have it wrong: it is not Satan that we must overcome; it is our own sinful human nature.

Satan is just a deceiver who befriends our sinful nature.

Satan's heart is our heart.

Satan's sin was to attempt to raise himself to the level of God—just like we do every single time that we sin.

For every sin is simply a statement that we believe our will for our life is better, smarter, easier, and more important than God's will for our life—we raise our beliefs above those of God.

When we sin, we raise ourselves and our desires above God and His desires.

Copyright 2013 Michael K. Pasque

In God's eyes, everything that Satan did we also do.

This is not to deny Satan's existence or his importance as a deceiving enemy of our heart; it just means that we should not focus upon him as if *he* were the problem.

This focus upon the real problem is critical because it brings us to a discussion of the purpose of the decision-points that God has structured into our lives.

God has designed every aspect of our lives down to the details of every minute of every day.

God has a tactical battle plan for our life that has as its prime motivator the drawing out (into the light) of the desire, the sin that we share with Satan.

The decision-points that God has orchestrated into our life are aimed at that need of ours to place ourselves as the focus of attention at the center of our life—that attempt to raise ourselves to be *"like the Most High." (Isaiah 14:14)*

Satan's sin is our sin.

It is the very basic sin that resides in *every* human heart from the moment of birth.

Our human nature demands that *we* be the focus of our attention.

It demands that we make all of the choices at the decision-points in our life and that those choices be oriented around us, not around loving, serving, and worshiping God by loving and serving one another.

Our human nature demands that we worship ourselves.

It also demands that we place ourselves repeatedly and continually at the center of our attention and that we also try to convince the rest of the people of the world to also place us at the center of their attention.

So, we go about our lives with our attention focused on ourselves—and most pointedly not on God—all the while trying to coax the world into joining us in our self-worship.

Copyright 2013 Michael K. Pasque

Precisely this is what the whole of a believer's life is spent trying to *overcome*.

We must—and this can only be done by inviting Christ into our hearts—refocus the attention of our hearts upon God by redirecting it off of ourselves.

The focusing of our attention on God is in fact our true deep heart desire, purpose, and eternity—it having been derailed by our selfish human nature.

When we—by the grace of God and the power of the death and resurrection of Jesus Christ—manage to focus our attention back on God, we begin our transformation into beings that focus their attention on God—we begin our transformation into the likeness of God's Son, Jesus, who has spent all of eternity with His attention subserviently and sacrificially focused on loving the Father.

The way that we focus our attention on God is (by His decree and design) by focusing our attention on the people that He brings into our life.

We, like His Son Jesus, must focus on others with subservient, sacrificial love being both the motivator and natural product of this effort.

Obviously, it cannot be both the motivator and the natural product of this effort unless someone else is involved.

In this case, that someone else is Jesus Christ resident in our hearts.

It is Jesus Christ who supplies the subservient, sacrificial love that motivates and empowers us to love one another.

Without Jesus, we are destined to spend our whole lives pursuing self-adoration and attempting to refocus the attention of the people in our life upon us.

In other words, we spend our lives just like Satan—who wants us to worship him just like he tried to get Jesus to worship Him in the desert.

The only solution to our problem is to focus the attention of our hearts on the Person upon whom they were created to focus upon—Jesus.

Copyright 2013 Michael K. Pasque

The only way to do this is in that critical period of time when for a passing brief moment we step down from the throne of our heart and ask Jesus (we must ask) to assume His rightful place upon the throne of our heart with sovereign dominion over our life.

At that moment our salvation is assured and our eternity is set...

And yet the battle continues.

> *Therefore, my dear friends, as you have always obeyed—not only in my presence, but now much more in my absence—continue to **work out your salvation** with fear and trembling, for it is God who works in you to will and to act according to his good purpose. (Philippians 2:12-13; emphasis added)*

Our salvation is assured and yet we must, with Jesus, *"work out"* the sanctification of our heart—the complete purging of all that is not Jesus—removing all of the *self*-garbage that we have accumulated over our lifetime.

In this process—the sanctification process—we are guided by God through a long series of carefully orchestrated decision-points by which we are drawn to our self-centeredness and must surrender—unfortunately over and over again—even the backcountry recesses of our heart kingdom to the sovereign dominion of Jesus.

Our life is like a long great war to free a kingdom with Jesus fighting battle after battle with us to slowly win over every part of our heart kingdom.

This life is, therefore, about *"the kingdom of God,"* which is, in fact, nothing less than the dominion of our heart.

> *Once, having been asked by the Pharisees when the kingdom of God would come, Jesus replied, "The kingdom of God does not come with*

Copyright 2013 Michael K. Pasque

your careful observation, nor will people say, 'Here it is,' or 'There it is,' because the kingdom of God is within you." (Luke 17:20-21; emphasis added)

Our life therefore becomes a long series of battles—of skirmishes—which are the decision-points God places in our lives to draw us to the battlefield of our self-centeredness—the point of which is to win the battle for the complete surrender of *self*, of our heart kingdom to Jesus.

And in that heart fight is found *"the kingdom of God."*

Copyright 2013 Michael K. Pasque

Day 36

How Do We Carry Out This Thought Control On A Day-To-Day Basis?
The Centrality Of Jesus In Our Daily Life

Satan's grand plan of attack is to direct our thoughts *away from* the One upon whom they should be directed.

In other words, instead of letting us focus continually upon Jesus—*which places us in a state in which we simply cannot sin*—Satan wants to refocus our attention upon those things in our life that we substitute for God: our idols.

This is his plan because he knows it works and he is good at it.

Our solution to our problem, therefore, must be to keep the focus of our attention on Jesus where it belongs.

One simple fact will assist us in this critical endeavor.

We must remember that everything or every one in this life that attracts us—including our idols—does so only by their ability to reflect a fleeting glimpse of our Savior.

No person or thing can attract the attention of our *hearts* except in the way that he, she, or it resembles—in one way or another—some facet of our Savior Jesus.

Can it be any other way?

Can our true deep heart yearn for anything other than its Creator?

Deep down, can we really yearn for anyone other than our Savior, our Lord, our God?

Copyright 2013 Michael K. Pasque

Once again, nothing—no thought or word or person or thing—can take the place of our Creator *in the deep recesses of our heart*, or they would in fact be our Savior, our Lord, and our God.

Our hearts are tuned to Jesus because Jesus created them.

He made our hearts that way.

Could He have made them any other way?

Not if He is God—which He is.

Think about it.

God, by definition must embody everything that is infinitely and perfectly knowledgeable, wise, beautiful, merciful, righteous, just, and loving.

By definition, we, as His created beings, absolutely *must* love God.

The bottom-line is clear: if we are attracted to something or someone, it is because they have somehow picked up the reflection of Jesus.

Every handsome man, every beautiful woman, every magnificent sunset, every great warrior, every beautiful flower, every great leader, every great story, every captivating song, every last minute rescue—they all get our attention because they have been endowed with a tiny spark of the raging fire that is the Person of Jesus Christ.

So rather than focus upon the tiny spark, the blurred reflection, the mere fragment of the whole, we should focus upon the only real deal.

We focus on our idols—and Satan knows this—because they reflect a tiny bit of that which we will experience when finally we stand in the presence of Jesus.

Think about it.

Our evil primary thoughts are almost always about our top ten idols.

They are almost always centered in the top ten things in our life that we substitute for God and that we repeatedly allow to grab some of our attention, some of that focus of our hearts that is reserved for God.

Copyright 2013 Michael K. Pasque

This is not by chance.

Our evil primary thoughts revolve around our top idols because we have allowed Satan and his minions repeated access to these areas of our heart.

We have empowered the enemy in the present by giving in to our idol-worshipping evil primary thoughts (with affirming secondary thoughts) in the past.

Our evil primary and secondary thoughts *always* displace God.

The only way to successfully abandon the bad primary thoughts is to fill our mind with good secondary thoughts.

Since our bad primary thoughts are all displacing Jesus and our resulting bad secondary thoughts about our bad primary thoughts are all displacing thoughts about Jesus, the key is *to think about Jesus*—to focus our thoughts and, therefore, our hearts and minds on Jesus.

This is easier to do if we remember that the idol that we were thinking about in the first place is just a shallow reflection of Jesus anyway.

Jesus is the great Wellspring of all that we desire.

Most certainly, if we love that idol, we will flip out over the real thing for which it is a mere surrogate.

Directly and solely upon Jesus is where our hearts desire to be focused.

So, when our minds are flooded with evil primary thought after evil primary thought, this is where we should go—to Jesus.

Jesus is the solution to this problem.

Do you think that there is any chance that we will be abandoned to sin if we try to direct our thoughts to Jesus?

No chance.

Copyright 2013 Michael K. Pasque

The really fun thing about this is that it can quickly and easily become habit-forming.

In other words, the more we think about Jesus, the more we think about Jesus.

We just have to get that snowball started on its trip down the hill.

Pretty soon, it gains momentum of its own—and the rest is easy.

This is by God's very special planning.

This is God's grace.

And it is always enough.

That is His promise.

> But he said to me, "My grace is sufficient for you, for my power is made perfect in weakness." Therefore I will boast all the more gladly about my weaknesses, so that Christ's power may rest on me. (2Corinthians 12:9)

So when we sweep that evil idol-worshipping primary thought out of our house, we must immediately fill it with thoughts of Jesus.

> "When an evil spirit comes out of a man, it goes through arid places seeking rest and does not find it. Then it says, 'I will return to the house I left.' When it arrives, it finds the house **unoccupied, swept clean** and **put in order**. Then it goes and takes with it seven other spirits more wicked than itself, and they go in and live there. And the final condition of that man is worse than the first. That is how it will be with this wicked generation." (Matthew 12:43-45; emphasis added)

Copyright 2013 Michael K. Pasque

If our minds, and thus our hearts, are full of good secondary thoughts of Jesus, the bad primary thoughts of our idols and any secondary thoughts that resulted from them are swept out and no further bad primary thoughts can enter.

The presence of these good secondary thoughts of Jesus lets those evil spirits know that there is no room in our life for their influence.

It is all a matter of focus.

It is all a matter of filling our minds with the very same Person who fills our hearts—Jesus.

Thus, victory is all a matter of learning to *rapidly refocus*.

The more we do it, the easier it becomes.

The more we do it, the more automatic it becomes.

If we respond to a bad idol-worshiping primary thought with secondary thoughts about Jesus, our house is full of the goodness of God and there is simply no room for the evil secondary thoughts that scheme, plot, and lust on behalf of our idols in response to the idol-oriented primary thought.

The evil secondary thoughts are displaced by the focusing of our secondary thoughts upon the real *power*, the real *wisdom*, the real *beauty* that is found only in Jesus Christ.

We must fill our minds with thoughts of the consistent goodness, fearful awesomeness, and captivating beauty of God.

We are told precisely this in scripture:

> *Finally, brothers, whatever is true, whatever is noble, whatever is right, whatever is pure, whatever is lovely, whatever is admirable—if anything is excellent or praiseworthy—think about such things. (Philippians 4:8)*

Copyright 2013 Michael K. Pasque

We are to think of and dwell upon *the past* with Jesus when He gave us those seminal moments in our life where we experienced His awesome presence, strength, and beauty.

We are to think of and dwell upon *the present* with Jesus—that He alone has provided us with our current status as an heir to the kingdom of God.

And we are to think of and dwell upon *our future* with Jesus and that He is our only hope—that eternal hope into which we have been saved.

By thinking of and dwelling upon Jesus, we are able to so fill our house with the goodness of God that there is simply no room for those evil spirits to come place more evil primary thoughts about our idols in our minds.

The refocusing of our heart's attention disempowers them.

So, how do we keep Jesus foremost in our thoughts?

Just look around.

Jesus is all around us in our daily life.

We just need to look around.

Jesus is that Hero.

He is our Champion.

He is that Prince whose dashing regal figure turns our head.

He is that beautiful sunset that captivates our wondering heart.

He is the deep purple, rich reds, and bright yellows of that thin crescent of sunrise set against the pitch-black darkness at the edge that separates earth from sky out our jet window at 30,000 feet in the air in the earliest moments of the dawn.

He is the richness of the deep vibrant colors adorning the intricacies of the flowers that surround us.

He is the beauty in a face.

He is the strength of the soldiers who defend us.

Copyright 2013 Michael K. Pasque

He is the Warrior King.

He is the downtrodden around us—who will conquer in the end.

He is the very definition of meekness—being both infinitely strong and, therefore, in his humiliation, infinitely humbled.

He is that knot in our throat when our hearts are captivated by a last minute save.

He is that tear in our eye when beyond all hope, justice triumphs over evil.

He is every thirst that is quenched.

He is every hunger that is sated.

He is our Hope.

He is our Joy.

He is that warm fire on a winter's eve.

He is that shelter from the driving storm.

He is that cool shade in the oppressive heat.

He is our Praise.

He has saved us.

He has lifted us up.

He is our final Victory.

It is *easy* to dwell upon the Person who so surrounds us and makes Himself apparent to us in so many ways every moment of every day of our life.

We need to dwell upon the fact that our Hero, our Champion, our Savior Jesus (along with the Father and the Holy Spirit) willingly gave up that which He cared most about for all eternity.

He (They) willingly broke the eternal fellowship of the Trinity—just for us.

Copyright 2013 Michael K. Pasque

We need to appreciate the fact that for us, Jesus made Himself to be everything that His Father (the one Person He wants most to please) hates the most—our bitter rebellious sin.

Instead of dwelling on secondary thoughts of our idols, we need to dwell on the fact that what Jesus has already done for us ensures an eternity of endless joy, infinite life, and perfect fulfillment—and all as if we never once plotted bitter rebellion against His pure and bright light righteousness.

And while we are at it, we can also dwell upon that which, by the work of Jesus on the cross, is specifically not ours: an eternity of loss, frustration, loneliness, heart-deep pain, and infinite and utter hopelessness:

> Therefore this is what the Sovereign LORD says: "My servants will eat, but you will go hungry; my servants will drink, but you will go thirsty; my servants will rejoice, but you will be put to shame.
>
> My servants will sing out of the joy of their hearts, but you will cry out from anguish of heart and wail in brokenness of spirit. You will leave your name to my chosen ones as a curse; the Sovereign LORD will put you to death, but to his servants he will give another name." (Isaiah 65:13-15)

And while filling our minds with nothing but thoughts of our One True Love, we will have no room for the primary thoughts that are founded in the lies and the nonsense of our idols.

Copyright 2013 Michael K. Pasque

Day 37

Is All This Secondary Thought Mumbo-Jumbo Really That Important?
An Eternally Lost Opportunity To Bring Glory To God

One of our biggest problems in walking daily with Jesus is that we, in our typically human fashion, tend to trivialize the many decision-points that God places in our lives each day.

There are so many of these decision-points in any day—let alone the massive summation of them in any human life—that we discount the significance of so many *seemingly small* individual choices.

We must, nonetheless, realize the impact of every single decision that we make.

For, like it or not, each one of these decision-points—big or small, important or trivial, exciting or mundane—represents a unique opportunity to bring glory to the focal point of our life and our only reason for existence—Jesus.

Each of these decision-points is critical.

There is no inefficiency found in God—ever.

Without each and every one of these decision-points—even the seemingly mundane—we would not be the perfect eternal children of God with whom God desires to spend eternity.

Their summation = perfection.

Their summation = us.

Copyright 2013 Michael K. Pasque

So, if even one of them—the smallest most trivial of all—were to be removed, we would not be whom God wants us to be.

Our eternal perfection would be in jeopardy.

Each decision-point is absolutely critical to the perfection of God's plan, God's perfect creation, God's perfect eternity—and Jesus's perfect bride: *us*!

Bad choices are not just bad in their very nature, but even further, they find extreme infamy in the fact that they represent an eternally forsaken chance to bring glory to the only One who deserves it—once forsaken, they are gone forever.

Each decision-point represents nothing less than a once-in-a-lifetime (in fact, a once-in-eternity) opportunity to glorify God, such that when it passes by it is gone forever and cannot be reclaimed—for eternity.

There are no *Mulligans*, no *do-overs*, in our secondary thought life.

In the eyes of eternity, every choice at every decision-point is *forever*—and gains its significance in precisely that fact.

Every choice either brings Glory to God *for eternity*, or it doesn't—and there are no second chances to make things right.

Thus every decision-point—no matter how seemingly trivial—will either delight the God of Creation or grieve His Holy Spirit—and in this fact, every one of these trivial decision-points take on monumental eternal importance.

Every decision-point matters and we must fight Satan's continual attempts to downplay the eternal importance of every choice that we make.

For it is *always* Satan who is that quiet voice that downplays a sin as something that is "small and insignificant," such that we not need worry ourselves about it.

They are all significant to God.

They are all disobedience.

Copyright 2013 Michael K. Pasque

They are all rebellion against the only One who really cares about us.

They are all treason against the Righteous King.

It is not the size of the sin that determines the amount of offense to God—*size* in this regard is a typically human designation—because all sin, even the tiniest of sin, is darkest rebellion and thus heinously offensive to a perfectly holy, pure-light God.

This is because *every* sin contends with and offends the perfection of the bright white light.

In other words, it is God's inherent holiness—not our human valuation—that determines the offensiveness of our bad choices at our life's decision-point choices.

And God's inherent holiness is always the same—always infinite—no matter the size of the sin.

So the affront to the Holy God is always the same, no matter how *trivial* the offending sin.

Since God is perfect, infinitely holy, even the tiniest of sins is as dark as the darkest black hole.

And this for all eternity.

Copyright 2013 Michael K. Pasque

Day 38

How Do We Defeat Besetting Sin?
Our Transformation By The Renewal Of Our Minds

The process of sanctification boils down to one thing: the development of a consistent perspective by which we can persistently defeat sin in our life.

Sin is rebellion against God and opposes everything that is written on our hearts regarding our deepest desire in life and the purpose of our creation.

Being made into the likeness of Jesus—the goal of our sanctification, the goal of our life—is the elimination of sin.

When we seek a metric by which the process of sanctification can be objectively assessed, sin—and in particular besetting sin—is an obvious first choice.

So, when we discuss the topic of defeating besetting sin, we are discussing the very foundation of our sanctification process.

This is what we who have accepted Christ as our Savior are all about in this life of ours.

Becoming more like Jesus is our only real goal—for in the attainment of that most primary of goals, we attain all that is the desire of our heart and the purpose of our creation: the ability to know, fellowship with, and subserviently and sacrificially love the Father as royal children—princes and princesses—of the eternal kingdom of God.

Copyright 2013 Michael K. Pasque

We cannot attain this deep heart desire or achieve our creation purpose any other way than by being transformed into the likeness of Jesus—the only man who has ever subserviently, sacrificially loved God.

So, the elimination of our besetting sin patterns is the critical part of our life that (we are promised) will have critical eternal consequences.

Our typically human first response to our acknowledgment of our need to eliminate sin is to try to do it all by ourselves.

This is our attempt to attain *self*-righteousness.

This, as we have discussed, is hopelessly destined to utter failure.

This process of elimination of besetting sin—this process of our sanctification—is no more dependent upon us (or our efforts) than is the process of our salvation.

We are not saved by our own efforts and we are not sanctified by our own efforts.

We have no capability to save ourselves and we have no ability to sanctify ourselves.

We have no capability to eliminate besetting sin by ourselves.

Sanctification by the elimination of besetting sin occurs only when the Spirit of Jesus Christ in our hearts acts through us—in the power of the cross of Christ—to change the way that we respond to the circumstances that are orchestrated into our life by God.

Our goal is to *abide* in Christ such that He can act in us and through us.

That is never our first choice.

Nor is it ever our 2nd through 100th choice.

Instead, we always go back to our old human ways and try to fix the problem ourselves.

And we fail.

Copyright 2013 Michael K. Pasque

And when we fail, we cinch up our belt and resolve to *just try harder*.

Just trying harder is, at best, a temporary fix in regard to *besetting* sin—the recurrent sin pattern that dominates our life and seems to repeatedly herald the defeat of our sanctification process.

Our best efforts in regard to the defeat of besetting sin may work for a while, but ultimately, sin *always* defeats our own human efforts.

Luckily, God has a different plan.

Jesus asks us to *abide* in Him.

Abiding in Jesus simply means actively taking Jesus and His *perspective* along with us as we travel through the carefully orchestrated days of our life.

We, by ourselves, simply cannot force ourselves to remember to take Jesus along.

Instead, God wants to change our whole *mind*.

He wants to change the way we think.

God wants to give us a whole new perspective with which we are to view the world and the events of our every day.

He wants to give us an utterly radical, all-encompassing change of perspective.

The Bible tells us that we are *"transformed by the renewing of [our] mind"* such that God's truth is substituted for the world's truth.

> Do not conform any longer to the pattern of this world, but be transformed by the **renewing of your mind**. Then you will be able to test and approve what God's will is—his good, pleasing and perfect will. (Romans 12:2; emphasis added)

Copyright 2013 Michael K. Pasque

This means that the truth of God permeates every *secondary* thought that we generate in response to the primary thoughts that are placed in our minds every moment of every day of our life.

I am sure that there is not now nor has there ever been a true Christian who would not gladly accept such a thing as the continuous presence of God's truth in our thoughts if it were offered by a sudden stroke of God's mighty hand.

The problem is obvious.

God has created the world such that there is no mechanism by which we can just suddenly substitute God's truth for the worldly perspective that has been pounded into our minds since the moment we took our first breath.

For some reason, God designed the whole system such that we must go through a long process—that process called sanctification—in which we gradually substitute the truth of God for the truth of the world.

Obviously, something about actually living that experience of that long sanctification process must be critical to preparing us for our eternity as sons and daughters of the kingdom of God.

That process, by God's specific design, matures our mind by the slow substitution of His truth followed by the fixation of it in our minds by the process of its repeated persevering application in our day-to-day life.

> *Therefore, since we have been justified through faith, we have peace with God through our Lord Jesus Christ, through whom we have gained access by faith into this **grace** in which we now stand. And we rejoice in the hope of the glory of God. Not only so, but we also rejoice in our sufferings, because we know that suffering **produces perseverance; perseverance, character;** and character, hope. (Romans 5:1-4; emphasis added)*

Copyright 2013 Michael K. Pasque

In other words, the goal is to apply God's perspective to the events of our life and thereby to, by perseverance, further solidify it in our mind such that it is easily, efficiently, and immediately applied in subsequent life events.

Perseverance must finish its work so that you may be mature and complete, not lacking anything. (James 1:4)

As we can all attest, this is a long, tiring, complex, and often painful process.

If you are like me, you have only one question: "My life sucks when I do things my way instead of God's way—so how do I speed up this process?"

And that brings us to the longest Psalm in the Bible, Psalm 119.

The reason that the longest Psalm in the Bible, Psalm 119, was written was to tell us that the defeat of recurrent sin in our heart can occur by only one mechanism: the renewing of our mind by the replacement of the world's so-called *truth* with the *real* truth of God.

What Psalm 119 repeatedly tells us, in an almost fatiguing number of different ways, is that the word of God—as recorded in the Bible—*is* that *real truth of God* that must become the perspective through which we view all of the circumstances, events, and relationships that God brings into our life.

It tells us the key to our sanctification.

That key to the process of our sanctification is that we, very simply, must read the Bible.

We must read it every day.

Then, we must think about what we have read.

Copyright 2013 Michael K. Pasque

We must fill our minds whenever we can with thoughts about that which we find in the written Word of God.

The Bible is therefore one of the primary keys to defeating besetting sin in the process of our sanctification.

The Bible is that real truth of God that must be substituted for the worldly perspective that has hounded us every moment of our life and permeates every thought, word, deed, occasion, event, thrill, fright, relationship, and love of our life.

For our *beliefs*—in other words, that which we hold as *truth*—generate all of our behavior.

Beliefs generate behavior.

Beliefs generate perspective and perspective generates, drives, and continually influences all behavior.

Perspective is what we bring to each new situation.

It is how we view each new set of circumstances in our daily life.

And most critically, at its most influential level, perspective determines how we regard each new primary thought—both good and evil—that is thrown into our mind every moment of every day of our life.

This is why the changing of our perspective (to resemble the eternally based perspective of Jesus) that comes about with the transformation of our minds in the process of our sanctification is so vitally important.

If we change perspective, we change our secondary thought reaction to our primary thoughts.

And, as we have reviewed, our secondary thoughts drive our behavior.

Thus, behavior in any particular situation is based upon how we view each situation, which is based on beliefs.

Copyright 2013 Michael K. Pasque

Beliefs generate behavior because beliefs generate perspective.

So, if we want to influence our sinful behavior, we need a change in perspective and that only comes about by way of a change of beliefs.

To change our beliefs, we must read the written Word of God and let it begin to act in our life.

This combination—behavior based on the written Word of God—is the only way to change our perspective.

We must substitute God's truth for the worldly truth that occupies our mind before He begins His sanctifying work.

And by this, we are then enabled to replace the worldly perspective with which we regard our primary thoughts (and therefore the events, circumstances, and relationships of our life) with God's eternal perspective.

This is the so-called *"renewal"* of our minds.

There is nothing easy about the substitution of God's truth for the worldly truth that has filled our every thought since birth.

This worldly truth *owns* our mind and its secondary thoughts.

It will not give up control of our mind without putting up a ferocious fight.

We cannot just wish it to be replaced.

We cannot just pray it into retirement.

We cannot just read the Bible *once* and have the worldly truth magically replaced.

Instead, by God's specific and purposeful plan, we must repeatedly and continually (see Psalm 119) read the Bible—preferably in the morning every day—so that it will permeate our thoughts as we face the events of each day.

Only our actual *real world* implementation of the written Word of God in dealing with the real-life events of our daily life (in the way that God wants us to

Copyright 2013 Michael K. Pasque

deal with them) can fix the truth-problem that pollutes our minds—and this is the process of the renewal of our minds.

The Bible says that we must *know* God.

This *knowing* of God can be defined as the sum accumulation of life events in which the written Word, the truth of God, is applied in and through our life.

The more we apply it, the more it permeates our mind and the more we then reapply it.

This is a cycle and we must build momentum in the cycle.

Like everything else in life, the more we do it, then the more we do it.

We need to replace our worldly mind with the thoughts of God.

In so doing, we replace our worldly perspective with the perspective of God.

In so doing, we replace our individual and very personal perspective with the eternal eyes of God.

And in so doing, we see things through God's eyes, through His perspective—filtered through His plan, His will, and His eternity.

We see things the way that God sees them.

We see these events, circumstances, and relationships the way that God sees them only after having substituted His perspective for ours.

And it is in this changing of our perspective that our only hope for changing our thoughts and behavior is found.

For now we *see* things differently.

We approach the same situation, the same circumstances, the same person that we have approached a thousand times before—but now we see things differently.

It is as if we are looking on a brand new scene.

It is as if we are speaking with a totally new friend.

It is as if we have never seen things this way before.

Copyright 2013 Michael K. Pasque

For now we see things God's way.

Our response—in thought and in action—will be completely different.

It must be.

Now, the old way of thinking and the old way of responding and the old behaviors that used to always fit in these situations—they just don't seem *logical* anymore.

The old way just doesn't *make sense* in this situation any more.

We find ourselves responding—behaving—differently.

It isn't because we are doing something different or better.

We certainly are not succeeding in avoiding sin because we are *just trying harder*.

We aren't using some mind trick to fool ourselves into a type of behavior.

We aren't influenced by our efforts to try harder to build good habits.

Instead, we change our thoughts and we change our behavior because God's way, in this new perspective that we have in our renewed minds, just seems like the right way to handle the situation, encounter, or relationship.

God's way, for the first time, just seems like the *logical* way—it just *makes sense* to do it His way.

Give me understanding, and I will keep your law and obey it with all my heart. (Psalm 119:34)

It seems like the logical way because we know that steps in the other direction take us away from where we want to go.

It seems like the logical way because we know that steps in the other direction will be less efficient, more painful, and delay the work of God in our life.

Copyright 2013 Michael K. Pasque

Something is obviously radically different—and we didn't have anything to do with it.

This change didn't come from the outside where we or someone else tried to coerce us into different behavior.

This change came from within.

This change is the Spirit of Jesus Christ acting through—very literally through—us.

And it all came about through a single action on our part.

The first step (and all of those that follow) must be *into* the written Word of God.

It is there that the transformation begins.

It is there that the renewal begins.

It is there that the knowledge of God is found.

It is there that the wisdom of God is found.

It is there that the perspective of God is found.

The Word of God is the truth that we are to substitute for the lies that Satan and his world have built into the foundation of knowledge from which our current perspective is generated.

It is in the written Word of God that we are, for the very first time, made aware of that which is written on our hearts—God's law.

And from God's law in our minds and in our hearts comes God's perspective, God's way of seeing things, and then God's way of doing things.

Rescue from besetting sin is the process of our sanctification and it is all by God.

But, God never performs this rescue by giving us more willpower.

Copyright 2013 Michael K. Pasque

Instead, it is always done by truth from the written word of God illuminating a lie that we have come to accept as fact—and that has become the root of besetting sin.

We don't even have to *just try harder* because God's choice has now become our first choice because we see the world's choice for what it is—less efficient, more costly, more painful, less logical—and this all from a little truth, a little understanding, a little of God's wisdom.

This change in our perspective by the illumination of God's truth on our situation is what makes this change permanent.

First we must know God's truth, then we must put it into action in real life situations, and then we receive the positive/negative feedback reinforcement (of many different kinds in many differing manners).

These are the three steps of the feedback process that initiates, progresses, and solidifies our sanctification.

Just trying harder is a temporary fix, while a real change in perspective supplies a *permanent* solution.

The renewing of our mind by God's truth changes the perspectives through which we interface with the real world.

The yoke is heavy.

And the yoke is light.

It's hard to turn over the direction of our life to the only Person who can get us where we are supposed to be.

And yet when we truly turn over the dominion of our heart to Jesus, the yoke is light—for His promise is that He *will* do it all because He has *already* done it.

Copyright 2013 Michael K. Pasque

Day 39

How Can I Be Saved?
A Brief Testimony: Changing Our Life And The Lives Of Others In 1,368 Words!

The *purpose* of our existence far exceeds simply living this life in this world.

The *deepest desire of our heart* far exceeds anything that can be sated in this life in this world.

God, the Creator of *this* world of ours, has also established an eternal kingdom. And He created us also as *eternal* beings.

It is the *purpose* of our creation and it is our *deepest heart desire* to spend eternity in God's kingdom—as a son or daughter, a prince or princess, a royal heir of that kingdom—in subservient, sacrificial loving fellowship with each other and with the three Persons of the Triune God.

God, the Creator of the kingdom, has firmly established how we can gain entrance into that eternal kingdom that encompasses our creation purpose and deepest heart desire.

Our only access to that kingdom and, therefore, to our creation purpose and deepest heart desire occurs during this life, while we are still alive.

It is our natural inclination to rebel against the God-decreed path by which one gains access to God's eternal kingdom and to believe that we are somehow empowered to change it if we want, to adapt it to our own set of values and desires.

Copyright 2013 Michael K. Pasque

Nonetheless, just because we choose to ignore God's way to enter into our creation purpose (because we do not like it or because we do not think it is fair) does not negate the fact that it *alone* will determine and rule our eternity.

Like it or not, we did not create the universe, are not God, and do not make the rules.

Like it or not, therefore, our Creator God's rules will apply to us regardless of whether we choose to ignore them and act like they will not affect us.

Eternity is a very long time.

10,000 years from now (we have been alive less than 100 years—can we even imagine 10,000!), we will not have even scratched the surface of eternity.

The way to enter into the eternal kingdom of God is simple and has as its foundation the fact that *He is perfectly righteous and holy*.

The only way that we can enter into an eternity of loving fellowship with a perfectly righteous and holy God (which, once again, is why we were created and the deepest desire of our heart, whether we like it or not) is to also be perfectly righteous and holy.

God's righteousness and holiness will not allow Him to share eternal fellowship with anyone who is not also perfectly righteous and holy.

This is, of course, a problem.

To be worthy of the eternal kingdom of God, we must be capable of love.

To be capable of love, we must have a free will.

Since love is the foundation of our creation purpose and our deepest heart desire, God has given us an independent free will.

In this life, God has given us the freedom to make all of our own free will choices.

God will not force our hand on anything, especially regarding the choice of the object(s) of our love.

Copyright 2013 Michael K. Pasque

Whom we love is 100% our choice.

Following the natural inclination of our nature, we have used our free will to rebel against God, which is the antithesis of loving God.

This rebellion is manifest in our lives on a daily basis and is called *sin*.

Since it only takes one sin to ruin *perfection*, there are none of us, therefore, who can, under our own steam, enter the eternal kingdom of God.

Everything about God is perfect—especially His righteousness and holiness.

So, the individuals with whom God will spend eternity must also be perfect in every manner—including righteousness and holiness.

Thus, we are back to our very obvious problem.

We are utterly helpless in regard to fixing this obvious problem.

In other words, our problem is unfixable by our own effort.

Trying to fix it by our own efforts is called *religion* and religion is not the answer.

God loves us.

He has, therefore, offered us a *real* solution to our problem.

God's love for us was proven infinite in its capacity by the infinite price He paid for the solution to our problem, for our redemption.

The *good news* of the gospel of Jesus Christ is that Jesus led, for us, the perfect life that qualifies us to spend eternity in the kingdom of God and offered it to pay the infinite cost of our unrighteousness by dying on the cross of Calvary the death that we have earned by our sinful rebellion.

God offers, as a free gift, the perfect righteousness and holiness that are needed to enter the loving fellowship of His eternal kingdom as a prince or a princess of that kingdom.

A gift does not become a gift just because it is offered.

For it to become a gift, it must be accepted.

Copyright 2013 Michael K. Pasque

> *This is _all_ that is required.*

We must simply accept the gift that God has already freely offered.

This gift will buy for us the eternity for which we were created and for which we long in the deep recesses of our heart.

To gain the eternal life as a prince or princess of the eternal kingdom of God, _all_ that we must do is _accept_ the gift.

We must admit that our sin has proven our inability to attain perfect righteousness and holiness by our own effort and accept the gift of the atonement for our sins that guarantees eternal life—all of which is made possible only by the sacrificial shedding of Christ's blood on the cross of Calvary.

If we simply, in the privacy of our own heart, *accept* the gift of Christ's redemption, then from that moment on, everything changes.

The cross of Christ saves everything that, until then, was hopelessly lost.

All of our sin—even that which we have not yet even committed—is immediately assigned to Jesus.

He thereby died the death we deserve.

And in the exchange, His righteousness is assigned to us.

We get what He deserves.

We gain eternal life by His death.

From that moment on, our life will begin to change more than we can imagine.

From that moment on, it is our *irrevocable* privilege to spend eternity frolicking through the adventure, beauty, passion, exhilaration, and joy of the eternity that God has planned for us—and we get to do that as if we never ever rebelled against the holiness of God.

This is God's incredible promise: that He will forget every single sin that we ever committed and look upon us as He looks upon His only Son Jesus.

Copyright 2013 Michael K. Pasque

This incredible gift waits only for our acceptance.

And yet, for the majority of us, it will remain unaccepted.

God will never force us to take His free gift.

It is ours to grasp or ours to refuse.

But never for a single second can we believe that the ease with which we can claim this incredible gift in some way lessens the hard reality that we will face if we turn it down.

God will not force this upon us.

He only wants people in His eternal kingdom who actually want to be there.

What do we have to lose in accepting this generous gift?

Nothing.

What do we have to gain?

Everything.

Very literally, everything.

Without Jesus, we get nothing.

Very literally, nothing.

With Jesus, we get everything.

Everything.

It is our choice.

This I know: right this minute it is our choice.

I cannot speak for the minute following this one.

Right here, right now, it is simply "Yes" or "no."

"Yes" or "No"?

There is no middle ground.

We can choose to simply not answer, but by not answering, by attempting to not commit ourselves one way or the other, by seeking to just fade quietly into the

Copyright 2013 Michael K. Pasque

scenery, by remaining falsely humble in our silence, by remaining silent at all, we most assuredly answer "No!"

So, until we actually say "yes," *OUR ANSWER IS "NO!"*

The option to not answer does not exist.

By not answering, we answer, and that, in the most pathetic fashion.

Just say, "Yes" and join us in eternity...

Copyright 2013 Michael K. Pasque

Day 40

Out Of The Valley Of The Shadow Of Death
In Summary: Knowing God

Our creation was a natural consequence of God's love.

In fact, God's love for us is the foundation of the entirety of the creation.

The subservient, sacrificial nature of God's love for us is demonstrated in every aspect of the creation (but most poignantly, of course, in the death of Jesus on the cross of Calvary).

In fact, God's subservient, sacrificial love for us motivated and guided every single decision that He made in the process of creating all that would ever be created.

His creation includes every position and movement of every subatomic particle in existence for every moment of time—for all eternity.

Thus, everything that we are (including our personality characteristics) and have and experience exists solely by the hand of our Creator—and God's love for us guided *every* aspect of everything He created, including us.

In our recognition of this fact—that everything that we are and have and experience is solely by the will of God—is found the humility with which we can love everyone sent into our life by God, including our enemies.

More specifically, it is only in the recognition that everything that we (and our enemy) are and have and experience is entirely God-ordained that we can turn the other cheek to the individual who just struck us, offer our shirt to the person who took our coat, lend to those who cannot repay, love our sworn enemies, rejoice

Copyright 2013 Michael K. Pasque

with those who rejoice, and mourn with those who mourn—all of which are encompassed by Jesus' request that we truly and unconditionally, subserviently and sacrificially, *love one another*.

The sovereignty of God and the fact that it is He who gives us everything that we are and have and experience thereby mandate that it is also He *alone* who can claim credit for every single aspect of our salvation, most assuredly including the very faith by which we are saved.

If God makes that call regarding who is saved and who is sanctified, why do we even go through all the trials of this life?

The answer is foundational: We must *"know"* God.

> *Now this is eternal life: that they may **know** you, the only true God, and Jesus Christ, whom you have sent. (John 17:3; emphasis added)*

There is no way to *"know"*—to understand, to comprehend, to experience—God without knowing the bright white, pure attributes of God.

In a pure white room with nothing to contrast the pure bright white of God's attributes, we are blind to them—and, thereby, we cannot know God.

In other words, there was nothing perfect about the state of Adam and Eve in the Garden of Eden because they could not *know* the fullness of God's attributes.

We cannot know, we cannot experience God without experiencing that which He is not—we need contrast to clearly, completely, and perfectly define God's attributes, to *know* God.

Specifically, we must live this life in the presence of evil, surrounded by those who will *not* join us in eternity, and with evil living in our hearts—all in order that we might *know* God.

Copyright 2013 Michael K. Pasque

By the awesomely omniscient and sovereign mind of God, we can be assured that the very best way that the outcome that God desires could be brought about is in fact exactly the way that it has happened, is happening, and will continue to happen.

God *will* have His perfect sons and daughters—the purpose of His creation—princes and princesses with whom the three Persons of the Triune Godhead will fellowship in perfect subservient, sacrificial love in the kingdom of God for all eternity.

> *As for God, his way is perfect; the word of the LORD is flawless.*
> *(Psalm 18:30a)*

That this is all occurring according to God's plan neither lessens the joy of the saved, not the anguish of the unsaved.

Instead, this knowledge should focus our attention like a laser upon every event of every day of our life.

Of this we can be sure:

There will come a singular moment in time during our life when our life actually hangs in the balance of a decision that faces us.

It will be *our life* versus another person's life.

It will, therefore, be *our life* versus Jesus.

That moment will determine the *success* of our life.

Our entire life will be judged by that moment in time.

If we choose our life, we will lose it.

And, we will lose everything.

We will lose everything for which we have worked our entire life.

If we choose to lose our life, we will gain it.

Copyright 2013 Michael K. Pasque

And, we will gain everything.

Everything for which we have labored our entire life will be carried into eternity with us.

The only problem with this monumental moment in time is that *it occurs every moment of every day of our life*.

Copyright 2013 Michael K. Pasque

www.ingramcontent.com/pod-product-compliance
Lightning Source LLC
Chambersburg PA
CBHW071948040426
42447CB00009B/1284